M000279673

'The reader, whether Jew or C
the meaning of the covenant, th
and the implications for both in
and very important book, esp
involved in ministry with Jew

John Armstrong
President, Reformation & Revival Ministries
Carol Stream, Illinois

'Jewish believers in Jesus have long been plagued with critical questions: "How are we to live our lives? Are we to worship in churches with our Gentile brothers and sisters or are we to commit ourselves to 'Messianic Judaism'? Indeed, is 'Messianic Judaism' the answer?"

The Gentile Church – as well as all Jewish believers – will agonise with Baruch as he lovingly and graciously explores the theological implications of 'Messianic Judaism', its applications to the lives of its adherents – and to the Church. This book is must reading for everyone who cares about the Jewish people.'

Stan Telchin
Stan Telchin Ministries, Florida

'Finally – a clear, contemporary exposition on evangelising the Jews. Baruch Maoz, a Jewish Christian converted over 35 years ago, and pastor of a solidly Reformed church in Israel, guides us sure-footedly through the major theological and practical questions and issues, explaining how Jews in the Messiah remain Jews, how the Mosaic covenant relates to Jewish evangelism, and how the Messianic Movement today inadvertently reaps harmful fruits. This long-needed book, written with mind and soul by one intimately acquainted with the subject, is packed with spiritual and practical instruction. It is a must read for all Christians and denominations involved in, or contemplating, Jewish evangelism.'

Dr. Joel R. Beeke,
Professor of Systematic Theology and Homiletics
Puritan Reformed Theological Seminary, Michigan

'The thrilling increase in recent years in the number of Jewish people coming to faith in Jesus their Messiah has posed significant theological and cultural challenges. Crucial issues in the current debate include Jewish identity, relationships with the pre-dominantly Gentile Church, as well as the Synagogue, and the place of Law in the life of the Jewish believer. At last a Jewish Christian has cogently argued for a radical biblical approach to such questions. Baruch Maoz, a pastor of a large and growing congregation in Israel, writes with passion and deep pastoral concern. He pays careful attention to cultural and theological nuances, as well as manifesting a deep awareness of the need of Jewish believers to retain their Jewish identity. For Baruch Maoz, the ultimate arbitrator in all questions of tradition, doctrine and practice is the Bible, both the Tenach and the New Covenant Scriptures. His exegesis is thorough, his methodology exemplary and his conclusions convincing, if sometimes controversial. This is essentail reading for Jewish believers in Jesus, Christian leaders, and all whose passion is the creation of the "one new man in Messiah"(Eph. 2:15).'

Rev. John Ross, Formerly General Secretary,
Christian Witness to Israel

'The title of this book succinctly captures its controlling thesis. Written primarily as a constructive critique of the Messianic Movement or Messianic Judaism and in light of the author's experience of more than 30 years as a minister of the gospel in Israel, it has far broader relevance. Within the present heightened dialogue between Christians and Jews in many settings worldwide, it highlights, in a fashion both compelling and winsome, considerations that are non-negotiable today, as always, in maintaining the integrity of the gospel of Jesus Christ and biblical Christianity. Even those who may differ from the author at points will benefit from his thorough searching of Scripture on these issues.'

Richard B. Gaffin, Jr.
Professor of Biblical and Systematic Theology,
Westminster Theological Seminary, Philadelphia

'This is a provocative book. It provokes thought on an impressively important subject, a division among believers in Jesus Christ. Pastor Maoz makes an impassioned plea for his brothers in the Messianic Jewish Movement to reconsider the direction they are taking. He sees the Movement as making an unintentional slide away from historic Christianity. He respectfully addresses the leaders and urges them to call a halt before it is too late.

Maoz does not speak from ignorance, but as a Jewish Christian who has watched the Movement from its beginnings. The heart of his indictment is this: the Movement has allowed rabbinic tradition to overshadow the Bible. In a laudable attempt to attract Jews to Christianity, they are in danger of losing the essence of the faith as it centers in Jesus Christ. How could that be? Aren't these leaders themselves earnest Christians? Maoz grants that, but calls our attention to extensive Biblical passages that warn about this very type of problem that faced the first century church. In doing so he reminds us that all of us who labour in the gospel are laying the groundwork for the church of tomorrow.

This book needed to be written. It is not an act of enmity but of love to call brothers to account for their principles. As a Gentile outside to this discussion I cannot anticipate its outcome. What I can say is this: leaders of the Messianic Jewish Movement owe it to themselves, to their people, and to the church at large to take these accusations seriously. Read it. Prayerfully meditate on it. And answer Pastor Maoz in the same spirit he has written to you. All of us will benefit from that kind of frank and loving exchange.'

Tom Wells
Pastor, The Kings Chapel, West Chester, Ohio

JUDAISM IS NOT JEWISH

A FRIENDLY CRITIQUE OF THE MESSIANIC MOVEMENT

BARUCH MAOZ

MENTOR

DEDICATED
To the glory of God,
to the beloved congregation I am privileged to serve
and to Paul Liberman, a Messianic leader,
who disagrees with most of what I have said in this
book but from whom I have learned a great deal.

Copyright © Baruch Maoz
ISBN 1 85792 787 7

Published in 2003. Reprinted in 2003
in the
Mentor Imprint
by
Christian Focus Publications Ltd,
Geanies House, Fearn,
Ross-shire, IV20 1TW,
Great Britain
and
Christian Witness to Israel,
166 Main Road, Sundridge,
Sevenoaks, Kent, TN14 6EL

www.christianfocus.com

Cover design by Alister MacInnes

Printed and bound by Bell & Bain, Glasgow

CONTENTS

SECTION B:
A PRACTICAL ASSESSMENT

PREFACE

Saying 'Thank you' is more than a duty; it is a moral privilege. There are many I need to thank for helping me along with this book, intentionally or otherwise. My first thanks go to the countless number of Messianic Jews from whose views, challenges and practices I have learned so much. Special thanks are due to those whose warmly held views I controvert here, and who by their sincere enthusiasm repeatedly reminded me that God is to be served wholeheartedly. Some of these people are mentioned in this book.

I also thank Rivka Nessim, my faithful and competent colleague, who played a large part in the final form of this book and in many of its details. Thanks are more than due to my loving and patient family and to the congregation of Grace and Truth in Rishon LeTsion, who have always and still bear with me so graciously. My earnest prayer is that this book will contribute in some small way to the glory of God and to the salvation of my beloved people.

AUTHOR'S FOREWORD

BEHOLD YOUR GOD:
Israel in the Light of Biblical Prophecy

INTRODUCTION

'Comfort, O comfort my people,' says your God.
'Speak kindly to Jerusalem
and call out to her that her warfare has ended,
that her iniquity has been removed,
that she has received of the Lord's hand
double for all her sins.'

A voice is calling: 'Clear the way for the Lord in the wilderness!
Make smooth in the desert a highway for our God!
Let every valley be lifted up,
and every mountain and hill be made low,
and let the rough ground become a plain,
and the rugged terrain a broad valley.
Then the glory of the Lord will be revealed
and all flesh will see it together,
for the mouth of the Lord has spoken.'

A voice says, 'Call out!'
Then he answered, 'What shall I call out?'
'All flesh is grass,
and all its loveliness is like the flower of the field.
The grass withers, the flower fades
when the breath of the Lord blows upon it;
Surely the people are grass!
The grass withers, the flower fades,
But the Word of our God stands forever.'

Get yourself up on a high mountain,
O Zion, bearer of good news.
Lift up your voice mightily,
O Jerusalem, bearer of good news;
Lift it up! Do not fear! Say to the cities of Judah,
'Behold your God!
Behold, the Lord will come with might,
with his arm ruling for him.
Behold his reward is with him,
and his recompense before him.
Like a shepherd he will tend his flock.
In his arm he will gather the lambs,
and carry them in his bosom.
He will gently lead the nursing ewes.'

Isaiah has devoted the greater part of 39 chapters to warning the people of impending doom because of their sin. From time to time a shaft of promised blessing has lightened the burden of his message, but, on the whole, it has been one of divine anger and its awful consequences.

In spite of God's undeserved kindness, Israel has sinned consistently. God is offended. Judgement has therefore been decreed and, unless the people repent, they can do nothing to avert it. Only a remnant shall remain. The country shall be devoured, the people exiled and the nations shall witness the punishment of God's elect nation. God is a holy God who should never be taken lightly. The whole earth is full of his glory.

Transported by the Spirit of God to a later date when

the judgement has already fallen, Isaiah now devotes the remainder of his message to comfort. It is our happy lot to briefly study the opening statements of the prophet's Book of Consolations. As should always be the case, we will first explore its content, and then apply the content to ourselves.

THE GRACE OF GOD

> *'Comfort, O Comfort my people,' says your God.*

Whom is the prophet addressing? No one in particular. Everyone in general. Whoever 'catches the message that God would have his people comforted should spread the good news' (Leopold).

> *'Speak kindly to Jerusalem and call out to her that her warfare has ended, that her iniquity has been removed, that she has received of the Lord's hand double for all her sins.'*

Addressing the people as if after judgement has fallen and they have experienced the full brunt of God's wrath, Isaiah is called upon to assure them that their unfaithfulness cannot annul the faithfulness of God. In spite of all their sin, they are still his people and he is still their God. He has not forsaken them nor become indifferent to their fate.

Israel, although called to a life of obedience, was constantly the object of undeserved grace. It was by grace that God called them into existence. By grace he raised up Moses, led the people out of Egypt and gave them his Law. The same grace continued while they rebelled against him in the wilderness. Having come into the land, they consistently sinned against him. Yet God in his grace sent prophets to warn them. Some they stoned. Others they simply ignored. None were ever heeded. They had been visited by God's righteous anger. But his grace continued with them. *'Comfort, O comfort my people,' says your God.*

How is Israel to be comforted? *Speak to her.* Later

on we read, *Call out!* However else Israel was to be comforted, the primary means which the prophet is called upon to employ is speech.

> *Get yourself up on a high mountain, O Zion, bearer of good news! Lift up your voice mightily, O Jerusalem, bearer of good news. Lift it up! Do not fear!*

The good news, of which we shall be hearing in a minute, is to be declared to the people. The remainder of this passage deals with the content of the message committed to the prophet and, through him, to whoever 'catches' it.

What is the prophet to say to the people? What could possibly comfort them in exile, when their land will be destroyed, their cities torn down, and they themselves so distant from their beloved homes and subject to the reign of a foreign king? *Speak kindly to Jerusalem and call out to her that her warfare has ended, that her iniquity has been removed, that she has received of the Lord's hands double for all her sins.* The good news is this: the then-present state of the people was indeed to be the just reward of their sin, but sin is not to be allowed to determine the fate of the people. God rules, and he will save them.

The people had rebelled against God. They had transformed their society into a money-grabbing, heartless one in which the strong devoured the weak. They had worshipped God as if all he should require was the blood of bulls and goats, and the people's habitual presence in the courts of his Temple. So long as they maintained their outward religiosity, they thought, he should be satisfied.

But God was not to be tampered with. Their punishment would come directly from his hand. He would not rest until they had borne the full weight of their due punishment. Once their *warfare* (a term used in the original text to indicate a set measure of exacted hardship) was ended, the same God who punished would also bring an end to the punishment. He would not be angry forever.

By suffering at the hand of God, Jerusalem's sins had been removed. She had received of the Lord's hand double for all her sins. Of course, the latter phrase is not to be taken as the voice of legal justice, let alone of a form of mathematical morality. It is the voice of merciful love, which now declares, 'I am more than satisfied. I require nothing more of you with regard to your sin.' The term *remove* in the original text indicates a full payment of all that is due because of sin (Lev. 26:41-43). God's justice is real and exacting. None should think otherwise. But his grace is no less real, none should forget.

THE GLORY OF GOD

> *A voice is calling: 'Clear the way for the Lord in the wilderness! Make smooth in the desert a highway for our God!'*

God was returning to his people. Note, please, that there is no indication of repentance or of worthiness on the part of the nation. In this passage Israel is altogether passive. It is God who acts. God's grace is sovereign, unilateral and uncontingent. It is God's grace and therefore it partakes of all the attributes of his essential Godhood.

God is returning to his people. Nothing can stand in his way. Neither the height of mountains, which shall be brought low, nor the depth of valleys, which shall be filled, can separate the people from the love of their God. He will come with all the power of his gracious majesty. He will return to them with all the richness of his love. *Clear the way in the wilderness! Make smooth in the desert a highway for our God.* Every obstacle shall be swept away. *Then the glory of the Lord will be revealed, and all flesh will see it together.*

There are many ways in which God could choose to be glorified, but he has chosen one. He has chosen to be glorified by the way he treats Israel. Having exacted the full burden of their punishment, he will now love them freely. The gifts and the calling of God are irrevocable.

To what end has God determined to work in such a manner in the history of Israel? *Then the glory of the Lord will be revealed, and all flesh will see it together.* All God's deeds are done for his own glory. When mankind truly comes to know him, they will know him as a God whose holiness is not to be compromised, or made light of. Sin in God's world will always be punished. But neither is his grace to be forgotten. He delights to choose the not many noble, not many wise. He delights to show his love to men in spite of their sin. God framed Israel's history in order to reveal himself to the world as he truly is. Israel will carry out that mission without fail, *for the mouth of the Lord has spoken.*

THE TRUSTWORTHINESS OF GOD

Once again, *a voice says, 'call out!'* Then he (presumably the prophet) answered, *'What shall I call out?'* The answer comes: call out that *all flesh is grass and all its loveliness like the flower of the field.* The reference here is not to the weakness of human existence but to the weightlessness of human effort and ability in contrast to those of God. 'The grass withers, the flower fades when the breath of the Lord blows upon it.' Nothing in this world can withstand God. No empire, however great. No nation, however determined. *Surely the people are grass.*

God is not weak. His purposes cannot be frustrated. His will shall be done. *The grass withers, the flower fades – but the Word of our God stands forever.* Isaiah does not call upon the people to put their trust in some uncertain intention or contingent goodwill, divine though it may be. They are to trust him whose Word can never fail and who will work his will among men without fail.

COMFORT FROM GOD

That being the case, the message of comfort is to be declared with a confidence worthy of its content and which, by the sheer strength of its confidence, will give God his due. *Get yourself up on a high mountain where you will be clearly seen and heard by all, O Jerusalem, bearer of good news.* Have you noticed? Jerusalem, who is to be the recipient of this message, is now described as its proclaimer. Is this an intimation of the remnant?

Lift up your voice mightily ...! Lift it up! Do not fear!

E. J. Young has an excellent statement here, which I cannot forbear to quote in full. He says of this passage, 'the words constitute a true picture of the manner in which the word of God is to be proclaimed to the world. The messenger is to be bold; he is to raise his voice that all may hear. The church is not to keep this message to herself but is to present it to Judah's cities with a holy boldness. She is not to pose as a seeker after truth, unsure of her message, but to declare in clear, firm and positive voice that her message is true. She must be vigorously and militantly evangelistic. Hesitation, timorousness, and trembling are out of place. There is no need to fear that the word of God would not be fulfilled, or that the message would prove to be untrue and embarrassment would result' (E. J. Young, *The Book of Isaiah*, Vol. III, W. M. Eerdmans Publishing Company, 1972, 1974, pp. 37-38).

What is to be proclaimed by Jerusalem and to whom? Allow me please to remind you that we are still dealing with Israel and its history in the hand of God. The addressees are clearly described in vs. 9 of this passage: *Say to the cities of Judah.* Israel remains the object of Isaiah's message, although the message is now being borne by a group described as 'Zion' and 'Jerusalem'.

JUDAISM IS NOT JEWISH

J U D A I S M   I S   N O T   J E W I S H

The message is pure and simple. In effect it is the same message we have been following throughout this passage: *Say to the cities of Judah, 'Behold your God!'* Look at him! Take notice of him. Note what he has done in your history! He forsook you when you sinned, just as he said he would. Now he is returning in mercy, just as he promised. *Behold, the Lord God will come with might, with his arm ruling for him,* as a mighty King whom none can withstand. *Behold, his reward is with him and his recompense is before him.*

All will receive from his hand their just deserts. Those who oppose his will and believe not the good news shall be destroyed from the presence of his glory. Those who believe shall experience his wonderful grace. *Like a shepherd he will tend his flock.* The picture is one of amazing tenderness. Mighty – yes, overwhelming – well, yes, in a very real sense. But overwhelming as only sovereign love can overwhelm. *Like a shepherd he will tend his flock. In his arm he will gather the lambs and carry them in his bosom. He will gently lead the nursing ewes.*

Have you ever seen a shepherd bend down, swoop a lamb into his arm and lovingly carry it to the pasture? At first the lamb is naturally terrified; suddenly it is swept off its feet, away from the familiar order of things and into the arms of this tall, strong creature who controls the herd without question. But a short while later the lamb is settled quietly in its benefactor's arms, enjoying his embrace and the warmth of his affection. Such will be the fate of Israel. God will swoop down with the irresistibility of his love, and make them his own.

CONCLUSION

Such is the message of Isaiah 40:1-11. Now what has this to do with us? A very great deal. We are those who have, in the quaint term of Leopold previously quoted, 'caught' the message. We know the grace of God in a fullness that can only be known in Christ.

| 16 |

We have learned from the history of Israel. We have learned pre-eminently from that part of Israel's history that has to do with the coming of the Messiah, his life, atoning death and justifying resurrection. We know that God is indeed not to be tampered with.

His hatred of sin is awful, and altogether just. His love is amazing and can never be suppressed. His power is beyond all resistance. He brings down mountains and lifts valleys, if that is what is necessary to fulfil his will. His will includes the salvation of Israel. Although they have sinned, they are still his people and he is their God.

We have a message to proclaim and we 'must not stay to play with shadows or pluck earthly flowers till [we our] work have done and rendered up account'. The vows of God are upon us and the end of our endeavours is secure. *The glory of the Lord will be revealed and all flesh shall see it together.* We should refuse every form of fear, reject every temptation, love God more than we love our ministries, our reputations or ourselves. We should work together to promote the glory of God through the promised salvation of Israel.

However vital our wellbeing may be, our primary task is and ever shall be to *cry out*, to call, to proclaim. Preaching the good news is our ultimate duty. Social and economic aid is often called for. Political encouragement may sometimes be necessary. But our task is to lift up our voice mightily.

Nor ought we to focus in our message on anything but the majesty of God's grace. *Behold your God* is the crux of our message. His mercy and faithful love are its corollaries. May we be faithful to our task.

FOREWORD

Trusting My Jewish Saviour
by *Stan Telchin*

Some months ago, I was asked to be a principal speaker at an International Conference on Jewish Evangelism. It was only after I had agreed to do so, that I was assigned my very challenging topic. It was: 'Trusting My Jewish Saviour'.

'Trusting my Jewish Saviour'? That was a subject I'd never really thought about. Certainly, it was one I had never spoken about. But that was the assignment I was given – and that is the assignment I accepted.

I want to share with you some of the things I learned as I prepared that message. My purpose in doing so is threefold: first: I want you to learn some important truths about me. Second: I want to encourage you to consider these truths – as they may apply to your life. But my overwhelming objective is to help you become even more effective in your outreach to Jewish people.

As I first thought about the subject 'Trusting my

Jewish Saviour' I realised that, like you, I have a whole list of things to trust him for: my salvation, my life, my family, my work, my health, my relationships, my ministry ... my finances. But later as I continued to think about this assignment, I realised that there is another fundamental and extremely important matter I am trusting him for. I am trusting him for my identity on earth!

Think about that word 'identity' for just a moment. If you had to define the word, what would you say? Do this, take a pen or pencil and write down how you would define your identity. Here's how I used to define it: I am a first generation Jewish American. Please note the order of what I have just said. I am not an American-Jew. I am a Jewish-American.

Why the emphasis? Because as soon as I was able to understand, I was taught that I was a Jew before I was anything else. Continually in the late 20s and early 30s as I grew up in a ghetto on the East Side of New York, I was reminded that I was a Jew!!!

Anti-Semitism was a very real part of American life in those years. Indeed, if anyone asked me my nationality, I knew they weren't asking if I was an American, they wanted to find out if I was Jewish! I would boldly say, 'I am a Jew!'

Over the years as I grew up, I did the things that most good Jewish boys did. I went to Talmud Torah – religious school. I became Bar Mitzvah at the age of 13.

That's when I joined a Zionist youth group. I was very active in it. With my family, I celebrated all of the Jewish holidays. Later, after serving in World War II for three years, I attended George Washington University in Washington, DC and was very involved with Hillel, the Jewish centre on campus. During my last two years in college, I was on the air with a weekly radio program called 'The Jewish Life Hour'.

Years later, I took a job on the staff of the United Jewish Appeal, which led to a job with the State of

Israel Bond Office, which led to a job with a public relations firm which handled Jewish organisations, among whom were Brandeis University and B'nai Brith. In 1955, after I went into business for myself, about 85 per cent of my clients were Jewish.

In time we moved into a Golden Ghetto, joined the best Synagogue in town, contributed generously to the United Jewish Appeal, belonged to a Jewish Country Club, gave money to Jewish causes, supported the Hebrew Home for the Aged and so on.

With all that service and giving, came honours. I was a trustee of this Jewish organisation, a board member of several others, I was Man of the Year for still another. It seemed as if the more money I gave the more honours I received. I understood all of that – but also understood 'I am a Jew and we Jews have to take care of our own'.

What I want you to see is that I was totally immersed in the Jewish community and in Jewish life. No matter what else I was, being Jewish was my identity.

Those of you who have read my books *Betrayed* and *Abandoned* know of the crisis that came into our home early in 1975, when my daughter called from college to tell me that she believed that Jesus is our Messiah.

You may remember my reaction. I felt betrayed. I felt that my daughter had just left us, the Jewish people, and had joined them, the Christians. The very last thing in the world that I wanted her to believe is that Jesus is the Jewish Messiah. 'If a Jew believes in Jesus' I thought, 'he loses his identity. He ceases to be a Jew and becomes a "Christian". Who would ever want to do that? Who would ever want to give up his identity as a Jew?' In order to win my daughter back, I set out to disprove the Messiahship of Jesus.

Over the months, as I searched the Scriptures to prove who he was NOT, I found out who he is! In spite of myself, soon I began to believe! No matter how hard I tried to tell myself that believing in Jesus was absolutely impossible for me. No matter how often I reminded myself about the Crusades and the Inquisition and the pogroms and the Holocaust – and of the hatred I had experienced as a child. I kept hearing on the inside of me: 'Yes, but it's true! Jesus really is the Messiah!' I would argue with myself proclaiming: 'My identity is at stake in this decision!'

'In view of all that I have experienced during my lifetime – in view of all the things I know about how we Jews have suffered at the hands of Christians over the centuries – how can I possibly consider leaving US and becoming part of THEM?' The struggle went on for months.

During these months, I continued to search the Scriptures. The time came when I could no longer deny Jesus' identity. Then new concerns arose. How will my wife Ethel and my children react if I accept Jesus as Lord? How will the rest of my family react? How will my neighbours react? How will my clients react? How will the United Jewish Appeal react? How will the rabbis and members of my synagogue react?

The overwhelming question I struggled with was this: 'If I accept Jesus as my Messiah and Lord, what will happen to my identity as a Jew?'

Despite these unanswered questions, my study of Scripture produced in me an overwhelming conviction that Jesus really is our Messiah – and on 3 July 1975, I confessed him as Lord of my life.

I did so recognising that the Jewish community would consider me a traitor. I did so recognising that many of my neighbours, clients and friends would turn their backs upon me. I did so recognising that the Jewish organisations for which I had worked would no longer welcome me.

For the first two years after my wife and I received Jesus as Lord of our lives, we attended a Messianic congregation every Friday night. I worked hard to help that congregation. I thought it was a way for me to retain my identity as a Jew and be a believer at the same time.

I remember in those early years the very ser
conversations I had with countless Jewish belie
from all over the country about how we are to live ᴜᴜᴜ
lives. Among the questions we asked were these: 'How
are we Jews to function in what is primarily a Gentile
world?' 'Do we remain separate from Gentile believers,
or do we worship with them?' 'If we are to worship
with them, will we have to join churches?' 'Won't this
lead to assimilation?' 'Mustn't this be avoided at all
costs?' 'As an alternative, should we strive to create a
synagogue for our worship?' 'If so, which kind:
Orthodox, Conservative or Reform?' 'If we establish
synagogues what will happen to our Gentile brothers
and sisters who want to worship with us? Won't this
make them feel like second class citizens?' 'If that
happens, won't we be violating Jesus' prayer that we
be one?' 'How will the non-believing Jewish community
react to Messianic synagogues?' 'Will such synagogues
attract other Jews or repel them?' Most importantly,
'How are we to reconcile Messianic synagogues with
the Word of God?'

As we talked about these things, dire predictions
were made. Again and again I heard people threaten:
'If we don't keep our families in a Messianic
congregation, our grandchildren will not be Jewish.'
One extreme statement was that, 'If we don't keep
the Law, we could wind up least in the family of God.'
Round and round the discussions went for more than
two years.

Then came the pronouncements: we will identify
ourselves as the Fourth Branch of Judaism: 'Messianic
Judaism'. We will establish 'Messianic Synagogues'.
We will proclaim our leaders to be 'Rabbis'. We will
declare that we are NOT Christians! We are Messianic
Jews!!!

Though I met some wonderful people in the
'Movement', who seemed fulfilled by it, I soon realised
that most of them had not been raised as 'Jews' or,
indeed, were not Jewish! And they were making a

very serious mistake: They were equating ALL of Jewish life with synagogue life. As I realised these things, I also realised that I was losing my joy.

Why? For many reasons that we need not discuss at this time. Suffice it to say that I was being encouraged to focus more on my 'Jewishness' than on my new life as a follower of Messiah Jesus! That is when I felt the Lord guiding me to leave the Movement. Afterwards, I thought: 'Well, Telchin, now you have really done it.'

'You took your feet out of the traditional Jewish community and put them into the Messianic Congregation.'

'Now you have taken your feet out of the Messianic Congregation.'

'So where will you put your feet now?'

'How will you retain your identity as a Jew – and as a believer?'

Sobering questions. The only answer I could come up with was that I had to set my feet upon the Rock. I had to put my total trust in the Word of God and in Jesus, my Messiah, Saviour and Lord. As I continued to study the Scriptures, the weeks stretched into months and the months into years. I came to understand a number of things that have brought me much peace. Let me share some of them with you.

I am a Jew. I was born a Jew. I have lived a Jewish life. And I will die a Jew. No one made me a Jew. No rabbi. No teacher. No organisation. My Jewishness was not conferred upon me by public opinion or by government edict. No one has the right or the power to take my identity as a Jew away from me, no matter how much they would like to do so. Even if it were possible for me to reject my Jewish identity and heritage, I would never do so. As a matter of fact, I am so comfortable and so secure in my Jewish identity that I am not threatened by the fears and anxieties of some who would question it.

But hear me on this: My Jewish identity is not based upon external form or actions. My Jewish identity is not based upon whether or not I attend a synagogue. My identity as a Jew is an inner reality. It is a God-given reality.

Accordingly, I am not to become embroiled in the futile tasks of trying to verify or justify my identity as a Jew to anyone. I don't have to prove my Jewishness. Not to other Jewish believers. Not to the Jewish community. Not to the United Jewish Appeal. Not to the State of Israel and not to the church.

More importantly, I learned that my 'Jewishness' is not the real issue. I can't imagine anyone rushing into the arms of the Lord because of my 'Jewishness'! It is my relationship with God that will provoke them to jealousy. 'If Jesus truly is my Saviour and the Lord of my life, my identity really needs to be in Him.'

As I continued to study the Scriptures, I found more and more confirmation of this truth. My study of the epistles brought me great peace. They focused my attention upon the Word of God and the promises of God. They taught me to feast on the Word of God. They also told me to meditate on God's Word.

One portion of Scripture on which I meditated was the Apostle Paul's statement in Romans 2:25. He wrote, 'Circumcision has value if you observe the Law, but if you break the Law, you have become as though you had not been circumcised.' As I thought about that truth, I substituted the word 'Jewish' for the word 'circumcision' and applied it to myself. 'Being Jewish has value if I observe the Law, but if I break the Law, I have become as though I was not Jewish.' I was truly stunned, as I struggled with that truth.

As I read Galatians 1:10, I was challenged in another way ... Paul wrote: *Am I now trying to win the approval of men, or of God?* As I meditated on this verse, I realised, with the Apostle, that if I am trying to please men, I will not be a faithful servant of the Messiah.

In his letter to the Ephesians, Paul said something else that was critically important to me: in Chapter 2 verse 14, writing of the fears and concerns, which existed among Jewish and Gentile believers of that time, Paul wrote: *For He Himself is our peace, who has made the two one and has destroyed the barrier, the dividing wall of hostility, by abolishing in His flesh the Law with its commandments and regulations. His purpose was to create in Himself one new man out of the two, thus making peace and in this one body to reconcile both of them to God through the cross, by which He put to death their hostility.*

When Paul wrote these words, he was addressing a misunderstanding of the Law. Today, for many Jewish believers, the issue is not the Law at all. It is our flesh. Our concern is more about ourselves and the Jewish community than about God!

Paul stressed that there is one body and one Spirit, one Lord, one faith, one baptism, one God and Father of all, who is over all and through all and in all. He challenged us not to be infants, tossed back and forth by waves and blown here and there by the teachings and concerns of men.

Instead, he urged us to speak the truth in love and to grow up into him who is our Head. In 2 Corinthians 5:16 Paul declared: *from now on we regard no one from a worldly point of view.* Oh, how that verse impacted me. I was guilty of regarding almost all men from a worldly point of view. Then Paul explained that if anyone is in the Messiah he is a new creation; the old has gone – the new has come! Old things have passed away. Behold! All things have become new!

We Jews and Gentiles – who are in the Messiah – are all new creations, unlike any creations, which ever existed before. We Jews and Gentiles who believe are equally new creations! In God's sight there is no difference between us. In our sight there is to be no difference. We were saved in the same way. We have the same mission to accomplish. We have the same responsibility while we are on earth, and we will all receive the same reward.

As a result of my study and prayer, I came to this understanding: celebrating my Jewishness is not what

God wants of me. Nowhere in his Word does he tell me to do this. But he does want me to be transformed into the image of his Son – who always did what his Father told him to do. I am to put off my old earthly concern for the approval of men as I rejoice in the approval of God. I am to put on the grace and peace, that God himself has provided for me. Every day of my life, I am to follow after that peace which passes understanding. I am to continually seek the wisdom that comes from above. I am to avoid wrath and anger and striving, as God's love nature becomes manifest in me. I don't have to dance to the drumbeats of 'custom' or of 'tradition' or of 'old hatred' or of 'fear'.

My God reigns! In him, I live and move and have my being! I am complete in him! There is nothing more to add! No 'ic' and no 'ism'! Nothing can be taken from me either. I am a child of the King. I am sealed in his love. He knows every hair on my head and every thought in my heart. He has forgiven me of all my hard-heartedness and sin. He has called me to be his ambassador. He has called me to proclaim his nature and his love. He wants me to walk in love and in unity. He wants me to live a life of integrity. He wants me to speak the truth in love. He wants me to walk in agreement with him and with others who are in agreement with him. He has shown me that I am not accountable or responsible for what other people think or do. I am only accountable for all that I think and do.

For fourteen years, he called me to be a pastor. For the past six years, I have served as an evangelist, to the Jew first, but also to the Gentile. He has equipped me to share the miracle of his love with all who have ears to hear. I rejoice over all of these things. I rejoice too, that when my earthly days are done, I will spend eternity with him and with all my brothers and sisters – Jews and Gentiles alike.

In view of all of these scriptural truths, in view of all that God has already done in my life, how could I not let my fleshly cares, fears and concerns about my identity as a Jew disappear? How could I not let my spirit soar in appreciation of his grace? How could I not totally trust my Jewish Saviour?

Now we come to the application of this message to your life. In all that I have written about myself, I have had you in mind. If you are a Jewish believer, I'm sure that, at one time or another, you have wrestled with Jewish identity issues even as I did. It may be that you are still struggling with them. If that is where you are today, then God has guided me to prepare this message specifically for you.

But my message also has value for you, if you are not Jewish. You may be struggling with different kinds of identity issues or you may know people who are. So here is your word of encouragement:

Just as God waited years for me to apply to my life the scriptural truths I have just shared with you ... so he is waiting for each believer to apply them to his or her life. Especially with regard to our very identity, each of us must know that we can totally trust our Jewish Saviour.

FOUNDATIONS

In the following pages, I propose to discuss the Messianic Movement. I wish to examine its assumptions, claims, practices and theory and to weigh them in the balance of biblical truth. I do so as an honest friend and brother. The longings that motivate the Messianic Movement, to know God better, to serve him better and to be more effective in addressing our nation with the gospel, throb in my heart as well. Since such an examination is inevitably a controversial subject, it is important that we lay down a number of agreed foundations from the outset.

1. *Biblical Assumptions*
Surely, all God-fearing individuals who believe that Jesus is the Saviour of the world agree that everything we do in the service of the gospel should be grounded in his Word (Lev. 11:44; 19; 20:2, 26) and directed at his glory (1 Cor. 10:31). Its reason, its logic, its mode and its goal should all be the product of God's commanded will. Human reason, human needs and human preferences should all be made subservient to the divine 'thus says the Lord' which commands

our obedience and governs our every act, especially with regard to worship. If we frame our actions without reference to the Word of God, it is because *there is no light* in us (Isa. 8:20). It is God's Word that brings light.

We are not free to do in the service of God whatever we deem wise, useful or effective (1 Sam. 13:8-14; 15:2-3, 9, 13-23). It is high time for us to confess that we are not wise enough to identify what is truly useful or effective in ultimate and spiritual terms – and that 'ultimate' is all that really matters. Appearances have often deceived us (1 Sam. 16:7). Short-term advantages have turned out to be long-term mistakes. What we have considered to be the very best has sometimes turned out to be the worst of all possibilities.

We are servants of God, conveying *his* message, doing *his* work and promoting *his* glory. God's work is to be done in God's way. There is no room for human ingenuity, except in the faithful and careful application of the Word of God in a manner that is true to its original meaning.

Nor is there any need to innovate – are we wiser than God (Rom. 16:27; 1 Tim. 1:17)? Have we a better perception of the circumstances to be addressed, of the challenges to be faced, of the pitfalls to be avoided or of the opportunities to be utilised? Of course not. We are but dust and our Lord is the eternally wise one (Prov. 8:14; Jude 25). Every act we undertake should therefore be an act of worship, an expression of loving obedience rather than of our vaunted wisdom.

Nowadays, gospel work is perceived as a means to meet human needs. Man needs forgiveness, salvation from hell, comfort in life, a sense of a loving community and the like. The gospel is often presented as the panacea for human ills and the resolution of all human problems. However much truth there is in such statements, that is not the biblical perspective. In the Bible, the chief reason for preaching the gospel is to glorify God (Isa. 40:2; Eph. 1:6). It is from this biblical perspective that I wish to conduct our discussion of the pros and cons of Messianic Judaism as against those of a Jewish Christian identity. However much we might disagree at the outcome, I am confident that we can and will agree on this basic foundation: whatever we do should be done to the glory of God and according to the Word of God.

In order to achieve this goal, we need to learn to think and to speak clearly. Of course, all such discussions must be carried out in love, but it will not do to cloud our intentions and to cloak our sincerest thoughts with words that can be taken to mean whatever our hearer wants to hear.

The only way we will grow is if we have the confidence to disagree with each other graciously, listen to each other kindly, argue our case before each other clearly and respectfully, and have the guts to examine our positions and correct them if they are discovered to be wrong. Barrett (Barrett C. K. and Martin Hengel, *Conflicts and Challenges in Early Christianity*, edited by Donald Hagner, published 1999 by Trinity Press International, Harrisburg PA) speaks of 'the importance in theology of saying exactly what you mean and not using compromise formulas that can be interpreted in more ways than one or attempting to let everyone have at least a bit of his own way. To become as a Jew to the Jews is good as a matter of social courtesy; as a way of salvation such occasional obedience would be worse than no obedience at all' (p. 74).

For this reason, we will endeavour in the course of this paper to measure the issues at stake from the perspective provided by the Word of God. Other considerations will be admitted only as secondary, and these should never be allowed to determine a course of action or formulate what purports to be a biblical response to the pressing and important questions troubling us. He has given us his Word as a light for our feet. The closer we adhere to it, the less likely are we to err by unintentionally compromising the truth.

I deny the right of any other consideration to impinge upon the authority of the Word of God. What is more, I am confident that most of my readers will agree with me. Together, therefore, we must question that modern theory of missions commonly known as 'the Church Growth Movement', originally formulated in the Fuller School of World Missions under the tutelage of Dr Donald McGavern. The assumptions that underlie that theory are largely anthropological and sociological, not biblical. Dr McGavern's school of thought claims that, if a certain method of proclaiming the gospel addresses a perceived human need, it should be used to promote the gospel. The fault with such a view rests in its focus: it has to do with human needs, human wishes, human cultural practices and human preferences rather than with obedience to God, subservience to his will, seeking his glory, and recognising his full and rightful rule over all that is. In other words, it is centred on man and human society instead of on God and his truth.

Such an approach lacks the biblical undergirdings of faith in an almighty, sovereign God who bends the hearts of men and women according to his will, in spite of their perceived needs, and sometimes contrary to them. It lacks a thoroughly biblical recognition of the depth of sin and its power over man, and of the nature of the saving work of the Holy Spirit in persuading sinners, granting them faith and repentance through regeneration, and in uniting them with the Saviour in his death and resurrection. If God can make the very stones cry out for him, can he not break through every barrier that the devil may set up to block the spread of the gospel? Can he not lay aside every contrived objection, however well founded, even for 2,000 years?

Salvation is, from beginning to end, an act of God, not a human achievement (Ps. 3:8; Jonah 2:9). None but God can impart it, and there is nothing we can do to make his action more effective. The very best we can do is to falteringly obey. We are to preach God's gospel in God's way, and trust him to do his own divine work in spite of our weakness. Any kind of 'faith' in Jesus, which is not the unmixed product of divine blessing on our labours, is not the faith that saves or sanctifies.

Regrettably, there is reason to fear that a significant proportion of Jews who profess faith in Jesus do not perceive him to be all that the Bible teaches. This might be an astonishing statement, but I am honestly concerned that there might be some among us who profess to have had their sins forgiven through Messiah, yet who have never come to a true recognition of their sinful nature. Such people have never repented, nor cast themselves on the mercy of God, who forgives sinners by his undeserved grace and transforms them by his irresistible power. In spite of their protestations to the contrary, they remain in their sins.

The gospel has become in the hands of some evangelists merely the best of all religious choices. It is disconcertingly possible that at least some Jews who profess to believe in Jesus have been impacted by a gospel shaped to meet man's conscious needs and hopes, that they have embraced a form of faith that has little to do with a biblical fear of God, which is the foundation of any true wisdom (Prov. 1:7). There is in their hearts no submission to God's objective will (Exod. 19:5; Deut. 13:4; 1 Sam. 15:22; John 14:15; 15:10, 14). There is no ongoing, committed struggle against sin, which aims to obscure the glory of God and to remove him from his throne.

I am not eager to argue with my brethren. But the concerns mentioned above leave me little choice. I must enter the fray and challenge assumptions that have regretfully become common among a growing number of those presently engaged in the evangelisation of the Jewish people.

I sincerely believe that it is wrong on the part of my

fellow Jewish believers in Jesus to define Jewishness in terms of the Mosaic Law or of rabbinicism, because rabbinic Judaism is not Jewish. I believe that it is equally wrong to import into our worship and the practice of our faith – lock, stock and barrel – customs that are the product of rabbinic religious culture. Rabbinicism is not biblical. Instead of being embraced, rabbinic Judaism should be challenged. It is high time that the rabbis' usurpation of Jewish national identity is brought to an end and that Jesus be crowned as the only true 'King of the Jews'. Nothing less is my goal and heart's cry as I write this book. Through it I hope to invite you to join me in biblical aspiration, in an effort to love God better and to serve him more faithfully.

2. Who Am I?

One issue I wish to lay to rest at the beginning of this discussion is my attitude to being Jewish: first, I am Jewish. I was born in the Jewish community of Boston, Massachusetts, to which my family immigrated after fleeing the pogroms in Russia. My maternal grandfather's name was Potashnick and he was a well-known cantor in the community of my hometown.

My parents met and married in Boston and my father worshipped in the conservative synagogue of the city of his choice (Dallas, Texas) until the day he died. After my parents were separated, my mother immigrated to Israel in 1953 with my younger brother and me. I was about ten years old.

I grew up in Israel, served in the army, met the delight of my earthly life and married her. In fact, ours was the first Jewish-Christian wedding ever to be held in Israel. It was attended by practically the whole of the Jewish-Christian community. Our three daughters have all served in the Israeli army. I was honourably released from military duties in 1985.

Second, I love being Jewish. My family greets the Sabbath each Friday night with a traditional Sabbath meal and we celebrate all the biblical and traditional feasts with gusto. If you think this constitutes a contradiction to my earlier statements, read on.

I sincerely believe that being Jewish is a calling from God (1 Cor. 7:24), and I gladly embrace it with gratitude. I also believe that the continued existence of an identifiable Jewish entity within the body of Messiah is a testimony to God's faithfulness, and that it will somehow be a means in the hands of God for Israel's conversion (Isa. 29:13-24), for which I long, pray and labour. As the text just referred to from Isaiah says, Israel's conversion is linked to a time when the nation takes note of a body of people *in his midst* which is recognisably both Jewish and the work of God's hands.

In his commentary on that passage, E. J. Young puts it this way: 'among the physical children of Jacob there will be found his true children, who are the work of God's hands'. Then, says the Lord, *those who are wayward in spirit will gain understanding; those who complain will receive instruction.* I also believe that the salvation of Israel is a promised future act of God's grace toward his covenant people (Rom. 11:26-27), and that it will be such a means of blessing to the world that Paul can find nothing else to which to compare it but *life from the dead* (Rom. 11:15).

So, I do not argue here against the right, need or legitimacy of a Jewish Christian entity living concurrently within the body of Messiah and as an integral part of our nation. I am privileged to serve a congregation of believers in Israel, which has long been in the forefront of open evangelism, social responsibility and the absorption of immigrants in the country. A high percentage of our congregation are Jewish and, since so many of them had been stripped of their national culture by the totalitarian communist regime that ruled the USSR, we have taught them the cultural practicalities of Jewishness. The issue I hope to raise in this book does not question the legitimacy of a distinctly Jewish-Christian entity. Rather, it has to do with the form many of my betters have chosen to accord that entity, and with the biblical arguments they raise in defence of that form.

Third, more than being Jewish, I love being a child of God's grace. The thought that all my sins have been forgiven because the Son of God loved me and gave himself for me never ceases to amaze. To think that, in spite of my terrible failures, God will glorify himself in me, bring me into his presence with great joy and transform me into the image of his Son, is something that I would find impossible to believe if the Bible did not give me solid reason to do so and the Spirit did not witness with my spirit that I am a child of God.

There is nothing in the entire world more important to me than to please God, love him more purely and carry out his will more faithfully. There are also very few things in the world that I desire more than that others – especially my own beloved people – would love the God of our fathers – Father, Son and Holy Spirit – and that they would join us in this pilgrimage through the present world, seeking to love and serve him with all their hearts, souls, minds and strength.

Fourth, there is absolutely no conflict between my being Jewish and my being Christian, in spite of the terrible and shameful history of relations between the Jewish people and many who bore the name of my Saviour. Anti-Semitism is as contrary to the teaching of the Bible as darkness is contrary to light. But, if the irrational ever occurred (that is more than a distinct possibility in this sin-crazed world) and I was forced to choose between my Jewishness and my Saviour, I would choose Jesus any day. In choosing Jesus I would be choosing God himself. Only he can save. Only he is worthy of total, unreserved and sacrificial devotion. Jewishness without the Saviour is like heaven without God.

As I said before, my faith in Jesus is not in conflict with my Jewish identity. Quite the contrary. True Jewishness is wrapped up in Jesus because he is the fulfiller of the promises to the fathers, the accomplisher of the covenant God made with the patriarchs and of the covenant he made with their sons when he led them out of Egypt. What now passes for Jewishness is not Jewish, it is a 2,000 yearlong aberration that demands rectification – but I will be dealing with these issues later in our discussion.

The main point I want to make here is that I am in full agreement with the basic tenets that motivate the movement I here criticise. The issue I wish to raise here is not that of Jewishness but of faithfulness to the Messiah. It is my firm conviction that the Messianic Jewish Movement has erred in important areas of the truth, and that the result of such errors is a misinformed spirituality that needs to be corrected by the Word of God. I am also disconcertedly convinced that the Messianic Movement has sparked a trend that will lead increasingly further from biblical truth.

3. *Definitions*

We had best get our terms clear from the outset. The term 'Messianic Jew' is used in this book over against the terms 'Jewish Christian' and 'Hebrew Christian'. Jewish Christians and Hebrew Christians define themselves as belonging to the Jewish people while they reject Judaism's claim to have the right to determine what is Jewish. They adhere, to varying degrees, to national customs formulated by Old Testament and rabbinic injunctions, but do so as a matter of national custom, not of religious obligation. They believe that Judaism as a religion constitutes a departure from the biblical norms. They consider it to be a religion that inevitably concludes in a rejection of Jesus and of the faith that he taught. Hebrew and Jewish Christians believe that the unity of the body of Messiah should have expression in congregational form, with mixed congregations of Jews and Gentiles, each living according to their respective customs at home but worshipping in a culture that does not exalt one culture over against another.

While Jewish and Hebrew Christians acknowledge that the gospel should be couched in terms that are both understandable and relevant to the body of people addressed by it, they do not believe that such conceptualisation should be allowed to affect the essence of the gospel. They believe that Jewish people in the Messiah are free from the Mosaic Law, while they are also free to keep those aspects of it that do not now obscure the gospel.

Messianic Jews, on the other hand, call for the implementation of a platform of what is commonly described as 'Messianic Judaism'. In its most consistent forms, the movement for Messianic Judaism (commonly know as 'the Messianic Movement', the term we shall adopt in the course of this discussion) insists upon the establishment of Messianic synagogues led and instructed by 'rabbis', encourages the use of traditional synagogue attire (kippot – head coverings, and talitot – prayer shawls), the prominent placement of a Torah scroll in the house of worship and at least some measure of adherence to rabbinic custom as a matter of religious duty. As such it is allowed to define modes of worship, and lifestyle, theological terminology, sometimes also dietary and dress codes. I will document my statements as we proceed. Messianic Judaism is that view of the gospel and of life in the presence of God, which is affirmed and practised by adherents of the Messianic Movement.

We have no argument with those who insist on the continuance of Jewish identity in Christ. Nor have we an argument with those who understand that Jewish custom is the language of their life and therefore the terms in which to express their biblical faith in Christ, so long as that language is informed by truly biblical injunctions.

The rationale of the Messianic Movement is, above all, its insistence upon the need, justification and wisdom of separate congregations for Jewish believers in Jesus, in which Jewish religious practice is adhered to in varying degrees of devotion. The goal – highly commendable in itself – is to create within the Jewish people a distinct entity that will be recognisably Jewish and, at the same time, true to the gospel and therefore uniquely capable of presenting the gospel to our nation. In order to achieve this goal it seeks to create a Jewish Messianic entity within the church.

In this book we shall examine the doctrinal grounds upon which that effort is formed, as well as some of its practical consequences.

Some have gone still further by arguing that the adoption of 'a Jewish lifestyle' is an obligation incumbent on all Jewish believers in Jesus, and that a 'Torah lifestyle' is the duty of all Jews who believe in Jesus. A still smaller number insist that Torah lifestyle is spiritually advantageous to Gentiles as well as to Jews.

Originally, the Messianic Movement embraced its distinctive points of view in an effort to insist upon the right and duty of Jews to believe in Jesus, which, they insist, Jews should do *as Jews*, that is to say, as members of the covenant people. All who choose to describe themselves by any of the terms mentioned above share this central purpose. The difference between them lies in the methods used in their efforts to preach the gospel, and therefore in the underlying presuppositions which guide them in the choice of those methods.

Inevitably, this paper deals with generalisations. There are exceptions to every rule and, happily, there are exceptions to the general rule described here as 'Messianic Jewish'. I know of such exceptions myself and welcome them most heartily. Nevertheless, the generalisations used in this paper faithfully describe the majority of those who adhere to the Messianic Movement, at least of the direction to which the views of the Movement inexorably lead.

This may easily be demonstrated by a visit to most Messianic congregations anywhere in the world, except in Israel (where most congregations are, in fact, Jewish-Christian even if they are generally designated as Messianic). In most Israeli 'Messianic' congregations, rabbinic lore plays a very small part in congregational life and, on the whole, is limited to the celebration of the traditionally Jewish feasts in a moderately traditional Jewish manner. This is done without according those terms an inherent religious significance except as they are taken to portray the person and work of Jesus – an issue we will discuss later. So, while Israeli congregations insist on being described as 'Messianic' when speaking in English (the Hebrew term 'Meshichi' includes both Jews and Gentiles), most of them are poles apart from the practices, and assumptions that underlie those practices in Messianic congregations overseas.

In Israel, the term 'Meshichi' serves to include all those who, in English, would be described as evangelical Christians, Jewish or otherwise, including Lutherans, Baptists, Anglicans, Pentecostals, Charismatics and others. American Messianic Jews mistakenly insist that the Hebrew term would best be translated as 'Messianist', or something of the kind. In terms of the semantic meaning of the Hebrew, they are correct. But in terms of the word's common use, they are wrong. Meshichi means, pure and simple, evangelical Christian. Notsri, on the other hand, means simply Christian – of any stripe.

The term 'Messianic Movement', as used in this book, is therefore not intended to include most Israeli congregations. Most of these were not formed on the basis of national distinctions, do not follow the practices of Diaspora Messianic Judaism and do not identify with most of the views of the Messianic Movement. Rabbinic lore plays a very small part in the congregational life of most Israeli 'Messianic' congregations and, on the whole, is limited to the celebration of the traditionally Jewish feasts in accordance with some traditional Jewish custom.

Having said that, it is necessary to recognise that there is a growing tendency among some Israeli congregations to emphasise their Jewishness in terms of the American-born Messianic Movement. In such cases, our conclusions are relevant to that community as well.

Section A:

A Theological Assessment

SHOULD WE PREACH
TO THE JEWISH PEOPLE?

The Jewish people need to hear the gospel. It is almost embarrassing to have to insist on this but, surely, it is more embarrassing to hear it questioned in spite of evangelicalism's long-term acquaintance with the Word of God. Time and time again the apostles addressed the people of Israel with the gospel, calling them to repent, to turn from their sins (Acts 2:38; 3:19; 8:22, etc.) and from their unbiblical religiosity (Acts 3:13-14; 5:28-29; 7:42; 10:28), and to submit to the Messiah God had sent the nation in accordance with his promises to the fathers.

You see, Jews are sinners too. Like Gentiles, they need forgiveness because, like Gentiles, they will perish in their sins unless granted salvation by virtue of the sacrifice of Messiah.

The apostles did not preach one gospel to the Jews and another to the Gentiles. Rather, they preached as did Paul to those in Damascus, in Jerusalem and throughout the region of Judea, the one and selfsame gospel that was later preached to the Gentiles, namely, *that they should repent and turn to God* (Acts 26:20).

Do we Jews need to turn to God? We most certainly do. Is Israel not the people who always served their Maker? We most certainly are not, as even a superficial survey of the Old Testament will clarify. We Jews need Jesus because we are sinners as much as anyone else. We need to be forgiven. We need to be converted (the old word for 'turned') from sin to God. We need to repent. We need a Saviour because we cannot save ourselves and no one else can do it for us. Jesus is that promised Saviour.

Nothing less than the outline given above is the gospel. Nothing less should be preached to the Jewish people or to any other body of sinners. How it is to be preached is another matter, but at least this much should be clear: the one gospel addresses Jew and Gentile alike. There is no difference, for *all have sinned and fall short of the glory of God* (Rom. 3:23).

The gospel is not 'come to Jesus and be happy'. It is not 'accept Jesus' or 'believe that he is the Messiah and you will find wonderful purpose in life'. It is, pure and simple, 'repent', acknowledge your rebellion against God and your inability to make sufficient amends to a perfectly holy Maker. Despair of yourself and turn to him in shame and in longing, with a keen awareness of your need. Cast yourself upon his grace and beg him for forgiveness (why have men forgotten to beg God for anything but healing, or a new car?). Trust in his love but do not take it for granted. Rely on him and be saved because he graciously promises to save all who call upon him *in spirit and in truth.*

It is not a matter of 'come fulfil your Jewishness' but of 'recognise your sinfulness, both as a human being and as a child of the covenant God made with your forefathers, Abraham, Isaac and Jacob, and admit your inability to do anything about it'. Acknowledge the fact that you are lost, without God and without hope in the world, unless God shows you mercy in Christ.

We Jews need to have that gospel proclaimed to us. We need the gospel as much as do the Gentiles.

HOW SHOULD WE PREACH THE GOSPEL TO THE JEWISH PEOPLE?

Should the gospel be preached in a different way to Jews? To some extent, yes, on condition that the *mode* of preaching is not allowed to modify the *content* of our message nor become paramount in relation to the message itself.

There is no sense in preaching in Hebrew, Greek or Aramaic just because the apostles did so, if our audience can only understand French, English or Swahili. The apostles accommodated the mode of their message to their hearers. Simon Peter did so in Jerusalem when he appealed to the covenant, the prophets and the promises (Acts 3:12-26). Paul did not preach in Athens (Acts 17:16-34) in the same way he preached in the synagogues of Southern Galatia (Acts 13:16-41), Asia or Europe. He used terms that showed the relevance of the gospel to his hearers and that could be understood by them. We should preach the gospel to the Hutus in a way that differs from how we preach it to the Danes, and to the modern

Mr Sophisticate in a way that differs from how we preach it to the despairing streetwise children of Brazil.

But it must always be the same gospel, couched in different terms and approached from different directions, but identifiably identical to all peoples.

Of course there is room for contextualising the way we present the gospel! Paul always began with the common grounds between his message and his hearers. Did the audience believe in an unknown God (Acts 17:23)? Then he would declare to them the revealed nature of that unknown God. Did they acknowledge a providential relationship between life and the Maker and Sustainer of all? Then he would appeal to that knowledge (Acts 17:24-25). Did they identify with the history of Israel (Acts 13:16-41)? Paul, as did Peter (Acts 2:16-36) and Stephen before him (Acts 7), would establish his witness on that common denominator.

But, please note, the terms in which the apostles couched their message were those that the gospel most readily addressed within the culture and the circumstances of their hearers. These, therefore, were the points that served as a starting point for the preaching of the gospel. Once the gospel was preached and believed, culture was subjected to a gradual transformation that utterly changed its inward parts, even if some outward aspects of that culture remained.

Where those aspects conflicted with the gospel (the use of idols, for example, the awe in which supposed holy places were approached, the attribution of deity to material objects, the separation of Jews from Gentiles or the superiority of being Jewish), they were blown to the wind, much like the books of sorcery were burned by the new believers in Ephesus.

The apostles did not stick out like a sore thumb in the cultures they addressed. Paul accommodated himself to his audience (1 Cor. 9:20), so long as this did not threaten the fabric of the gospel (Gal. 2:5). For us that means that we preach to the Jews primarily from the Old Testament, that we will appeal to them through the promises given to the fathers. We will present Jesus as the fulfilment of Old Testament promise, hope, ritual, symbol and history. It does not mean that we will embrace Jewish religious custom or that we will fashion our worship in primarily cultural Jewish terms.

As we shall see later on, there is a very important difference between evangelism and congregational life. There is also a big difference between religious authority as represented by rabbinicism, and cultural mores represented by customs of the Jewish consensus. Paul and the other apostles did not embrace the respective cultures they visited. They did not identify with those cultures. They moved comfortably from one culture to another without hesitation (1 Cor. 9:19-23). They were Jews to the Jews, Gentiles to the Gentiles, as under the Law to those who were under the Law and as without Law to those who had no knowledge of the Mosaic Law.

'Ah. But the Jews are special!' I can hear you say and, to some extent, I agree. But does this mean that the restraint I mentioned above is lifted? Does it mean that we preach a different gospel when we address the Jewish people? Absolutely not. The gospel – the very same gospel – is *to the Jew first and also to the Gentile* (Rom. 1:16). Peter preached to Cornelius (Acts 10) exactly what he preached to his fellow Jews in Jerusalem, and both groups were accepted on the same grounds (Acts. 11:17-18). This must be extremely clear, otherwise we will find ourselves inadvertently wandering into strange fields, corrupting the gospel by modifications that are meant to further its cause but in fact distort and hinder it.

A Jew to the Jews
One of the failings of the Messianic Movement can be seen in the inconsistency of its claims in relation to Paul's statement that he became a Jew to the Jews (1 Cor. 9:20). The Movement frequently explains to

objectors that its motive is purely evangelistic. But the Movement's arguments far exceed those relating to evangelistic considerations: many Messianic Jews argue that Jews in Messiah *must*, as a matter of faithfulness to God, remain Jews, and that the means to do so is by adherence to rabbinic custom – without defining the nature of that adherence. Is it indeed a matter of religious obligation or are we Jewish believers merely embracing the cultural symbols by which our people identify themselves? Paul vociferously opposed among his converts and fellow Christians any tendencies to impose religious or national custom, as happened, for example, in the churches of Galatia. However, in modern times, Jewish Christians worshipping in churches are under tremendous pressure from Messianic Jews to leave their churches and join the Movement. Gentile Christians are sometimes encouraged to believe that joining a Messianic congregation accords one some spiritual advantage – it is 'closer to New Testament Christianity', at the very least.

Hengel writes that the conflict between an emerging 'normative (that is to say, rabbinic – BM) Judaism' and the Messianic Movement represented by the followers of Jesus centred on 'the relation between messianic redemption and the traditional validity of the temple and the Torah', with the latter two more or less comprising 'the heart of the Jewish faith'. 'Faith (*emuna*) and obedience were no longer directed primarily to the Law, which was delivered to Israel on Sinai, but to a messianic person... It is no longer Moses and the Law that mediates between God and humanity, but the Messiah, Jesus, the bringer of the new covenant (cf. Jer. 31)' (pp. 10-11).

As aptly summarised by Hengel's editor in his concluding remarks, 'the basic issue between Judaism and Christianity is "Christ and Torah, indeed, Christ or Torah. This remains the basic issue' (p. 82). And so it does today.

This is so much the case that, as Hengel indicates (p. 11), the High Priest ordered the execution, by stoning, of James, the brother of the Lord and by all accounts a Law-abiding leader, and other Jewish Christians 'as offenders of the Law' (hos paranomesanton Josephus, Ant. 20 200). In other words, Judaism rightly understood faith in Jesus to be a contradiction of continued obedience to the Torah, even when such a faith was professed by those who continued in dutiful practice of the Torah.

Their practice was, in fact, contradicted by their faith in Jesus, and the rabbis were quicker to recognise this than was the early church. Rabbinicism recognises an incipient, inevitable contradiction between practising the Torah and seeking to combine such practice with any kind of religious faith in Jesus. In that sense, rabbinicism is more biblical than modern-day adherents to Messianic Judaism. The adherents of that movement are blind to the contradiction because they are so focused on being recognised as Jewish that they have failed to reflect sufficiently on the greatness and the finality of the person and work of Jesus.

That biblically motivated understanding on the part of the rabbis is precisely why the rabbis today refuse to recognise Messianic Jews as practising a legitimate form of Judaism, and why they find it so difficult to believe the sincerity of those Messianic Jews who affirm both a faith in Jesus as Saviour and faith in the Law as a means of spiritual growth or as an expression of spiritual vitality. If being accepted by the Jewish people is the major issue, Messianic Jews will have no choice but to continually erode their biblical convictions concerning Jesus, until they finally turn their back to Messiah and embrace a wholly rabbinic Judaism. It is a matter of grave concern to note that such tendencies are increasingly evident among some Messianic Jewish groups, and their numbers are growing. Very few Messianic congregations anywhere ever hear a sermon on the doctrine of the Trinity.

In this regard Barrett (p. 69) rightly states, '[T]he Son of God ... makes compromise impossible and he himself constitutes the alternative to compromise. One does not ask, "can we give a little here and gain a little there?" One asks, "What does it mean to have Christ the Son of God as Lord and Redeemer?" When the question is so put, there is no doubt what the answer will be.' Jesus is our all in all. He is not required to 'give' one whit. If at all, it is our Jewishness that must 'give'.

The Argument from Galatians: Righteous People Live by Faith

Paul wrote his letter to the Galatians addressing just such a situation. Some in Galatia were insisting that believers are bound by virtue of their faith in Messiah to keep the Mosaic Law – all of it. Many today claim that the issue was not whether believers are free from the Law, but whether Gentile Christians should be required to keep it, or whether obedience to the Law was necessary for salvation. There are three considerations we need to take into account in our reply, each of which will be proven as we proceed in our review of the letter to the Galatians:

First, Paul's presentation of his position is based on universal principles that have to do with the gospel itself, not with matters relating to the Gentiles or to the Jews. Second, Paul takes Peter and himself as illustrations of and evidence to his point of view – and Paul and Peter were undeniably Jewish. Third, he cannot be discussing the way of salvation, because the issue at stake is not how to be saved but how those who are in Christ should live. Those who arrived from Jerusalem and taught the necessity of keeping the Mosaic Law addressed Christians (Acts 15:1), not people outside of the pale of grace. So saved here means 'enter in to the fullness of salvation'. Let us summarise Paul's argument in his letter to the Galatians:

The issue controls the Apostle's thinking from the moment go: someone was trying to convince believers in Messiah to accept the yoke of the Mosaic Law. It is immaterial here whether they were Jewish or Gentile. To do so is what Paul calls without reserve *another gospel*. To preach such a gospel is to incur the anger of God and to be in danger of condemnation from him (1:6-9).

Paul refers to his own *previous way of life in Judaism* (1:13) to his former advancement *in Judaism* and to his former great zeal *for the traditions of my fathers* (1:14). Note that he speaks of these as a thing of the past and juxtaposes such former commitments with the present by use of the word *but* in verse 15, going on to say, *but when God, who set me apart from birth and called me by his grace, was pleased to reveal his Son in me...* (1:15-16). Former adherences had a terminus, an end. Their end came when God chose *to reveal his Son* in Paul. From that moment on they became a thing of the past.

He did not then return to Jerusalem, to relearn his traditions in light of what he had discovered. Instead, he went to Arabia, visiting Jerusalem only three years later, after he had come to a mature understanding of the faith of Jesus. There he received apostolic approval for the gospel he preached (1:17-24), that gospel which introduced him to a wholly new set of loyalties. Judaism and Jewish religious traditions were now things of the past.

Years later, Peter, Barnabas and Paul were in Antioch, when the city received a visit from a group of men who had apparently been sent by James (2:11). Their mandate from James is not stated, but it seems like they exceeded it. Clearly, their presence intimidated Peter and Barnabas. Prior to the group's arrival, the two had practised open table fellowship with Gentile believers in the city. Now they withdrew, in accordance with Jewish religious custom. Paul was infuriated when he saw this and took them to task because, as he put it, *they were not walking according to the truth of the Gospel* (2:14). Paul's rebuke to Peter and Barnabas obviously implies that the two had acted wrongly when they reassumed a specific aspect of Judaism: the avoidance of table fellowship with Gentiles, when non-kosher food was served or likely to be served. In fact, he does not hesitate to say that their behaviour contradicted the gospel.

In acting as if they were still bound by those limitations Peter and Barnabas were *not walking according to the truth of the Gospel*. This will become clearer as we proceed in our study of the letter. Paul embarrassed the two by publicly stating that, before the group arrived from Jerusalem, when they – or at least Peter – were leading lives more consistent with the gospel, they lived like Gentiles (2:14). This shows the kind of life Peter led until he came under pressure from the Jerusalem emissaries. He did not live as a Jew. He *lived like a Gentile*.

Paul then begins his theological argument: *We*, he says, that is to say, he, Peter and Barnabas, *who are Jews by birth* (2:15-26), have stopped looking to the Law. Instead, we *have put our faith in Messiah Jesus* (2:16).

Rebuilding What We Have Destroyed
At this point some exclaim, 'That is just the point! Paul is not arguing against the keeping of the Mosaic Law as such, but against those who insist that the keeping of the Law is necessary for justification'. Not quite. Whatever the group from Jerusalem might have said to the Galatians, they did not challenge Peter and Barnabas about the way one is justified by God, but as to how they two, and the Gentiles with whom they fellowshipped, should live as believers in Messiah. The issue of justification, as we commonly understand the term, could have never entered the picture because

they and the Gentiles with whom they had table fellowship were already known to be justified.

The biblical view of salvation always considers the new birth, faith, justification and sanctification as a whole, made up of inseparable parts. You cannot be born again without being justified, and you cannot be justified without being sanctified (Rom. 8:28-30). True, sanctification is something that becomes increasingly evident as one grows in Messiah, but the extent to which our sanctification becomes visible is a measure of our justification. All the justified are *saints, sanctified in Messiah Jesus* (1 Cor. 1:2). We will see this more clearly as we continue our overview of Paul's letter to the Galatians.

Let us return to Paul's argument in 2:17-21. What does Paul say there? In verse 18 he talks about rebuilding what he had previously *destroyed*. What is he talking about? Very simply, he is telling us that if he returned to keeping the Law (for whatever purpose, because no qualifying purpose is stated) after having stopped doing so (presumably, he, like Peter, had been *living as a Gentile*), he would be re-establishing the authority of the Law over his life. But he had turned away from the Law to Messiah! Through the Law he had become *dead to the Law* because the Law had pronounced a death sentence upon him. No, he had been *crucified with Messiah*. He had died to the Law in the death of Messiah and risen to a new life by faith in the Son of God who loved him and gave himself for him.

That glorious sacrifice was not only for his justification. It served to secure a justification that embraced the whole of salvation, including sanctification and ultimate glorification in the presence of God for all eternity. Therefore, to set the Mosaic Law back on its feet in terms of its authority to command Paul's lifestyle is to *set aside the grace of God. If righteousness could be gained through the Law, then Messiah died in vain!* (21). A horrible thought.

Paul's opening words in chapter 3 are very strong. He is convinced that the re-establishment of the Mosaic Law constitutes *another Gospel* and that it threatens the glory of Messiah as well as the salvation of the believers. He therefore calls the Galatians *foolish* for following the wishes of the group from Jerusalem, and claims they have been *bewitched* (3:1).

What kind of inconsistency have they accepted, he asks, demanding to learn from them *just one thing: did you receive the Spirit by observing the Law*? (3:2). Obviously not. *Or by believing what you have heard?* Obviously, yes. Well, then, *Are you so foolish? After beginning with the Spirit, are you now trying to attain your goal by human effort?!* Why should you think that you could be sanctified by any other means than that by which you were forgiven of your sins? Why should you think that justification is granted on the basis of faith and that sanctification – spiritual advance in salvation – is achieved by the keeping of the Law? *Does God give you his Spirit and work miracles among you because you observe the Law or because you believe what you heard?* (3:4).

Abraham

Abraham, Paul insists, illustrates his point. *He believed God and it was reckoned to him as righteousness* (3:6). So it is not Law-keepers who are considered to be Abraham's sons, but *those who believe* (3:7, 9). On the other hand, those who rely on the Law *are under a curse* because they cannot possibly *do everything written in the Book of the Law* (3:10). No one can (3:11). It is precisely from that curse, which the Law imposes upon all who do not keep it perfectly, that Messiah came to deliver us by becoming a curse for us. Righteous people live by faith, not by keeping the Law (3:11), because there is a fundamental contradiction between keeping the Law and believing (3:12), and faith is the essence of true spirituality.

Faith, not the Law, is necessary. That is why Abraham was not required to keep a Law – any law –

but to have faith. The Mosaic Law, which *was introduced 400 years later, does not set aside the covenant previously established,* because to do so would be tantamount to doing away with the promise (3:17). The Mosaic Law is not essential to godliness, but faith is. That is why the inheritance depends on faith and not on the Law (3:18). Not that the Law opposes the promises of God, but the Law cannot give anyone a part in those promises, whether justification, sanctification or the nearness of God. The Scripture declares the whole world to be a prisoner of sin, incapable of obtaining the promise through keeping the Law, so that *the promise by faith in Jesus the Messiah might be given to those who believe* (3:22).

The Mosaic Law kept us *in custody ... being shut up to the faith which was later to be revealed* (3:23), but *now that faith has come, we* (all believers, including Jewish Christians) *are no longer under the supervision of the Law* (3:25). Note again: Paul, the Jew, who is making this argument, includes himself in his statements by using the explicit terms 'we' and 'us'. All who have faith in Jesus are the sons of God quite apart from keeping the Mosaic Law, and there is in this respect no difference between Jew and Gentile, because *there is neither Jew nor Gentile, slave nor free, male nor female, for you are all one in Messiah* (26-28).

The Tutor

Paul illustrates this further from the traditions of the ancient Roman world. Children were not then considered as possessing rights until they came of age. In terms of civil privileges they were like slaves (4:1) and were subject to tutors and guides until the time set by their fathers. *So also we* (again, Paul includes himself), *while we were children, were in slavery... But when the fullness of the time had come God sent his Son... that we might receive the adoption as sons* (4:2-5), including the Holy Spirit (4:6-7), who assures us of our sonship and of our close relations with God.

So then, Paul asks, how is it, *that you are turning back to those 'weak and miserable principles'? Do you wish to be enslaved by them all over again? You are observing special days and months and seasons and years...* (4:9-10). It is worth noting what he is describing here as *'weak and miserable principles'*. He is describing the Laws of the covenant God made with Israel at Sinai. If it were not in Scripture, I would never have dared to say it, but since it is in Scripture, you and I dare not ignore it!

I plead with you, brothers, says Paul, and you can assume he is writing to a purely Gentile audience if you wish, but take note of what he says. He is seeking to persuade his listeners to leave off keeping the Mosaic Law and he says to them: *I plead with you, brothers, become like me, for I became like you* (4:12). What is he talking about?

In their effort to prove that Paul kept the Law, Messianic Jews tend to forget the full text of 1 Corinthians 9:20-21. Let's look at it for a moment because it will help us understand what Paul meant in the letter to the Galatians. Paul not only chose to adopt Jewish custom when it served his purpose among his own people, but he also lived *as without Law*, that is to say, as not under the Torah, in order to win Gentiles. Since most of his labours for the gospel were in Gentile contexts, it is fair to say that he, like Peter, *lived like a Gentile* (Gal. 2:14) for most of the time. 1 Corinthians 9:20 can in no way be construed as biblical justification for the Messianic Movement's efforts to create Messianic Judaism.

Become Like Me
That is what he is talking about when he says to the Galatians: *I plead with you, brothers, become like me* (4:12). Although I am free from the Law, in certain situations I am willing to abide by its requirements. However, I do not do so as a matter of religious duty but merely as a means to communicate the gospel.

Paul is deeply concerned about the Galatians, because they are being persuaded to keep the Law as a matter of religious duty: *My dear children, for whom I am in the pains of childbirth until Christ is formed in you. How I wish I could be with you now and change my tone, because I am perplexed about you!* (4:19-20). Paul is calling on the Galatians to learn from his example and to recognise that they are free from the obligation to keep the Mosaic Law. The very thought that they might not recognise this evokes in him grave concern.

He then turns to a further illustration, this time from earlier biblical history. Abraham had two sons, only one of which was the child of promise and therefore his legitimate heir. The other was illegitimate, born to a female slave as a product of his wife's unbelieving manipulations. But both were sons of Abraham. Couldn't they learn to live together and somehow share the promise? *What does the scripture say? 'Get rid of the slave woman and her son, for the slave woman's son will never share in the inheritance with the free woman's son'* (4:30). There is now no room for faith and grace to live in harmony with Law and Law-keeping. So then, *it was for freedom that Christ set us free* (not for us to submit to any new bondage). *Stand firm and do not let yourselves be burdened again by a yoke of slavery* (5:1).

This is a serious matter, insists the Apostle. It threatens the very heart of the gospel, because any introduction of a works principle into salvation by grace will inevitably corrupt one's understanding of grace – and it does not matter if we are talking about salvation obtained, maintained or enhanced.

Often such corruption will be a slow, imperceptible process, but it always takes place. Where works of any kind are deemed contributory to one's standing with God or nearness to him, works always displace grace. Paul's words are sharper than a sword: *Mark my words: I, Paul, tell you that if you let yourselves be circumcised, Messiah will be of no value to you at all.*

Again I declare to every man who lets himself be circumcised that he is [thereby] obligated to obey the whole Law (5:2-3). You cannot accept the Law piecemeal. It is all of a whole. Take it or leave it, but don't think you can use it for sanctification and not for justification, that you can keep kosher and celebrate the feasts as a matter of religious duty while excusing yourself on other issues such as mixed cloths, the wearing of *tsitsit* and the practice of ritual purity. There is an unbreakable link between all such uses of the Mosaic Law, just as there is between all aspects of the Mosaic Law.

Faith and Grace

That is why Paul goes on to say, *you who are trying to be justified by Law have been alienated from Messiah. You have fallen away from grace* (5:4). Why should Paul make such a statement? Why should he talk to believers about justification? These people belong to the church in Galatia. They have already been justified and received the Spirit. He describes them in chapter 4:6-8 as those who now *have the rights of sons*. God sent the Spirit of his Son into their hearts, *the Spirit who calls out, 'Abba, Father'*. Formerly they *did not know God*, but now they know him, rather, he acknowledges them. Now he writes to them about justification!

That is just the point. Their willingness to accept the yoke of the Mosaic Law indicates that they have been *alienated, fallen from grace*. Instead of trusting God for sanctifying grace, they are trying to achieve it by keeping the Law.

In their efforts, following their conversion, to achieve a greater spirituality through the keeping of the Mosaic Law, they had undergone the very process that, I insisted in the previous paragraph, was inevitable. Let me repeat what I said there: 'You can't accept the Law piecemeal, it is all of a whole. Take it or leave it, but don't think you can use it for sanctification and not for justification, that you can keep kosher and celebrate the feasts as a matter of religious duty while excusing yourself on other issues such as mixed cloths, the wearing of tsitsit and the practices of ritual purity. There is an unbreakable link between all such uses of the Mosaic Law, just as there is between all aspects of the Mosaic Law.'

In contrast with those who seek spiritual growth by keeping the Mosaic Law, says Paul, *by faith we eagerly await through the Spirit the righteousness for which we hope* (5:5). Once again, although converted, justified and greatly blessed by God, Paul speaks of his ultimate sanctification and that of his fellow believers (*we*) in terms of a *righteousness* (another word for justification), which they *await through the Spirit*. Why, '*await*'? Well, how else are they to obtain it? Full justification is a matter for the future because it includes our ultimate salvation, when we enter the presence of God and are transformed into his glorious image. *In the Messiah Jesus neither circumcision nor uncircumcision has any value.* The only thing that counts is faith expressing itself through love (5:6).

Paul then goes on in verses 6-15 to ask the Galatian Christians (remember, we are not here opposing the view that the Galatians were primarily Gentiles) and to warn them: they had begun to run well; who had interrupted their race and kept them from obeying the truth?

What is the Apostle talking about? Quite simply, he is talking about those who insisted that the Galatians were obliged to keep the Mosaic Law. In so doing they were obstructing the Galatians' run in the path of truth. In verse 10 he says that such a view of the Law throws the believer *into confusion*. In verse 11 he makes it very clear that no one can claim that the Apostle himself taught the Gentiles to be circumcised (he would hardly need to teach that to Jews). At least one principle we can derive from this statement: any effort to persuade Gentiles to keep the Mosaic Law is a deviation from the truth (5:7-9).

The Real Offence

For Paul, a believer's attitude to the Mosaic Law is no small issue. He has already indicated that it affects the gospel itself. Now he warns in this regard that *a little yeast works through the whole batch of dough* (5:9), that is to say, a minor error, or an error held by a small number of people, will have grave consequences.

Paul enlarges on this point in verses 11-12: as we have seen, the Apostle insists in verse 11 that he does not teach anyone to be circumcised. In other words, he does not call upon Gentiles to become Jewish. If he did, he would not have been persecuted, because the *offence of the cross* would have been removed from the minds of the Jewish people.

Now, that is an important statement. Paul is telling us that, already at that early time, the message of the gospel carried within itself an offence to the Jewish people, that it was repugnant to them. It is worth noting that Paul speaks in such terms long before the church adopted an anti-Semitic stance – before the Crusades, before forced conversions and before the Holocaust.

The real offence of the gospel in the eyes of a Jewish person has nothing to do with the obvious moral failure in Christianity's relations with the Jewish people. It has to do with what the gospel is in and of itself, with what it must always remain. Paul refuses to remove the offence of the cross by agreeing to preach it in a way that would satisfy Jews, because that would constitute an alteration of the substance of the gospel.

The real offence of the cross is its declaration that man can do nothing to save himself or earn any kind of standing with God, and that he is wholly dependent on God for any aspect of his salvation, be it forgiveness of sins or sanctification. That is just what the defenders of the Mosaic Law did not understand. It is what Jews as well as Gentiles do not like. Having *begun* [preaching forgiveness] *through the Spirit*, the proponents of the Mosaic Law were now teaching advancement in spiritual matters by Law-keeping. Such a view subverts the gospel because it attributes something to man. That is why Paul is so vehement in his opposition to it: *As for those agitators, I wish they would go the whole way and emasculate themselves* (5:12).

Law in the Christian life

Of course, to say that believers are no longer subject to the Mosaic Law is not to say that they are free to live as they please. The essence of the Law, its moral aspects, remain intact and find fulfilment in the process of salvation by grace through faith rather than in the doctrine of sanctification by works. As the ancients (who were wiser than we) put it, the moral aspects of the Law now serve as a guide for Christian living, while the whole remains a revelation of God and teaches us about him.

The freedom purchased for us by the blood of Messiah inevitably leads to *faith working through love* (5:6). *The whole Law is summed up in a single command: Love your neighbour as yourself.* So, life by the Spirit does not lead to gratifying the flesh but to a life of *love, joy, peace, patience, kindness, goodness, faithfulness and gentleness* (5:22-23). A life led by the Spirit rather than by the Mosaic Law will lead to the ongoing crucifixion of the sinful nature with all its passions and desires. That is what it means to belong to Jesus the Messiah (5:24): *those who are led by the Spirit are not under Law* (5:18), and yet they wholly fulfil the righteousness of the Law (see Rom. 8:1-3) *by the power of the Spirit who leads them.* On the other hand, those who live by the flesh, in an effort to keep the Law, will be subject to all the sinful motivations described in verses 19-21. *Those who live like this will not inherit the kingdom of God* (5:21).

Following some practical guidance at the beginning of chapter six, Paul returns to his subject: *Do not be deceived: God is not mocked; for what a man sows, this he will also reap. The one who sows to his own flesh shall*

JUDAISM IS NOT JEWISH

from the flesh reap corruption, but the one who sows to the Spirit shall from the Spirit reap eternal life (6:7-8). Paul is again contrasting efforts to keep the Mosaic Law with a faith that expresses itself through love and relies on the merits of Messiah alone to procure salvation in all its aspects: forgiveness, sanctification, joy, hope and ultimate glorification.

Barrett summarises the issues discussed by Paul in his letter to the Galatians as follows:

'Paul is arguing not merely that Gentiles are not to be obliged to observe the rules of purity; it is wrong for Jews, who also are justified by faith and not by works, to insist that such rules should be observed in order that they may be able to join in a meal' (p. 64).

In other words, Paul is discussing the freedom of Christian fellowship, the unity of Christian obligation to God and to one another, and the utter freedom of all who own the name of Jesus as Messiah and Saviour from any duties which were formerly recognised as binding either because they were imposed by the Torah or by rabbinic dictates. Paul preached a 'radical gospel of radically unconditional grace' (Barrett, p. 72).

That gospel was the ground of relations between man and God, and between one man and another regardless of national, social or religious background.

Well then, Paul's statements in his letter to the Galatians are as clear as a bell. We should heed the sound of its message ringing in our ears.

YES, BUT HOW ABOUT THE
EVANGELISTIC OPPORTUNITY?

Our concern should be to preach the gospel to the Jewish people, rather than to convince them that we Jewish Christians are still Jewish in spite of our faith in Jesus. I am very much aware of the fact that one of the major objections Jews raise in these days to the gospel is that their Jewishness excuses them from its claims, and that the threat it constitutes to their national identity is too real for them to ignore. We should not allow this to deflect us from our God-given calling to preach the gospel. God is able to turn the hardest of hearts and to rob the most obstinate of the ploys they might use in an effort to silence those who would preach the gospel to them.

Our focus should be where the Bible puts it: on the authority of the Word of God, the horror and bondage of sin, the inability of man to please God, the need of an atoning sacrifice, the saving work of the Holy Spirit, and the kind of life forgiven people should, and are enabled to lead for the glory of God. Instead of busying ourselves with Jewishness, we should be glorying in the one marvellous body of Messiah in which Jews and Gentiles are equal, in the hope of eternal life in the presence of God, and in the sustaining grace of a God who cannot and will not fail his erring children. Those are the issues with which the Bible is occupied. They should occupy our hearts and minds too. The most effective way to evangelise is to maintain a biblical emphasis and to focus on what the Bible makes the focus of its message.

It is time to get out of our trenches and go on the offensive. We do not need to defend our Jewishness. We need to proclaim Jesus. When we regain the confidence of our biblical convictions, when we begin to live courageously as disciples of Jesus, we are far more likely to command the respect and earn the attention of our people than we have so far succeeded in doing by equivocating about the gospel and subjecting ourselves to the obedience of what is a false religion engendered by the Pharisees. Evangelism will be best promoted by a clear message, not by one obscured by the trappings of Christ-denying Judaism.

Jesus said, *I will build my church and the gates of Hades shall not overpower it* (Matt. 16:18). The picture is a vivid one: the hordes of Hades have fled for refuge to the darkness of the pit, barred the gates and are now hoping for the best. But the army of King Jesus has arrived and is battering those gates with the Word of God. Will the gates hold? Will Satan's host be secure? Will even one of those appointed to salvation, now taken captive by Satan to do his will, remain in the hands of the enemy?

We need not wait until the end of the commercials or until the series end in order to find the answer to that question. The climax of history is already spelled out for us in Scripture. These gates will collapse under the blows of God-centred evangelism, and hell will be vanquished. Not one of those given to the Son by the

Father will be lost. All will be introduced to the presence of God with exceeding joy and all will obtain eternal life. *I have sworn by myself, the word has gone forth from my mouth in righteousness and will not turn back, that to me every knee will bow, every tongue will swear allegiance. They will say of me, Only in the Lord are righteousness and strength* (Isa. 45:23-24).

The Scriptures are full of such statements. The pessimism of modern-day evangelicalism finds no basis in Scripture because the Word of God is a fundamentally optimistic message. The book of Revelation was given in times of painful trial to assure the church yet again that God will make everything new, that the dwelling of God will be with men and that he will live with them. The redeemed will be his people and God himself will be their God. He will wipe every tear from their eyes. *There shall no longer be any more mourning or crying or pain,* for the old order of things will unquestionably pass away and God will make *all things new* (Rev. 21:3-5). The redeemed of the Lord will number ten thousand thousands, and their song of worship will be like the sound of mighty thunder, rolling over eternity to the praise, honour and glory of him who reigns in mercy and in love and whose wonder and beauty more than fills the universe.

God is sure to conquer and will do so by the gospel – without our improvements. He made the world by his word: he spoke and it was done. God the Son upholds the world by the word of his power. Nature itself functions by the power of his word: *He sends forth his command to the earth; his word runs very swiftly. He spreads the snow like wool; he scatters the frost like ashes. He casts forth his ice as fragments; who can stand before his cold? He sends forth his word and melts them; he causes his wind to blow and the waters flow* (Ps. 147:15-18). *Praise the Lord from the earth, sea monsters and all deeps; fire and hail, snow and clouds; stormy wind, fulfilling his word; mountains and all hills; fruit trees and all cedars; beasts and all cattle; creeping things and winged fowl; kings of the earth and all peoples; princes and all judges of the earth; both young men and virgins; old men and children* (Ps. 148:7-12).

God also saves by his word: *Fools, because of their rebellious way, and because of their iniquities, were afflicted. Their soul abhorred all kinds of food; and they drew near to the gates of death. Then they cried out to the Lord in their trouble; he saved them out of their distresses. He sent his word and healed them, and delivered them from their destructions. Let them give thanks to the Lord for his loving kindness, and for his wonders to the sons of men! Let them also offer sacrifices of thanksgiving, and tell of his works with joyful singing* (Ps. 107:17-22).

Jesus stood before the grave of Lazarus, dead for four days in the spring heat of the Middle East and commanded: *Lazarus, come out.* At the sound of the Saviour's word, the dead man stirred, rose from among the dead and came out of the grave, with the grave clothes still on him! Such is the message we preach. It is the *power of God.* Its words have a divine ability to demolish strongholds, arguments and every pretension that sets itself up against the knowledge of God, taking captive every thought and making it obedient to Christ (2 Cor. 10:4-5) because God is active in his word. The gospel is a message that has a life of its own because it is God's word, alive and active (Heb. 4:12). As Paul put it, *it is the power of God for salvation* (Rom. 1:16).

God will triumph in the world through the preaching of the gospel. Such preaching is the means by which he lays hold of men and women, young and old, releases them from bondage to Satan, and transforms them into a redeemed and sanctified people. The kingdoms of this world will unquestionably become the kingdom of God and of his Christ, and that through the intervention of God and the preaching of the gospel. That is why preaching – faithful preaching – is so crucial to the kingdom.

It is God who converts the sinner, not us. Evangelism is simply the faithful preaching of the gospel. That is why Paul consciously avoided displays of professional eloquence and of human wisdom when he preached. He preferred *a demonstration of the Spirit's power* (1 Cor. 2:4) so that the conversions that occurred in response to his preaching were not spurious products of human effort but the enduring fruit of God's powerful working in the hearts and minds of his hearers (ibid. v. 5).

That is the logic behind Paul's thanking God for the Thessalonians' conversion and for the spiritual and moral consequences that inevitably followed, rather than praising them for the wisdom that led them to make the right choice (1 Thess. 1:2-3). It is on those grounds that Paul could say to the Thessalonian Christians, *But we should always give thanks to God for you, brethren beloved of the Lord, because God has chosen you from the beginning for salvation through sanctification by the Spirit and faith in the truth. And it was for this he called you through our gospel, that you may gain the glory of our Lord Jesus Christ* (2 Thess. 2:13-14).

Peter reiterates this very conviction when he speaks of his readers as having been *born again to a living hope through the resurrection of Jesus Christ from the dead* (1 Pet. 1:3). How did God achieve this? Peter replies: *you have been born again not of seed which is perishable but imperishable, that is, through the living and abiding word of God ... and this is the word which was preached to you* (1 Pet. 1:23, 25). God changes individuals, communities and whole nations by the preaching of his Word, accompanied by the working of his Spirit; for the Word of God is the Spirit's sword (Eph. 6:17), by which he vanquishes Satan's opposition, frees his captives and gives life to the dead.

Once converted, we discover the power of the Spirit through the Word in the everyday of our lives. We are made increasingly spiritually and morally wiser by the Word (Ps. 119:7), encouraged and made joyful (v. 8) by it. By the Word we are kept from sin (Ps. 119:1, 4), enlightened (Ps. 119:180) and strengthened (v. 28). God moves according to his Word and through it in the lives of those who belong to him, warning them against sin (Ps. 119:9-10), teaching them the path of righteousness (Ps. 119:30) and evoking in their innermost being a desire for the things that belong to heaven (Ps. 119:97). In this way God sets the redeemed sinner on the path to eternal glory. He preserves sinners in that path, secures their safe arrival and succours them along the way by his Word.

Jesus taught his disciples how important it is that his words reside in them (John 15:7, 10). How is that done if not, among other means, by coming under the sound of the gospel as it is preached in church? The Spirit works by the Word and through it. He cleanses stumbling Christians by the washing of the water through the Word (Eph. 5:26), and they, in turn, sanctify themselves by obeying the truth proclaimed in the Word (2 Pet. 1:22).

God will overcome every opposition to his rule that Satan can throw in his way and he will do so by blessing the preaching of his Word. He converts sinners to himself through preaching, that is to say, through evangelism. The book of Revelation portrays Christ as overcoming Satan by his Word (Rev. 19:17-21 – note the sword in the mouth of our Lord). There is no room for doubt that he shall reign and every knee shall bow before him and, to the glory of God the Father, all will own Jesus as Lord.

Faithful, believing, Spirit-filled preaching of the Word of God is the means by which God prepares us for eternity. Having sanctified ourselves through obedience to the truth, we are given repeated foretastes of heaven as we contemplate the truths of God's Word and have lain out before us the wonders of heaven. The Word of the Lord teaches us to pray, informs, instils and stirs our hope, drives us to further action on behalf of the kingdom, and assures us of God's blessing as we labour for him. We Jewish Christians need to preach the gospel to ourselves, so that we are moved to trust it and live by it and by the power of God.

DO JEWS REMAIN JEWS ONCE THEY ARE CONVERTED TO MESSIAH?

Of course we do! Why should we not? If Jesus is indeed the Messiah promised to our forefathers, then there is no reason on earth (in heaven, or under the earth) why Jews should cease to be Jews in consequence of their faith in him. On the contrary, Jewishness seems to have been confirmed by that faith rather than weakened or in any way compromised by it.

To the extent that Jewishness is defined by the Bible, believing in Jesus is a very Jewish thing. It is rabbinic Judaism that is not Jewish, and that is why we should refuse to bend the knee to rabbinic dictum just because a large number of our people have done so for many years. History will yet prove that the rabbis were wrong and that Jesus is truly the Messiah of Israel because history is in God's hands not in the hands of the rabbis.

The apostles assumed that the faith they proclaimed was Jewish. They were taken by surprise when a growing number of Gentiles embraced it, and there arose a furious discussion whether or not these Gentiles should be expected to undergo a complete religious Jewish conversion and join the nation of Israel (Acts 10-11). After all, they now believed in the God of Israel and had been redeemed by the Son of Israel's hope.

Nor did any of the Jewish religious leaders of the day question the right of the Jewish disciples of Jesus to be considered Jewish. That came years later, when the rabbinic authorities succeeded in taking over the nation's machinery of self-identity and posited themselves as the sole arbiters of what Jewishness is to be. The conflict over whether or not Jesus is the promised Messiah was initially altogether an internal Jewish affair (Acts 18:15; 23:6-9, etc.).

The apostles addressed the nation with the gospel as Jews, not merely as human beings: *Men of Judea and you who live in Jerusalem* (Acts 2:14); *Men of Israel* (Acts 3:12; 13:16). They argued from the Hebrew Scriptures (Acts 2; 3:18-26; 7; 13:16-41, etc.). But the message was always the same: *Repent therefore and return, that your sins may be wiped away* (Acts 3:19); *Let it be known to you, brethren, that through him forgiveness of sins is proclaimed* (Acts 13:38).

The gospel is not a negation of Jewishness, but an affirmation of it, just as it is not a negation of Gentile identity but an affirmation of it and of God's love to them. So, Jews need not cease to be Jews in order to follow Messiah (1 Cor. 7:18). Neither should Gentiles be expected to embrace Judaism or Jewish national culture in consequence of their faith in Jesus (1 Cor. 7:18). We were bought with a price and should not, therefore, become the slaves of men (v. 23) (rabbis are, of course, men). Instead, we should each remain in that *condition* in which we were *called* (vv. 20, 24), serving the Lord as faithfully as he enables within that *condition*. In case there is any room for doubt as to what the Apostle meant, he spells it out in the opening verses of this section of his letter: *was any man called circumcised? Let him not become uncircumcised. Has anyone been called in uncircumcision? Let him not be circumcised. Circumcision is nothing and uncircumcision is nothing* (vv. 18-19).

Jews in Messiah remain Jews, and Gentiles in Messiah remain Gentiles. Both believe the gospel and are saved. Both enjoy forgiveness of sin and are baptised by the Spirit into one single body, whether Jews or Greeks, slaves or free, and both are *made to drink of that one Spirit* (1 Cor. 12:13). Jews do not cease to be Jews any more than Gentiles cease to be Gentiles, however much the Gentiles partake of the promises of God to Israel.

People sometimes mistakenly tell us that we Jewish believers in Messiah are 'Christians and nothing else'. This is as patently untrue of us as it is of anyone else. We are all also human beings, men or women, married, single or widowed, educated or unlearned, rich or poor, Swiss or American, and Jews or Gentiles. Following our conversion, every aspect of what God has made us to be should come into full fruition and serve as a channel for our loving obedience to God in every aspect of our lives.

The issue we are discussing in this book is not just what we are but how to express our being in the context of worship and obedience. There, my being married or single, poor or rich, Jewish or Gentile, should make no essential difference even if it requires, for example, worship in a different language or using different music. There is nothing inherently more biblical or spiritual in our various languages or customs. These are not to be allowed to affect the content of our worship.

IS IT IMPORTANT FOR JEWS IN
MESSIAH TO REMAIN JEWS?

It most definitely is, although we have no right to condemn any who choose to opt out of the Jewish nation, intermingle with the Gentiles and lose their Jewish identity, at least not on religious grounds, even though the loss of any Jew to the nation is painful.

On the other hand, we should unhesitatingly reject the opinion of those who, on purported biblical grounds, deny the right of Jews to remain such in Messiah, or who have themselves chosen that option for purportedly biblical reasons.

The Embarrassing Historical Facts
This has been the position of the church for almost two millennia. The church insisted that Jews who believe in Jesus are 'no longer Jewish'. The Fourth Century Confession of Faith of the church of Constantinople requires professed Jewish converts to declare: 'I do here and now renounce every rite and

observance of the Jewish religion, detesting all its most solemn ceremonies and tenets of faith that in former days I kept and held'. In other public statements, Jewish converts were required to affirm, 'I altogether... shun all intercourse with other Jews and [will] have the circle of my friends only among honest Christians', 'Nor [will I] associate with the cursed Jews who remain unbaptised'. They were called upon to promise that they would never return 'to the vomit of my former error or associate with the wicked Jews. In every respect I will lead the Christian life and associate with Christians'. As far as the family members are concerned, 'we will not on any pretext, either ourselves or our descendants, choose wives from among our own race, but in the case of both sexes we will always link ourselves with Christians'. Such stringent, unchristian language bespeaks an antagonism that must be thoroughly cleansed from the church. It also serves to insist that there is a contradiction between being Jewish and believing in the Jewish Messiah.

On this point, the synagogue has heartily agreed with the church. Indeed, short of some form of biblical theism, this is probably the only area in which church and synagogue have ever agreed. Jews who professed to have been converted to Messiah were expected by the church to disavow their national customs and effectively sever themselves from their own people, while the synagogue refused them the right to be recognised as Jews except in theory. Church edicts forbade them to wed other Jews, even if they were converts, and Jewish rabbinic edicts created situations in which Jewish believers in Jesus could no longer be effective members of their Jewish communities. There were times when Jewish converts had to prove the sincerity of their faith by eating pork in public. The rabbis created as high and as firm a barrier between Jewishness and the gospel as they possibly could, and the church gleefully but foolishly co-operated.

As a result, some Jewish converts endeavoured to prove their loyalty to their new religion by becoming enemies of their people. A shameful chapter was written in the history of Jewish-Christian relations, one that still awaits an honest historian's thorough research (Rausch, pp 16-17; Parkes, Appendix 394-400).

Any insistence upon discontinuity between Jewish identity and faith in Jesus inherently implies a discontinuity between the Old Testament and the New. In other words, the claim that loyalty to Jesus requires a rejection of one's Jewish identity is to imply that Jesus is not the Messiah promised to Israel. If he is not Israel's Messiah, he is no Messiah at all, for no other Messiah is spoken of in either the Old or New Testament!

There are no biblical grounds to require or encourage Jews to reject their national identity in order to serve God. That is why Rausch was so right to quote Fanny Peltz, a Jewish Christian, who stated that 'in accepting Jesus, I was not giving up anything Jewish!' (Rausch, p. 87). But, please note, we are speaking here of Jewishness as a *national* identity. When we speak of a *religious* identity, we must admit that we are Christians because Judaism is not biblical while the true message of Christianity is.

The rabbis claim that a change of religion necessarily leads to a loss of national identity, and the majority of our people have bought in to that theory. But it is wrong, and it is contrary to the rabbis' own Halacha (religious dictum), which states, 'Af al pi shechatah – yisrael hu' ('although he has sinned, he still belongs to Israel'). We need to challenge the rabbinic tyranny over our people, not submit to it.

History has rendered the cause of Messiah a great disservice. The anti-Semitism to which the nominal church succumbed imposed on converts a denial of their Jewishness. As we have said, this is a logical contradiction because the new-found faith of the converts was faith in him who was sent in fulfilment of divine promises given to Israel. It is but one expression of so-called 'Replacement Theology', of the nominal Christian church, which castigated Israel for its own sins while repeating them a hundredfold. I need not elaborate here. Anyone who is interested in the question of Jewish Christian identity is abundantly aware of the shameful history, the blot of which still has not been erased. So-called 'Christian anti-Semites' – a logical contradiction in terms – persecuted the Jews while doing all in their power to obliterate every trace of Jewishness in their own faith and practice. Regretfully, remnants of anti-Jewish sentiment are still to be found in many Christian pulpits and commentaries even among evangelicals.

To the Jew First But Also to the Greek
But the gospel is *for the Jew first,* and only then, *also* for non-Jews (Rom. 1:16). In making that statement, Paul was not discussing the chronological order of things. He considered it important to describe the nature of the gospel in order to explain why he was eager to preach it in Rome, and that is what he does in this justly famous verse.

Paul describes the gospel as *God's power to save.* It is in the nature of the gospel to save in a way that differs greatly from other purported 'ways' to salvation offered by the various religions of the world. Ultimately, all the other religions leave the matter of man's salvation in man's own hands. He must make up for his sins. He must pray earnestly and convincingly enough. He must make pilgrimages and placate his god by offering the right sacrifices.

Not so according to the gospel. The gospel is the great divider between the redeemed and the lost, for the gospel is not a way by which man can save himself, but *the power of God for salvation.* It is in the nature of the gospel that God is the one who saves. No wonder Paul was *not ashamed* of such a message! If God saves, then those he saved are saved beyond doubt or question.

There is more. Whom does the gospel save? *All kinds of men*, says Paul, *everyone who believes*. It is in the nature of the gospel to address everyone, just as it is in its nature to save.

Paul has another important statement to make about the nature of the gospel of which he is not ashamed and which he is so eager to preach in Rome: not only is it God's power to save, and to save everyone who believes, but it is so *to the Jew first*. That, too, has to do with the nature of the gospel because the message of God's kindness did not appear suddenly out of the blue. It is the fulfilment of Old Testament promise, the accomplishment of all that the Old Testament stands for.

What does this statement *to the Jew first,* mean? It means that the gospel is most obviously, most directly and most intentionally relevant to the Jewish people, and only then to the rest of the world. As Peter put it when he addressed his Jewish audience in Acts 3 11-26: *The things that God announced beforehand by the mouth of all the prophets ... he has thus fulfilled. Repent therefore ... that he may send Jesus, the Messiah appointed for you... It is you who are the sons of the prophets and of the covenant which God made with your fathers ... for you first God raised up his servant, and sent him to bless you by turning every one of you from your wicked ways.*

The point, I think, is this: the Abrahamic covenant still stands. The Mosaic covenant, that covenant which God made with the Jewish nation when he led them out of Egypt, has now been replaced by the new covenant that was promised in Jeremiah 31. On the other hand, the Abrahamic covenant has never been replaced. It forms the basis for the coming of Messiah (Gal. 3). Jesus came in fulfilment of that covenant in order to redeem the elect within the nation (Rom. 9:6-13; 11:1-5), as well as those among the Gentiles whom the Father has appointed to salvation.

The gifts and the callings of God are irrevocable. God will yet work savingly within the Jewish nation, so that *all Israel*[1] will be saved, as it is written: *The deliverer will come from Zion. He will remove ungodliness from Jacob* (Rom. 11:26).

The continuance of visible, identifiably Jewish Christians within the body of Messiah is therefore in no conflict with the gospel. A denial of the right of such an existence is tantamount to a denial of the Old Testament basis for the New Testament faith. The continued existence of an identifiable body of Jewish Christians within the nation of Israel is a testimony to both the church and to the nation that God remains true to his covenantal undertakings, even when Israel has failed to do likewise. It is a vivid expression of the wonder of God's grace.

In addition to reasons that issue directly from the Scriptures, there is at least one other reason why it is important for Jewish Christians to remain an integral part of their nation. The Jewish people must hear the gospel and see it lived out before them. That can be done most effectively by fellow Jews, who live and speak in the cultural language of the people, and who are able to address the nation from within. We Jewish Christians are no strangers to our people. We share in the experience of their joys and sorrows, struggle for the same national hopes, and bear the same scars of Christian and so-called Christian persecution of our forefathers. We feel the anguish of the Holocaust. We are fellows and partners with our Jewish people in their present struggles, including the struggle against assimilation and the loss of Jewish identity.

---

1. Without entering upon a lengthy discussion, which is not germane to our discussion, suffice it to state the following. *All Israel* is not the whole Jewish nation, but that remnant within the nation whom God appointed to salvation. Paul discusses this issue in his two previous chapters. See my more extended discussion of Romans 9–11 in Appendices B and C.

God has not forsaken Israel, nor will he. He loves our people by grace, and we love our people because they are ours and we theirs, no matter what they do or how they treat us, and regardless whether they acknowledge us or not. We labour for their welfare and will work and pray for their ultimate good, which we know can only be found in the Messiah.

HOW CAN JEWS IN MESSIAH REMAIN JEWS WITHOUT DENYING THE GOSPEL?

This is a crucial question, often based on the mistaken assumption already discussed, that there is some kind of contradiction between being Jewish and believing in Jesus. To put it plainly, there is no inner contradiction between being Jewish and believing in Jesus. Hopefully, none of my readers think otherwise. The question arises from a concern lest the way Jewish Christians express themselves as Jews in Christ may be in conflict with the gospel. That is what we must now explore.

National Culture
Obviously, the only way in which Jews in Messiah can identifiably be members of their nation is by the same means employed by other Jews in doing so: by practising the cultural norms adhered to by the majority of the people, adhering to the national consensus which defines, expresses and maintains

the nation's identity. On the other hand, it is their Christian duty to challenge any part of that consensus that conflicts with the gospel.

We Jewish Christians are Jewish by nationality, by race and by national custom.

We belong to the Jewish people by more than an accident of birth or the consequence of our education. We are Jews by choice, by virtue of our heartfelt and premeditated identification with our people in all aspects of their life – except their rejection of Jesus.

At present, there is an unresolved tension between our national and our spiritual identities. This tension has come about because most of our people continue to deny that Jesus is Israel's much-awaited Promised One.

Both he and his message are rejected. This tension cannot be resolved by our adopting rabbinic dictum as a way of life, or by returning to the yoke of the Torah as if Messiah had not yet come. The tension will only be resolved when our people turn to God, repent, and believe all that the Hebrew Bible and the New Testament say of Jesus. At that time, Israel will turn its back to a large part of its own national custom, because it stands in contradiction to the gospel and constitutes a rejection of the Jesus they will then adore.

Jeff Wasserman writes, 'When, at the age of twenty, I became a believer in Jesus as Messiah, I strained to find reference points in Christianity that were in any way familiar to me' (p. 1). On the one hand, if he had been made familiar at childhood with those truly Jewish themes of God – sin, grace, covenant, sacrifice, Messiah, forgiveness and so on – he would have found many of the major 'reference points in Christianity' exactly what he was looking for.

But Jeff was looking for something else. He was looking for familiar externals, rituals and customs. That is where he and many Messianic Jews have erred. What is really important can not be found in national religious customs but in the essence of the faith that a church or a nation professes.

Why should Jeff be surprised not to find familiar reference points between the faith he now professed and the customs of that faith in which he was brought up? Judaism, as developed over the last 2,000 years, is a denial of the gospel, a conscious, premeditated rejection of Christ. Jeff is simply wrong when he says, 'it was with a sense of mourning that I abandoned my Jewish heritage ... and set aside all that I had been in order to apprehend what I had become in Christ' (p. 2). He did not need to abandon his Jewishness in order to apprehend God's gifts in Christ.

It is amazing to note what Jeff means by 'elements of ... Gentile background'. On page 9 (footnote No. 1) he mentions 'a sombreness in worship, magic-style incantations in Jesus' name, a pantheon of divine beings that included a very powerful devil, and an influential Mary'. One wonders into what kind of church Jeff had wandered! Apart from sobriety, which should be found in every congregation that worships God, the features that offended Jeff would offend every biblical Christian. As to sobriety, is that a distinctly Gentile attitude of worship? If it is, Lord, make me a Gentile that I might fear and love you, as I ought!

Jeff goes on to describe what he believes is characteristically Jewish worship: 'joyful celebration of God's presence and favour and a strong consciousness of the need for human repentance in the face of the one and only God'. This is an idealised version of common Jewish worship, so much so that the average Jew would be hard put to recognise his synagogue services in Jeff's description. Most Jewish religious services are characterised by very little reverence. Latecomers rush through their prayers, and others follow suit in order to have time to talk with their business partner or client. Small talk, gossip and chatter are often heard throughout the service. It is not uncommon for the Rabbi to repeatedly call for silence. There is generally no sense of joyful celebration and no sense of the need for repentance. God is absent from the thoughts of many.

If truth were told, the tension between our national and spiritual identities is nothing compared to that under which our people presently labour. Ours is the product of history, in the course of which our people rejected him who is the goal and culmination of everything truly Jewish, while those who professed to be our co-religionists harassed and persecuted our people in a most unbecoming manner. But the terrible tension under which our people, Israel, live is the product of a calling to which they subscribe and yet refuse to follow, a duty which is the ultimate product of their Jewishness yet which they refuse to carry out. It is not without reason that the pressing question, 'who is a Jew?' keeps rising in Israel. The Jewish people will never know the God of their fathers until they come to know Messiah, Jesus of Nazareth, God who came to live and die among men for their salvation.

Throughout Jewish history since the destruction of the Temple in AD 70, the synagogue has served as the Jewish community centre, and rabbinic custom was the glue that kept the nation together. It is now generally assumed that Jews will be Jews by virtue of their adherence to biblical and rabbinic traditions, and that they will visit the synagogue (or temple, in some cases in America) at least once or twice a year, most notably on the Day of Atonement.

Every nation in the world expresses and maintains its identity by way of its cultural mores. Religious concepts have helped to formulate a substantial part of these but, in the process, they have lost a good deal of their original religious significance. For example, Paul was willing to allow the eating of meat sold in the market-place (1 Cor. 10:25), although he knew that most of such meat was supplied to the market from the altars of nearby pagan temples. Merely eating such meat carried no religious meaning. As soon as anyone attached a religious significance to the eating, Paul forbade it (1 Cor. 10:28). In other words, the same act was allowed or forbidden, depending on whether or not any religious significance was attached to it.

Paul had no difficulty maintaining traditional Jewish custom so long as it was not viewed as a matter of religious obligation. He *became* (amazingly, that is the term used) a Jew to his fellow Jews, while insisting upon his liberty to become a Gentile to the Gentiles (1 Cor. 9:20). This liberty makes it doubly clear that Paul no longer considered himself obliged to practise the Judaism of his day. Otherwise he would not have needed to become a Jew to his fellow Jews, nor a Gentile to Gentiles.

Paul refused to countenance Jewish custom when, by taking on a religious significance, it impinged upon the gospel. As we say, he did not even hesitate to enter into major controversy with the chief of the apostles when he considered the gospel to be at stake (Gal. 2). It is worth noting that Paul led people out of the synagogue, never into it. There is no biblical evidence that would lead us to think that Paul's converts continued to attend synagogues, or that they established their own once they left. Quite to the contrary, the congregations Paul founded were not called synagogues. He coined a new term for them: 'churches'. Only James, probably writing to a Jewish Christian congregation that continued to labour under the misconception that guided the messengers to Galatia (Acts 15:1, 5; Gal. 2:4, 12-13) and who therefore insisted on the necessity of maintaining the national traditions, used the term *synagogue*.

There is no doubt that the gospel can be at risk when it comes to the practice of some Jewish mores, particularly those which retain distinctly religious overtones. Fasting, for instance, on the Day of Atonement for the forgiveness of sins is a denial of the sufficiency of Christ. Giving to the church in order to obtain merit in the eyes of God is a contradiction of grace. But fasting and giving are not, in themselves, unacceptable. We must learn to distinguish between cultural mores and religious obligations.

In matters of morality and religion, none but God has the right to bind a believer's conscience. In matters of religion, the sole authority we may recognise is God's, speaking to us through his Word. In matters of national culture, Jews are as free to be Jewish as are the Swedes to be Swedish or the Hottentots to be Hottentots.

There are two major sources for the formulation of Jewish cultural mores: 1) the Old Testament, especially the Mosaic covenant, and 2) the traditions of the rabbis. Let us examine these separately.

1. THE MOSAIC COVENANT

Dan Juster tell us (*Roots*, p. vii), that the Messianic Jewish Movement is 'a movement among Jewish and non-Jewish followers of Jesus of Nazareth who believe that it is proper and desirable for Jewish followers of Jesus to recognise and identify with their Jewishness'. In spite of Juster's proviso that follows ('This Jewish lifestyle is to be maintained only as it is consistent with the whole of biblical teaching'), Messianic Jews who subscribe to a lifestyle consistent with this view regularly transgress the teachings of the Scripture. The reason for this is partly because Dan and those who agree with him never spelled out the meaning of the terms 'proper and desirable'. Perhaps they did not define it in their own minds.

Michael Schiffman affirms that believers may keep the Law 'as a part of a godly life-style' (Michael Schiffman, *The Return of the Remnant: The Rebirth of Messianic Judaism*, Lederer Messianic Publishers, Baltimore, 1992, 1996, p. 69). Jeff Wasserman (p. 62) reports, 'more than half of the [Messianic] congregational leaders who responded to my survey asserted the mandatory nature of Torah observance for Messianic Jews'. Jeff (p. 96) confirms these facts in a survey he conducted himself: 'Half of the congregations surveyed asserted that not only was observance of elements of the Mosaic Law permissible and recommended for Messianic Jews, but up to 23% thought it mandatory. Advocates cite effective discipleship as the outcome of Torah observance' (p. 97). He comments, 'for these Messianic Jews, Torah observance becomes the essential element in discipleship' (p. 98). On the same page he affirms, '30% of those surveyed recommend Torah observance for Gentiles'.

Focusing on Jesus
One of the great errors of the Messianic Movement is the fact that it has placed Jewishness at the centre of its life. That is where Jesus should be, no one and nothing else. He alone deserves to be the focus of our attention, devotion and commitment. He alone has the right to our hearts. A congregation or an individual that focuses on cultivating, defending, promoting and insisting upon Jewishness has chosen to ignore the high calling of God in Messiah Jesus, because it has placed its focus where it should not be.

Paul has some important things to say in this regard in his letters to the Philippians, chapter three. He had more to boast of with regard to Jewishness than most of us can legitimately claim for ourselves: he was a Jew whose father had him circumcised according to tradition on the eighth day. He came from the royal tribe of Benjamin that gave Israel its first king and capital. He was a *Hebrew of the Hebrews*. As far as keeping the Law, he was a Pharisee, a member of the strictest sect of Judaism in his day. We know from another source that his teacher was one of the most revered rabbis in the history of Israel, Rabban Gamliel the Great.

Paul was so zealous for God that he took it upon himself to persecute the small body of believers in Jesus that had recently come into being, and he persecuted them with both relish and determination. As to righteousness that any man can achieve by Law-keeping, no one could charge him of falling short. But he considered all these advantages worth losing *for the sake of Messiah* (Phil. 3:7), for whom he actually did lose them all (v. 8). Instead of busying himself with his Jewishness, he was taken up *with the surpassing value of knowing Messiah Jesus* his Lord (v. 8). As a result, he began to look upon his Jewishness as *rubbish* (the actual Greek word is not used in polite company – v. 8 again). He did not seek any form of righteousness *derived from the Law, but that which is through faith in Messiah, the righteousness that comes from God on the basis of faith* (vv. 9-10).

Note here that Paul contrasts faith with keeping the Law. As he has repeatedly stated in this passage, Paul left the Law and put his faith in Messiah. Consequently, rather than being taken up with Jewish things, his attention was constantly engaged with Jesus: *that I may know him, and the power of his resurrection, and the fellowship of his sufferings, being conformed to his death in order that I might attain to the resurrection from the dead* (vv. 10-11).

He was so focused on Jesus that he describes his attitude in terms taken from the Roman sports arena, from the famous chariot races the Romans loved so much. Like a charioteer nearing the end of the race, running neck-to-neck with others, he tells us that he is stretching forward with all his strength, bent on being the first to cross the line and, maximally reducing any friction that could slow down the horses, he has become one with the panting beasts, one with their pounding gallop and the screeching, groaning wheels of his chariot. He stretches forward *for the prize of the upward call of God in Messiah Jesus (v. 14),* because that is why God laid hold of him (v. 12).

The Messianic Movement's focus on Jewishness, the Law and rabbinic tradition has dispossessed Jesus, removing him from the central place, where he should be. In that sense it is non-Pauline and less than biblical.

Like Paul, we should be wholly taken up with Jesus, who he is, what he taught, what he did on earth, how he vanquished Satan by his death and celebrated his victory by his resurrection. We should be enamoured with his ascension, his present glory, the wonder of his return and his ultimate, eternal vindication when he hands the kingdom back to the Father. In short, we should be in love with Jesus, not with Jewishness.

The Mosaic covenant is undoubtedly a major influence in Jewish national culture. It is also a focal point in Judaism. In the former, it is the primary influence that shaped Jewish national culture. In the latter, and as interpreted by the rabbis, it is the very essence of Judaism. According to Judaism, God may only be approached through the Torah, and the Torah may only be approached through the rabbis. That is what Judaism is all about. Richard Longnecker (*Christology*, p. 41) quotes W. E. Davies who explained:

'... Judaism came to place more and more emphasis on the Torah, that is, the demand uttered on Sinai, which was itself a gift, the figure of Moses being a colossus because he mediated the Torah. The Church, as it looked back to the new Exodus wrought in Christ, first remembered not the demand but the person of Jesus Christ, through whom the new Exodus was wrought, and who thus came to have for the Church the significance of Torah. That is why, ultimately, the tradition of Judaism culminates in the Mishnah, a code of *halachot* (interpretative rules, which become dictum – BM), and in Christianity in the Gospels, where all is subservient to Jesus as Lord.'

Ariel Berkowitz (Prologue p. xvii) offers his own view of Judaism: 'we want to introduce you to a wonderful, loving, giving, gracious and beneficent friend'. In view of the high-handedness of rabbinic Judaism and the stark demands of God's holy Law, one would assume that Ariel is referring to him whom God sent to free us from what Peter described as *a yoke which neither we nor our fathers were able to bear* (Acts 15:10). But, no. Ariel's amazing invitation is of an altogether different nature: 'we want to introduce you to a wonderful, loving, giving, gracious and beneficent friend – the Torah'. Even my good friend, Paul Liberman, errs in this matter. He says, 'If a Gentile really wants to be like his Messiah, he should become ...' what? Holier? Kinder? Pure in heart? No – 'he should become more interested in biblical Judaism' (Liberman, p. 49)!

The early church considered Jesus to have taken the place of the Torah. Now a growing number of adherents of the Messianic Movement think that the Torah or rabbinic Judaism can fill in the life of believers the place that only Jesus can fill. Perhaps I might be forgiven if I quote from Martin Luther, who said in a sermon on John 2:23-24 (Luther's Works, Vol. XXII, Sermons on John 1–4, Concordia Publishing House, c. 1957, p. 254-261):

'I am to adhere to Messiah alone; he has taught me neither too much nor too little. He has taught me to know God the Father, has revealed himself to me, and has also acquainted me with the Holy Spirit. He has also instructed me how to live and how to die, and has told me what to hope for. What more do I want? And if anyone wishes to teach me anything new, I must say to him: I will not believe it, dear preacher, dear St. Ambrose, dear St. Augustine. For anything that goes beyond and above the man who is called Christ is not genuine. It is still flesh and blood, and Christ has warned us against relying on that. He himself did not trust himself to any man'.

The New Testament teaches that all may approach God through Messiah, and that there is no room for human intervention between God and his creature, be that human rabbi, priest or pope. *There is but one mediator between God and men – Jesus* (1 Tim. 2:5). In a truly New Testament faith, Jesus has indeed replaced the Torah, and there is therefore no room for it with respect to any part of spirituality. That is why early Jewish Christians spoke of Jesus as the Nomos (Greek for 'law', see the Shepherd of Hermas, 8.3.2 and Danielou, p. 163 ff.). In the famous first-century dialogue between Trypho – a Jew – and Justin Martyr, Trypho hears Justin speak of Jesus as 'another covenant', 'a new law' and 'God's covenant'. Clement of Rome learned from the early Jewish Christians to speak of Jesus as the 'Law and the Word', as 'another law', 'the eternal and final law'. Clement of Alexandria tells us that the new Law 'is the Son of God'.

Jesus himself never challenged the Torah, although he frequently challenged interpretations of the Torah created by that tradition to which some Messianic Jewish teachers would have us submit. Hagner (p. 89) reminds us: 'the difference between the rabbis and Jesus in their attitude to the Law cannot be denied. It is basically this difference that led to the death of Jesus'.

The Pharisees had little difficulty with Jesus declaring himself to be the Messiah, but they could not accept his questioning their interpretations of the Torah. The repeated charge against Paul had to do with his attitude to the traditions, not with his views of Jesus. To submit to such interpretations and traditions now is tantamount to taking issue with Jesus and siding with the Pharisees. Will we now turn our backs on him and reinstate the Torah or traditional rabbinic interpretations?

Not on your life! The conflict between Judaism and the message of Messiah is not merely one of fulfilment over against expectation. It is between Messiah and misguided rabbinical insistence on the Torah, between redemption by divine grace and the stubborn belief that one can keep the Law and thereby achieve divine approbation, between the divine authority of the Son of God and that of the rabbis.

The message of Messiah is not the fulfilment of rabbinic Judaism. It is its replacement, because Judaism as interpreted by the rabbis is not Jewish. The message of Messiah is the fulfilment of all truly biblical hopes that are nourished in the bosom of God's promises to Israel, not those formed by the rabbis in the painful crucible of Jewish existence or the distorting vision of a distinctly Jewish version of human sinfulness. It is a message for all mankind, brought to the world through the Jewish people, about a Jewish Saviour for all nations of the world. It is not about Jewish distinctives but about the glory of God in the face of Jesus, the Messiah.

THE MESSAGE OF THE
LETTER TO THE HEBREWS

Jesus and Moses Compared

The writer to the Hebrews reminds us of a truth we have but briefly observed. The Mosaic Law was a glorious *shadow* of what was to come (Col. 2:17; Heb. 8:5; 10:1). In its place we now have a great, eternal, perfect and utterly sinless High Priest (Heb. 4:14–5:10; 7:23-28). We should *hold on to our confession* of his accomplished redemption *and not return to the elementary principles* that led us to him (Heb. 4:14; 10:23).

Jesus is greater than Aaron (5:6), greater than Moses (3:3, 5-6), greater than Abraham, greater than all the angels of heaven put together (1:4*). To which of the angels did he ever say, 'You are my son, today I have begotten you'?* (1:5). Does God not command with regard to Messiah, *let all the angels of God worship him* (1:6)? God subjected the world to Jesus, not to any of the angels (2:5-8). When our people and others of the world rebelled against him God said to him, *Sit at my right hand until I make your enemies a footstool for your feet* (1:13).

We therefore ought to be very careful how we relate to Jesus, *lest we drift away* from the truths he proclaimed (2:1). If the Torah, delivered to our forefathers through intermediaries, was not to be altered and every transgression of it was duly punished, *how shall we escape* if we neglect the glorious, eternal salvation Messiah has purchased by his blood?

The good news of this salvation was first described by our Lord, then declared and confirmed to us by his disciples, who personally heard him speak those gracious words and saw him execute those wonderful acts. What is more, God bore witness to them with signs and wonders and by gifts of the Holy Spirit according to his own will (1:4–3:19).

God addresses Moses as a faithful servant, but he calls Jesus his *Son* (Heb. 3:1-6). Moses was appointed by God to oversee his house (3:5), but God appointed Jesus over Moses (3:6). God brought our fathers into the land by the hand of Joshua, but he told them that the land was not their ultimate possession (4:8): there was and is more to divine blessing than material, political, economic or social achievements. The *eternal rest* that comes from the knowledge of sins forgiven and the broken power of sin over us, from having the image of God restored in us and the favour of God eternally upon us, may only be had in Jesus (4:1-11).

So, *let us leave off the elementary first truths* (a phrase we should be familiar with from Paul's letter to the Galatians) *and go on to perfection* (6:1). Let us take care lest anything we do in the course of our efforts to retain our Jewishness conflicts in any way with the message of our Saviour. Otherwise, we might end up, like Esau, at the place of no return (Heb. 6:1-9).

I have no doubt that the majority of my fellow Jewish believers in Jesus wish for nothing more than to be uncompromisingly faithful (Heb. 6:9-12). I witness their zeal, their devotion, their sacrifice, and their sincere love for God and his Messiah, and covet the same for myself. That is precisely why I am writing this book: I am convinced that many have been drawn into a path they had no intention to walk and that, once the implications are made clear, they will reject the errors that have crept into their thinking and stand up for Messiah and his truth. Are you one of these?

Jesus' Priesthood
Abraham, as it were, paid tithes through Melchizedek to the Lord Messiah, whose priesthood accomplishes far more than the priesthood of Aaron ever could (Heb. 7:1-10). The Temple in which Jesus serves supersedes the tabernacle and any of the temples in which our fathers worshipped (9:11, 24). His sacrifice is *able to perfect all those who come to God by him* (10:14). His priesthood lasts forever (7:17, 21, 24) and is compassionate, powerful and untainted by sin or any human weakness (7:26). Of course, in earthly terms he is not a priest at all because he came from the royal seed of David, not the priestly family of Aaron (Heb. 7:11). His is a *new priesthood*, implying the removal of the shadow that was the Torah to make way for the *newer, better covenant* of grace (7:11–8:7).

Now, if the first covenant, made with our fathers at Sinai, *was faultless, there would be no occasion sought for a second one* (Heb. 8:7). But God found fault with our people as well as with his own covenant (Heb. 8:8). Therefore, he promised (in Jer. 31) a new covenant, which was to be unlike the one he made with our fathers when he led them by the hand out of Egypt.

Our fathers did not continue in that covenant because they were as sinful as any man (Jer. 31:32; Heb. 8:10) and because there was nothing in that covenant that could ensure they would continue. God therefore promised (and has brought in Messiah) a very different covenant (Jer. 31:33-34; Heb. 8:10-12). It has the power to ensure its continuance: he put the covenant in our minds, made it a part of our inmost beings and wrote it on our hearts.

The knowledge of God that we have in Messiah is direct, real, transforming. By promising such a *new* covenant (that is the very word Jeremiah uses) he has made the first obsolete (Heb. 8:13). Indeed, at the time the letter to the Hebrews was being written, the former covenant was already becoming *obsolete, ready to disappear* because the inexorable process of history was, under the hand of God, leading to the destruction of the Temple and to a cessation of the temple ritual (Heb. 8:7-13).

Now, the first covenant had its own procedures, furniture and context (Heb. 9:1-2). God was veiled from the people. None but the High Priest could access his presence – and even he could do so only one day a year, *never without sacrificing for his own sin and for that of the people* (9:7). *That is how the Holy Spirit signified that the way to the presence of God had not yet opened* (9:8). The continual need to offer sacrifices also reminded the people that *those gifts and sacrifices could never perfectly cleanse the consciences of those who worshipped under the old administration* (9:9). Instead, the people had a hope that was nourished by food and drink regulations, various washings, and such like, all of which were imposed until the time of reformation arrived (9:1-10).

The work of Messiah is much fuller, much better than the Torah because he brought with him all those *good things to come* which the Torah could only promise (Heb. 9:11): a greater and more perfect tabernacle, a better sacrifice and an eternal redemption that cannot be undone, including a complete and lasting cleansing of sinners' troubled consciences (9:11-14). That is precisely why Jesus is *the mediator of a new covenant,* which replaces the previous one (9:15).

Jewish Christians need to understand: our

forefathers and we transgressed the Torah and broke covenant with God (Heb. 8:9). How, then, could we *receive the eternal inheritance* (9:15)? Well, a covenant is, in this respect, like a will. The writer of the will must die before we can inherit anything. So Messiah died to ensure that we would partake of the promise. He now appears in the presence of God for us (9:24). Next time he comes, it will be to accord us, who eagerly await him, salvation in the fullest sense of the term (9:15-27).

As we have said, the *Law* is only a *shadow* (Heb. 10:1). As such, it *cannot perfect* those who approach God according to its commandments. Evidence of this may be found in the need to offer repeated sacrifices. Jesus is the perfect sacrifice, by which *we have been sanctified* (10:10). He offered himself in our place, and then *sat down*. His work is completed, because, by his one and single sacrifice, he did what the Torah could never do: *he has perfected for all time those who are sanctified* (10:14).

It is worth noting that Hebrews uses the term *sanctified* to describe salvation, a use which serves to support what we said earlier, when we reviewed the letter to the Galatians: salvation is more than just forgiveness of sins. It is a moral and spiritual transformation that God achieves for and in us, and which is as secure as forgiveness of sins. Jesus, not the Torah, secures both forgiveness and ultimate sanctification.

Evidence to this finished work of Messiah can be found in the nature of the promise given in relation to the new covenant. Jeremiah speaks of an internalisation of the Law of God, that is to say, a change in the bend of our wills, so that we willingly choose to glorify God (Heb. 10:15-18). Has that happened to you? Do you now desire, as you never desired before, to live for God and to do his will? If so, God has done in you what he promised to do some day in the hearts of his people. You are redeemed, forgiven, a partaker of the eternal inheritance!

So let us not let go of what we have received. Let us keep on keeping on! God is true and so should we be. Let's take great care lest we trample under our feet the blood by which we were bought. Remember: God is a terrible avenger. Do not draw away from your confidence in Messiah. Focus on him alone. You do not have to prove to anyone that you are Jewish and you must not compromise the gospel in an effort to do so. We – you and I – need the strength to endure so that, having done the will of God, we will in fact receive what he promised (Heb. 10:19-39).

Faith
Faith is not rejoicing in what we have, but in remaining faithful because of what lies in the future. Look at the list of great heroes of the faith in our Bible: Noah, Abraham, Joseph, Moses and all the others – did they trust because of what they had? Of course not. They suffered immensely, waiting in confidence and all the while paying a high price for their faith (Heb. 11). With such an audience, witnessing as it were our own race, *let us run the race God has set before us* with more fortitude than some of us have shown so far. Let us *fix our eyes on Jesus* rather than on the Torah or on our Jewishness. *Remember what he endured* for you – and remember that *you have not paid the ultimate price*.

The rabbis claim that you are not Jewish? So what? Does that make them right or grant them the victory? Your family, cherished and warmly loved by you, turn their backs to you and think you have become some kind of 'Jesus freak'? So what? Is that a price too high to pay for what you have received in Messiah? Your very suffering is a merciful act of God, shaping you to partake of his holiness. We should not shirk suffering and rejection but be willing to bear it, and demonstrate by such willingness the non-negotiable truthfulness of the message we proclaim (Heb. 12:1-17).

The implications of your choice in this matter are

tremendous. I've said it and I'll say it again: the giving of the Torah was accompanied with terrifying manifestations in order to emphasise the dire consequences of disobedience. But in coming to Messiah we have not come to a smoking mountain, to the sounds of trumpet blast and the like. We have come to something far more substantial: *to Mount Zion and to the city of the living God, to the heavenly Jerusalem and to myriads of angels, to the general assembly and church of the firstborn who are enrolled in heaven, to God, the judge of all, to the spirits of righteous men made perfect – to Jesus, the mediator of a new covenant, and to the sprinkled blood, which speaks better than the blood of Abel* (Heb. 12:18-29).

Just be sure that, in your tendency to focus on your Jewishness, you do not refuse him who is speaking. Rather, having received so much from God through Messiah, let us show how much we are grateful by maintaining an honest stand in the face of opposition. If need be, let's go with Jesus *outside the camp, bearing his reproach,* because our hearts are not fixed on what we can have on hand, in the here and now of this world. We are *seeking the city that is to come* (Heb. 13:12-14).

The Weakness of the Torah?
The Torah was *added* (Gal. 3:19) *until* (Heb. 9:10); its commandments are *weak and beggarly* in terms of what they are able to accomplish (Heb. 9:1-20; Gal. 4:9) due to our own sinful hearts (Rom. 8:3). Of course, the Law is not weak and beggarly in itself. Only in light of the magnificence of Messiah's work the Law appears to be so weak.

A thousand candles are a great light, but what are they in comparison to the light of the world? While serving in the army in Israel, we would sometimes use large projectors to view the border and reveal suspicious movements at night. The strength of these projectors was measured in 'candles' and the strength of one was equal to 10,000,000 candles. When they were turned on, everything in their beam became visible, even on the darkest night. But when the sun was up, no one knew if the projector was on or off, unless we looked at the switchboard. That is what it is like when the Torah is held up to the light of Jesus. Jesus outshines the Torah by an infinite measure.

The Torah cannot save or comfort. It cannot assure sin-sick hearts of God's good will. It cannot secure salvation or promote true holiness that arises from the heart, it cannot give the Spirit and it cannot sanctify. Jesus can do all that and a great deal more, and only he can. We should trust him.

When Paul spoke of the Mosaic covenant as a *ministry of death* (2 Cor. 3:7), he was not referring to the Torah's nature but to what it inevitably is because of our inherently sinful weakness. That weakness constantly drives us to disobey the Torah, or to transform it into what it was never meant to be – a means of salvation, sanctification or some other spiritual advantage, which, we claim, 'draws us closer to God' (Shoshana Feher, *Passing Over Easter: Constructing the Boundaries of Messianic Judaism,* Alta Mira Press, Walnut Creek, 1998, p. 111).

That is how the rabbis thought, and that is the growing tendency in the Messianic Movement. Ariel Berkowitz writes, 'all who are currently learning to apply the Torah to their lives are experiencing deep-seated and profound spiritual growth, and by teaching you to keep the Torah [they are] ushering you into new depths of intimacy with your God' (*Berkowitz,* Prologue, pp. xvi, xvii). Such a view of rabbinicism runs contrary to the testimony of Scripture.

The Law was given to teach us our utter inability, to lead us to the kind of despair with ourselves that will teach us to cry out to God for salvation, sanctification, spiritual reality and his nearness. But these spiritual benefits are given by grace and not by keeping the Law. Let us *cast out the bondwoman and*

*her son, for the son of the bondwoman shall not be an heir
with the son of the free woman* (Gal. 4:21-30).

Both And?

But why? Why can't we adhere at the same time to
both the keeping of the Torah and to the new covenant
brought in by Messiah? The answer is to be found in
what we have already learned. As we saw in our study
of Galatians, the covenant no longer binds our nation
as a covenant. It has accomplished its role as
schoolmaster, tutor and guide by leading us to
Messiah. We are *no longer under a tutor* (Gal. 3:25).

That is the implication of Paul's point in 2
Corinthians 3, where he contrasts the Torah with the
Spirit (a contrast with which we should already be
familiar) and indicates that the Torah, which was
divine truth *engraved on stones* (v. 7), never more than
that, however glorious the truths it proclaimed, cannot
do what the Spirit does, because the Spirit *gives life*
(v. 6).

Indeed, Paul insists that Moses covered his face so
that the people would not see the true and wonderful
glory of God that shone on Moses' face. That glory was
of a fading kind (v. 8). This, too, the people were not to
see. But the ministry of the Spirit, saving and
transforming individuals into the moral image of their
Creator is *even more* glorious (v. 8 again). *For if the
ministry of condemnation* (the Torah) *has glory, much more
does the ministry of righteousness abound in glory* (v. 9),
because the Torah can only demand righteousness,
while the Spirit provides it through regeneration and
his sanctifying influences. *Indeed, what had glory* (the
Torah), *in this case has no glory on account of the glory
that surpasses it, for if that which fades away was with
glory, much more that which remains is in glory* (v. 10-11).

Much the same kind of argument is made by
Jeremiah in the 31st chapter of his book, verses 31-
34, when he says that, unlike the earlier covenant
made at Sinai, the new covenant is not capable of

being broken, because God himself will inscribe it on the hearts of his people, make them wholly his and will be fully and gloriously their God, so that all will truly know him – beginning with the least among them. The grounds of all this: *I will forgive their iniquity and their sin I will remember no more* (v. 34).

Those who have tasted of the grace of God in the gospel will immediately recognise their saving experience in this description by Jeremiah. Nothing less than the saving work of the Holy Spirit is described, applying the atonement obtained by the death of Messiah and working out in the redeemed those essential ingredients of salvation: the joy of sins forgiven, a love for God and his truth, a heartfelt desire to do his will regardless of the cost, an intimacy in prayer they never knew before. The Torah can provide none of these realities. So why return to the shadows, images and promises when the reality taught by those shadows has arrived and images and hope inculcated by those promises have now been fulfilled?

One of my correspondents insisted, 'for us who have faith in the promises of God, in the salvation through Jesus, we know that there are many circumstances in which it is pleasing to God that we go beyond the boundaries established by the Torah (kosher meat laws, for example), if it will benefit the fellowship with our Gentile brothers/sisters, just as Peter and Paul did'. I confess myself disturbed by such a statement. If we are bound in any sense to keep the Torah, then we are bound fully and have no right to exercise judgement as to when that duty can be suspended. God's Law is not an elastic boundary which men may move when they deem suitable – for whatever reason. The very possibility that we may conceive of God's commandments in such a way threatens the fabric of our obedience to God and transforms our Law-keeping into a relativistic sham.

A greater than the temple is here (Matt. 12:6). The Mosaic covenantal arrangements went no further than the ritualistic symbols that were to be conducted in the temple, all of which pointed forward to the substance that is in Jesus. Those rituals and symbols were the intriguing *shadow* that *could not make perfect* (Heb. 9:9), and of which Messiah is the glorious reality (Heb. 8:5; 10:1).

They themselves are not the reality and can in no way convey that reality. In Messiah we have a better hope (Heb. 7:19), a better covenant (Heb. 7:22), a better High Priest, a more excellent ministry (Heb. 8:6), a better sacrifice (Heb. 9:23) and a better resurrection (Heb. 11:35). How, then, can Ariel Berkowitz claim that the Torah is capable of 'hitting the mark of man's needs, including his need to know who God is and what his righteousness looks like' (Berkowitz, p. 7-8)? That is something only Jesus can do, because only in the light of the cross can we begin to understand the awesomeness of God's righteousness and find the true provision for man's great need.

Living the Jewish Way
Of course, Ole Kvarme is right when he insists that 'to be a Jew is to live as a Jew' (Kvarme, *Israel and Yeshua*, p. 16). His words echo the central message of the Messianic Movement, as well as my own heart. But to live as a Jew is not to deny the full and perfect work of Messiah, or to obscure it in any manner. Nor does it mean that we worship as Jews do today. The rabbis have created an unbridgeable gap between the gospel and what they and our nation recognise to be Jewish. We must worship as Christians, as disciples of Messiah, while retaining our national identity. If that is not acceptable to the rabbis, so be it. If our people reject us for doing so, that is not too high a price to pay. We owe Jesus for more than we owe our beloved people or ourselves.

Ole goes on to spell out what he understands by living as a Jew, quoting an unnamed Israeli professor:

'to be a Jew is to accept Jewish history... The historical consciousness is a distinct element of Jewish identity, and the historical experience of the people has helped to shape its culture, customs and faith. To accept Jewish history is not only to rejoice in the victories of David and the Maccabees but, more than anything else, to carry the burden of centuries of suffering and the pain of the holocaust' (Kvarme, p. 16).

We agree, and since the Jewish people are still very much alive and kicking, being Jewish is not only bearing the burden of the past, but also that of the present and the future. This is something that no man can take from us, however much he tries.

To the extent that the consensus of national Jewish custom today retains the influence of the Mosaic covenant, in the national festivals for example (and not all of these are biblical), Jews in Messiah are free to adhere to that consensus. We are Jewish and therefore naturally adhere to our national customs. But we are not free to do so as a matter of religious obligation, because to do so is to act as if Messiah had never come, or as if he came and made no difference. Subservience to the Mosaic covenant is tantamount to a denial of Messiah (Gal. 2:18-21; 5:3-4) because it assumes that the keeping of the Mosaic covenant is part of the righteousness that should typify (Jewish) Christian obedience, for whatever purpose.

It was *for freedom that Messiah has set us free* (Gal. 5:1). We must *continue standing* in that freedom for the glory of God and for a testimony to the finished work of Messiah. One of the problems with acting as if we are subject to the Law is the message we convey to those who witness our lifestyles. Do we show that Jesus is the goal of the Law, and that, having been brought to that goal, we are no longer subservient to it? Or does our lifestyle state the opposite of what our lips affirm? Are we redeemed by the grace of God or are we not?

The issue at stake is the completeness of the work of Messiah and his sufficiency in a believer's life. By his sacrifice (Rom 8:1-4), Jesus procured for us an entire salvation, and assured it in us by the gift of his Spirit (Heb. 7:25; 10:14). That salvation includes our sanctification and growth in grace. Unlike the Torah, Jesus is truly able to save (Acts 13:39; Rom. 8:3; Gal. 2:15-21; Heb. 9–10). Having begun in the Spirit, is it possible to achieve spiritual advancement by the flesh (Gal. 3:3), that is to say, by the keeping of the Torah? Of course not! How can anything be added to what Messiah has done? How can it be thought that believers can obtain anything through any other means but by the blood and Spirit of Messiah?

Did Paul Keep the Law?
As we have seen, in his letter to the Galatians, Paul was not addressing the tendency toward legalistic observance of the Mosaic covenant for righteousness. He was concerned to challenge any kind of Torah-keeping (see 2:18-21; 3:3, 5-6, 10, 23-25, 27; 4:1-11, 21-31; 5:1, 6-12, 16-19). Messianic interpreters, with others, wrongly limit the meaning of the term 'righteousness' to what theologians like to call 'justification', that is to say, that initial forgiveness of sins and the attribution of Messiah's righteousness to a believer, which attribution introduces an individual to salvation. That is not what Paul meant when he used that term in his letter to the Galatians, nor is it always what other NT writers meant. Righteousness encompasses the whole of the Christian life. It is sanctification, godliness and spirituality, joy, moral conquest, and a hope that can never be disappointed.

Salvation is not merely the initial attribution of Messiah's righteousness at the beginning of a life of faith, but the growing impartation of that righteousness and its increasing expression (*from glory to glory, 2 Cor. 3:18*). It is the ongoing work of the Spirit in applying the finished work of Messiah to a believer's life. None whose life is not *righteous* may legitimately claim to be a Christian. He is a lost soul in need of Messiah. (See, for example, Acts 10:35; Rom. 1:17; 2:26; 5:17, 21; 6:13; 8:4; 2 Cor. 5:21; Eph. 4:24; 5:9; Phil. 1:11; 1 Tim. 6:11; 2 Tim. 2:22; Heb. 12:11; James 3:18.) Many such passages could be multiplied. They all make a simple but important point: sanctification is the inevitable and natural result of justification. Converted people are not merely forgiven, they are transformed, and that transformation is a necessary ingredient of their salvation.

Some claim that Paul remained zealous for the Torah, as were the thousands of Jews in Jerusalem who believed in Jesus (Acts 21:18-23). This is incorrect, although Paul certainly maintained his Jewish identity. Fealty to the Torah could not sit well with one who did not hesitate to be a Gentile to the Gentiles (1 Cor. 9:20). Why else would he insist that the observance of days, holy days, months, weeks and years is a matter for the flesh and for the now-defunct *rudimentary principles of the world* (Col. 2:16-19)? He goes so far as to say that those who insist upon the Jewish festivals are *not holding fast to the head* (Col. 2:19). This raises the uncomfortable question as to whether or not those who claim a faith in Messiah and, at the same time, seek to achieve in the realm of the Spirit by Torah-keeping, might have heard the gospel in vain (Gal. 4:10) – no small issue!

Messianic Views of the Torah
While I was engaged in writing this book I was challenged by Paul Liberman, whom I love and respect, with the claim that 'no recognised Messianic Jewish leader teaches that keeping the Torah is a duty before God or that it conveys any kind of spiritual advantage'. I wish that were true! I have already given evidence to the contrary (p. 85), and here is some more:

Dan Juster is a well-known and much respected leader in the Jewish Messianic community. Speaking of the Mosaic Law he tells us (in *Jewish Roots*) that

> 'God chose Israel to be a nation of priests, a national mediator between God and the nations of the world. She was to bring the nations to God and God to the nations. How? By being a nation under God, under his rule or Covenant, so that life would be blessed, just and healthy... And he has never changed his purposes' (*Roots*, p. 9).
>
> Only 'the sacrificial dimensions of the Law have been replaced by Yeshua's sacrifice' (*Roots*, p. 39). 'Since Torah is essential to Judaism, a Messianic Jew must gain an accurate understanding of Torah' (*Roots,* p. 14). 'Paul also maintained the validity of the Law as uniquely related to Israel's continued religious national identity and special witness as a people' (*Roots*, p. 90).

The confusion between national and religious identity is a significant factor in Dan's thinking. Such confusion is common in the Messianic Movement as a whole. The Torah is thought of as constituting 'God's external standards of righteousness' (*Roots*, p. 52), among which Dan includes the maintenance of a strictly kosher kitchen, wearing fringes (*Roots*, p. 56) and celebrating the biblical holidays (*Roots*, p. 57).

Ariel Berkowitz, who publishes a magazine that is distributed worldwide, and has written a great deal for the Messianic Movement, goes further. He states: 'In the same way that Yeshua is your life, the words of Torah are your life' (*Torah Rediscovered,* First Fruits of Zion Press, Littleton, Colorado, p. 145). 'As you live the Torah, Messiah himself will stand up in you and through you for all to see' (Berkowitz, p. 146). So, it is not by believing in and obeying Jesus that the righteousness of the Law is fulfilled in us (Rom. 8:3-4), but as we keep the Law, we partake of Jesus, who is seen in us! 'The words of the Torah are now our life. When we practice Torah ... we are also participating in our new life – the life of God' (*Berkowitz*, p. 39). The Torah community, created by obedience to the Torah, is the place where life reigns instead of death. It is the place of safety ... the place of blessing and life' (*Berkowitz*, p. 28).

David Stern makes similar statements. He insists, 'the Torah is in force and is to be observed' (*Messianic Jewish Manifesto,* Jewish New Testament Publications, Jerusalem, Israel, p. 102). In his *Jewish New Testament* he translates Hebrews 7:12 as 'there must of necessity be a transformation of Torah' and explains in his *Manifesto,* 'A transformation of Torah does not imply its abolition' only that it is 'adjusted'. David further argues in his *Manifesto* p. 160, that the dietary laws are still in force and that 'nothing in Galatians 2:11-14 can be construed to imply that the Jewish dietary law shall not be observed'. Indeed, 'when the Jewish people become obedient and cease to break the covenant, God will fulfil his promise to bless them as a nation' (*Manifesto* p. 100).

So, not conversion is here called for, or faith in Jesus, but an observance of the Torah. Then 'God will fulfil his promise to bless [Israel] as a nation'. By way of contrast, the writer to the Hebrews says: *On the one hand, there is a setting aside of a former commandment because of its weakness and uselessness (for the Law made nothing perfect), and on the other hand there is the bringing in of a better hope through which we draw near to God. So ... Jesus has become the guarantee of a better covenant* (Heb. 7:18-22).

Dan Juster concludes, the Law is 'irrevocable' (*Messianic Judaism,* p. 29). 'It is now by his Spirit that we are guided to do God's will' (that is to say, to keep the Torah) and 'in this we are transformed step by step into the likeness of Messiah' (ibid.).

Grace or Works?
Such statements substitute Jesus and his finished work on the cross with the Mosaic Law and obedience

to it. My dear friends, who are leaders in the Messianic Movement, attribute to human effort what the Bible attributes exclusively to the grace of God, so that he alone will receive the glory. This is to supplant the gospel with a doctrine of human works.

Of course, such is not the intention of any among the above quoted authors, or of their followers. They have no wish to modify the gospel. They are honest, godly men. But the direction in which their statements inexorably lead impacts the gospel in a way that will ultimately render it unrecognisable.

Either Paul was zealous for the Torah or he was not. Either the Torah filled his vision, or Messiah did. Either we obtain a full, complete and perfect salvation through Jesus' death, or Jesus just starts us on the road, and the rest is up to us. One view is the gospel, the other is not.

Some Messianic congregations, working under the assumption that the people of Israel are still bound by the Mosaic covenant, insist that there are aspects of that covenant which ought no longer be kept. Such congregations have opted for what could be described as a selective obedience. However, selective obedience is no obedience at all, for to break one of the commandments is to be guilty of breaking them all (Jam. 2:10). Either we *are* bound by the covenant or we are not. If we are bound in any sense, then we have no right to exercise judgement as to when that duty can be suspended.

God's Law is not an elastic boundary that men may move whenever they deem it suitable – for whatever good reason. The very possibility that we might learn to think of God's commandments in such a way threatens the fabric of our moral obedience and transforms our Law-keeping into a relativistic sham. Yet most – no, all – Messianic congregations fail to obey the covenant fully. All consciously and knowingly moderate its commandments.

Paul and the writer to the Hebrews clearly insisted

that the ceremonies of the Torah should not be kept as a means of salvation or as the way to spiritual progress. Torah-keeping in that sense forms no part of our religion, whether we are Jewish or Gentile. The rabbinic assumption that Jewish national identity and any form of religious duty are one and the same is correct only in the sense that Jews, as Jews, are under obligation to believe in Jesus because he is the promised Lord Messiah. Rabbinic Judaism is not Jewish. It constitutes a determined denial of the lordship of Jesus, and its most fundamental concepts are contrary to biblical teaching.

Judaism's view of God does not admit the Trinity. Nor does it accord God other glories that are due to his name. Instead, he is presented as subject to the dictums of the rabbis, effectively absent from the world he made, except in the wider movements of history, and dependent on the good works of the nation for the accomplishment of his purposes. Sin is no more and no less than an overt transgression of the Mosaic Law, or of rabbinic tradition. The services of a prostitute, for instance, may be engaged so long as this is not done in the city of his residence. Obedience does not require the heart's involvement – although that is much to be desired – it is enough to carry out the external commandments of the Law as interpreted by the rabbis. Salvation by grace and through a sacrifice is not needed. All one needs to do is to outweigh one's bad deeds with good ones, and the blessing of God is assured. Gentiles are, at best, sons of Noah, who have no place in the world to come although 'all Israel have their place in the world to come'.

Of course, since Judaism is so eclectic, one can always find a quote or two that proves the opposite. However, the convictions described above are shared by the majority of rabbis and by the overwhelming majority of the Jewish religious population. In each of these points Judaism contradicts the Gospel.

Spirituality and the Law

As we have seen, some insist that they find 'joy', even 'life' by obeying the covenant. Apparently, their experience differs from that of the apostles, who described the covenant as *a yoke which neither our fathers nor we have been able to bear* (Acts 15:10) and who insisted that Messiah had done what covenant-keeping could never have done (Rom. 8:1-4; Heb. 9:8-12; 10:1-18).

Covenant-keeping can bring joy only when one toys at keeping the commandments and does not sincerely and fully observe them. When one picks and chooses, Torah-keeping becomes an interesting diversion. But when it is kept with the religious devotion that any commandment of God deserves, it becomes what it was intended to be – an exposure of our inability and of our sinfulness, subjecting us to the curse due to us because of our failures, and thereby driving us to Messiah. That is what Paul meant when he spoke of the inability of the Law to impart life or secure from condemnation, *weak as it was through the flesh* (Rom. 8:3).

Having said as much, I wonder: since when has joy become a legitimate goal in the Christian life? Please note: I am not questioning the duty of those who love the Lord to rejoice in him. Nor am I claiming that a sullen, morose attitude is evidence of biblical spirituality. Nevertheless I ask, can the mere fact that something brings us joy legitimatise a course of action? Ought we not to find joy in contemplating the Lord himself, in bringing to our minds recognition of his glory, revelling in his boundless mercy, thrilling in the wonder of his love?

Since when may those who love him introduce into his service duties he has not commanded? Have we forgotten that the introduction of fire, which the Lord had not commanded, and an unwarranted but well-meaning touch of the ark both brought death? If the lighting of Sabbath candles and the wearing of prayer shawls are allowable in the worship of God because they 'bring joy', why not introduce icons, incense and other such implements if they likewise rejoice the hearts of those who use them?

We must not worship God in terms of the Mosaic covenant because we must not worship him as if the Messiah has never come, never died, never rose and never freed us from the ceremonial stipulations of the covenant God made with our people through Moses. Paul insists upon stating that it is impossible to live consistently in the Spirit and to keep the Torah at the same time (Rom. 7:6; Gal. 3:2, 5, 18). *The requirement of the Law [is] fulfilled in us, who do not walk according to the flesh but according to the Spirit* (Rom. 8:4). But those who seek to keep the Law are under its condemnation.

THE PURPOSE OF THE
MOSAIC COVENANT

The Mosaic covenant served in order to distinguish Israel from the pagan nations among whom it lived, specifically to distance the people from contemporary pagan practices (such as cooking a calf in its mother's milk). Note! There is no kashrus in the Bible, only a forbidding of certain foods and the practice of cooking a calf in its mother's milk. There is not even a prohibition to eat milk with meat. After all, that is what Abraham served the angels who visited him on their way to Sodom. Those covenantal stipulations served as a tutor serves a child, until he is of age to go to school (Gal. 3:24), preserving our national identity in terms of a covenant until Messiah came and instituted a new covenantal relationship (Jer. 31:31).

God's covenant with Israel, commonly described as 'the Torah', was never meant to be a means by which individuals could justify themselves before God or obtain any spiritual advantage. On the contrary, it taught Israel her total inability to satisfy the exacting, perfect standards of God (Rom. 3:20). Jesus is the goal of the Torah (Rom. 10:4), for the Torah evokes in us a desperate search for one to stand in the gap on our behalf to do for us what we cannot do for ourselves (Rom. 8:1-4). The Torah also taught that salvation was all of one piece. It was impossible to claim a right standing with God unless one was *sanctified* – made holy – and the Torah taught that none could be holy apart from God's grace because to offend at any one point was to offend in all (Jas. 2:10). Yet who could but offend?

Now that Messiah has come, the goal has been reached: We *are no longer under a tutor* (Gal. 3:25) and there is no longer need or room to maintain religious differences between Jews and Gentiles (Gal. 3:25-29). In religious terms, we are all one. None of us is subject any longer to the Torah as a national covenant. We are free.

As followers of the Messiah, we Jewish Christians are not free to obscure the freedom we have in Christ through his sacrifice (Gal. 3:23–4:11, 21-31), for to do so is a tacit denial of that freedom for which Christ died. It was *for freedom that Christ set us free* (Gal. 5:1). We must *keep standing* in that freedom for the glory of God and as a testimony to the finished work of Christ. If we live as if we are still subject to the Torah, we convey a false message by our lifestyle. We may verbally claim that Jesus is the goal of the Law, and that we have now been brought to that goal, but our lives constitute a denial of our words.

The Mosaic Code – the Torah – was wholly and exclusively composed of obligations meant for Israel alone. Beyond the ceremonial and civil aspects of the Law, there were moral obligations which are eternal reflections of the nature of God himself: the proscription of lying, stealing, murder and such like; the duty and privilege to love God with all of one's being; and the duty and joy of loving one's fellow human as one loves one's self. Joseph knew – without the Mosaic covenant – that he should not commit adultery, and that to do so would be to sin against God (Gen.

39:9). God punished lasciviousness and crass materialism in Sodom without reservation long before the covenant was promulgated at Sinai. Sabbath was an eternal duty in which man was instructed to emulate his Creator, resting in the finished work of the Eternal One who loved him so freely. The day was blessed and sanctified to God from the sixth day of creation. The principle of one day in seven remains our joy and duty today, and so shall be for all eternity.

Yes, I Am Free, But...
Some Messianic Jews insist that they fully recognise the fact that Jesus fulfilled the Law and that we are therefore no longer subject to it. But, they insist, they have chosen to keep the Law in order to affirm their Jewishness. In the excellent words of Stan Telchin, in the Introduction to this book: 'We have not been called to affirm our Jewishness. We have been called to be transformed into the image of our Lord Jesus.' Instead of being occupied with elements of Jewishness as a focus of our congregational life, we should be focusing on him, on living for him, on learning his word in its wider aspects and in seeking the gracious help of the Spirit to become more like Jesus. Moreover, what kind of Jewishness are we affirming by obeying rabbinic religious decree? It is certainly not the biblical Jewishness that leads to Christ!

So, then, Jewish Christians are free from the Mosaic covenant, but are free to keep it so long as they abstain from those aspects of it that are contrary to the original meaning of Scripture and from anything which contradicts the gospel. If they choose to keep any aspects of the Mosaic covenant as such, they are duty bound to make it clear that the Law is secondary to Messiah. Regretfully, such a message is seldom clear among Messianic Jews who insist that Jews in Messiah are under religious (i.e. spiritual) obligation to adhere to those aspects of the Mosaic covenant that the Messianic Movement has selectively chosen to consider binding.

We find some in the Messianic Movement (such as Dan Juster, David Stern, Ariel Berkowitz, Joseph Shulam and Rich Nichol), who recommend or even call upon Gentiles to adhere to the Mosaic Law. David tells us in his *Manifesto* (p. 178 and following): 'If a Gentile Christian wants to identify fully with the Jewish people, the New Testament allows him to become a Jew. He should accept the whole Torah as understood by the form of Judaism to which he is converting.'

This is nothing short of astounding. Paul's choice of words in the letter to the Galatians is so strong that I dare quote only portions of them: for a Gentile to become a Jew is to desert Messiah for a *different Gospel* (Gal. 1:6), which is *really no Gospel at all* (1:7), not to be *straightforward about the truth* (2:14), to make Messiah *a minister of sin* (2:17), to *act foolishly* (3:3), to be *severed from Messiah* (5:4), to have *fallen from grace* (5:4). Conversion to Judaism is never an option that a Gentile follower of Jesus may consider. His love for Messiah, his devotion to God and his gratitude for the salvation procured for him at so great a price should preserve him from allowing the thought ever to enter his mind.

Why on earth would he think otherwise? Peter tells us that the recipients of his letters, although mostly Gentile, are sharers in the ancestral prerogatives of Israel in accordance with the divine purpose, which was formulated before the world began (1 Pet. 2:1-10). Scan his two letters. There is not the slightest intimation that Gentiles may or could in any way be advantaged by keeping the Torah or becoming Jewish. There is nothing Jewish to be seen in Peter's letters, just the grace of God in Jesus. See what Paul has to say in his letter to the Ephesians:

'He broke down the barrier of the dividing wall by abolishing in his flesh the enmity, the Law of commandments in ordinances' (2:14, 15).

EPHESIANS – ONE IN MESSIAH

You and We

God has blessed us – Jews and Gentiles in Christ – *with every spiritual and heavenly blessing in Christ,* just as he had us all in his mind before he made the world and intended us to be *holy in his presence* (Eph. 1:3-4). He lovingly destined us in advance to be adopted through Jesus because of his sheer good will, so that we would be *to the praise of his glory through grace, given us freely in Jesus, in whom we have redemption through his death, the forgiveness of our sins according to the measure of his grace* (vv. 5-6). He lavished that grace on us all with utter wisdom, *revealing the mystery of his will to us,* a mystery shaped by his sheer good will and conceived in himself (vv. 7-9): *to sum up everything in Christ – everything in heaven and earth* (v.10).

In Jesus *we all have also obtained an inheritance* through him who causes everything to work according to his will, so that we (Jews), who were *the first to hope in Messiah,* should be to the praise of his glory. In him, you (Gentiles) have also, as a pledge, been *sealed by the promised Holy Spirit* when you heard the gospel and believed it (1:11-14).

That is why, after hearing of your faith and love in Jesus, I have been giving continual thanks for you when I prayed, that God will enlighten you to understand the hope of his calling to you both as Jews and as Gentiles in Christ, how rich are the joys we inherit from him together in Messiah, what enormous power is involved in our lives – the same power that raised Jesus from the dead and placed him *far above everything* in all ages, including future ones. That same power made Jesus to be *the head of his Body, the church,* which is *the fullness of him who fills all in all* (1:12-23).

You (Gentiles) were *dead in your sins* (2:1-2), and so were we Jews – *by nature children of wrath* just like everyone else (v. 3). But God loved us while we were all in our sin and gave us all new life in Messiah. You have been *saved by grace* (vv. 4-5). He *seated us in the heavenly places with Messiah* to show in the eternal future how glorious is his grace toward us all in the Messiah, Jesus (vv. 6-7).

You have been *saved by grace through faith,* and grace gave you faith, so that no one could boast that he achieved salvation by something he did or by the way he responded to the message of the gospel (vv. 8-9). God crafted us in his mercy by Messiah so that we would live as we should, fulfilling our eternal duties (v. 10).

So, remember that *you were formerly Gentiles,* despised by those who considered themselves the covenant people of God (2:11). You used to be *without a Messiah, excluded from the community of Israel, strangers to the covenants of promise, without hope or God in the world.* Dear reader, note: 'used to be' means that this is true no longer. See verse 19 onwards in the next paragraph. But now you have been brought near by the sacrifice of Messiah. The dividing wall between Jews and Gentiles is now *broken down* by him who united you Gentiles and us Jews, destroyed the enmity created by the Torah and made of us two *one new man.* *He established peace* between us and *reconciled us both* by the same single means – the death of Messiah – to himself, also destroying the righteous enmity that God had toward us both vv. (13-16).

Messiah preached peace with God and with our fellow man, both to Gentiles, *who were distant,* and to Jews, *who were near.* Through Messiah we *both have access to God by the same Spirit* to the one and self-same Father. So, you Gentiles are no longer any different from us Jews in terms of belonging to God's family and with regard to all the blessing and privileges that flow from that status. You are founded *on the foundation of the apostles and prophets,* with Jesus as *the cornerstone* (2:19-22).

That is why I, Paul, *am the prisoner of Jesus for your sakes* – if you have heard about the divine task graciously assigned to me on your behalf. *The mystery* was revealed to me so that I might make it known. In the past it was hidden, but no longer, and it is this: that the Gentiles share with the Jews in the inheritance and the promises, and belong to *the same body,* all this in Jesus the Messiah and through the gospel (not the Torah) (3:1-6).

This privilege was given to me, the least worthy of all: *to preach to the Gentiles the unfathomable riches of Messiah* and *to bring to light* (how) ... *the mystery, which for ages has been hidden in God who created all things* and which I described above, is now to be worked out (3:7-9).

This is no new thing. It is not a departure from the intention of the Torah or from the promises of the prophets. Rather, it is in full accordance with God's eternal purposes with regard to the Messiah (vv. 10-11).

Living It Out in Reality
It is amazing to note that, in calling Jews and Gentiles to live out their newfound unity in Messiah, Paul

makes no reference at all to the keeping of Jewish traditions or of the Torah. He merely calls upon both Jews and Gentiles not to live like Gentiles – that is to say – in sin (4:17-32). The new practices he enumerates and which they are to inculcate are: loving truthfulness, self-control, honesty with regard to material possessions, kindness in human relations, a high work ethic, liberality toward those in need, purity of speech, moral sensitivity, which will assist in abstaining from grieving the Spirit, tender forgiveness, and kindness (Eph. 4:17-31; see also 5:3-6, 9). The standard Paul sets is, again, not the Torah, but the example of Messiah himself (4:32; see also 5:23-24, 25-28, 29), for Jesus is the new Law. Indeed, Paul says, to imitate Jesus is to imitate God himself (Eph. 5:1-2).

Ariel Berkowitz insists: 'the relationship of the non-Jewish person to the Torah is one of permission and encouragement ... they are entitled to follow Torah' (*Berkowitz*, pp. 64, 69). Apart from what we have already said above, what would happen if all the Gentiles in the world, or all the Christian Gentiles, began to observe the Torah? In what way – according to Messianic Jewish views – would Israel be distinct from the other nations? Claude Montefiore (pp. 303-305) was right when he stated, 'Judaism's institutions and laws and embodiment are ... national.'

There is a further issue here. On what grounds do we distinguish between the duties of Jews in Messiah and those of Gentiles who share the same faith? A Jew may be circumcised (Timothy was) but a Gentile may never. (Titus was not, in spite of the pressure put on Paul. The Apostle refused to budge even for kindness' sake, because he wanted to defend the truth.) How, then, can Ariel make this kind of recommendation or David state that 'the elements of Torah which apply to Gentiles under the New Covenant are not the same as those which apply to Jews' (Manifesto, p. 156)? There is not an inkling of such a difference in all of the New Testament.

In terms of spiritual realities and spiritual benefits, there is absolutely no difference between Jews and Gentiles, as there is none between males and females, freemen or slaves. *No difference* because the barrier, the dividing wall which distinguished Jews and Gentiles, has been broken down with respect to everything that relates to life in the Spirit. That is one of the reasons why Jews who believe in Jesus should not observe the Mosaic Law as a matter of religious duty. To do so is to rebuild what Messiah has destroyed and to act as if everything that distinguishes a Jew from a Gentile is still in force!

There is an inconsistency incipient in the Messianic approach to Gentile Christians described above and their relation to the Mosaic Law. If keeping the Law is not necessary for the spiritual health of Gentiles, why is it necessary for Jews? Either the Mosaic Law conveys some spiritual advantages or it does not. If it does, all the followers of Jesus, whether Jewish or Gentile, are obliged to keep it because we are all bound to be the utmost for God, and to strive after the highest level of spirituality possible.

The Essence of the Law
Paul, in fact, speaks in Romans of Gentiles keeping the Law. In chapter 2 he speaks of Gentiles, who *do not have the Law* (v. 14), that is to say, have not been brought into the covenant God made with our forefathers at Sinai and perhaps do not even know about the laws of that covenant. Yet he says that they *do instinctively the things of the law... They show the work of the law written in their hearts* (vv. 14-15). Paul is telling us that the Law of God is also to be found outside of the covenant of Sinai, and that non-Jews are at least unconsciously cognisant of it quite apart from an acquaintance with the Mosaic covenant.

In fact, in the previous chapter Paul states that even determined sinners are aware of the Law, at least to the extent that *they know the ordinance of God, that those who practice such things* (the sins he described in the preceding section) *are worthy of death* (Rom. 1:32). What is Paul talking about? Do the Gentiles instinctively wear a *tsitsit*, keep a kosher kitchen and celebrate Passover? Of course not! Paul is speaking of the moral aspects of the Law, such as are to be found in the Ten Commandments, which are universally and eternally binding. He is talking about not lying and stealing, about faithfulness between a husband and a wife, about not coveting, and about the duty to give each man his due.

That is how Pharaoh and Abimelech knew the difference between right and wrong (Gen. 12:13-19; 26:6-11). That is how Joseph knew that he should not have another man's wife (Gen. 39:6-9). That is why Jesus could permit the eating of non-kosher foods (Mark 7:18-19), contradicting the Law, although Moses had very different things to say about dietary restrictions.

Jesus taught that the preservation and promulgation of the spirit of the Mosaic Law sometimes required its literal transgression, and that is sometimes how the Law was kept. So Jeremiah, the priest, bought land (Jer. 32: 6-15) although the priests were not entitled by the Torah to do so. Once the Law becomes an end in itself, it fails to fulfil its important function of leading us to Messiah.

The moral aspects of the Mosaic Law are to be kept, and not only by Christians or by Jewish Christians. All men are bound to God's moral Law and ever shall be. That is why the Ten Commandments have special status in the context of the Mosaic covenant. They are a summary of the eternal, moral Law of God, a reflection of the image of God that is in every man.

That is why they, rather than other parts of the Law, were written by the finger of God. That is why they and no other parts of the Law were placed in the ark. All mankind is bound to the moral Law of God because to break that law is to disfigure the image of God in man, to rebel against God himself.

The moral Law is a revelation of the glory and the holiness of God, to which all men are obliged to aspire, and by which all will be measured. It is in the light of that Law that we learn that we are sinners in need of saving grace. God's revelation of his holiness and of the holiness he demands of man was most clearly enunciated to our forefathers from Sinai, encapsulated in a specific covenantal form that included various rituals and civil arrangements that were commanded for a time, until Messiah came.

The civil and ritual aspects of the Law are not essential to the Law itself. They pass away. They are the shadow, not the substance. They were the signposts pointing to Messiah, his atoning death and the need for atonement: Messiah's power to transform us and the need for such a transformation. So, David could transgress the ritual aspects of the Law when he and his men ate some of the bread taken from the table of showbread in the tabernacle (1 Sam. 21) although this was ritualistically forbidden (Lev. 24:3-9). Ritual was never a crucial part of the Law. Priests could work on the Sabbath in the tabernacle and in the temple without being charged with doing what is unlawful. They trimmed the lights, cleared the ashes from the altar, carried wood to renew the fire and generally watched over their charges. That is how Paul could say, *circumcision is nothing and uncircumcision is nothing. What matters is the keeping of the commandments of God* (1 Cor. 7:19). That is the burden of the prophetic message. Ritualistic emphasis at the expense of moral adherence is an abomination in God's sight.

The eternal Law of God abides quite apart from the passing away of its civil and ritualistic elements. None of us is now free to steal, lie or engage in sexual promiscuity. All men are bound to love and honour God. That Law bound humanity as a whole, even if it was not formally promulgated, from the creation of the world. It will continue to obligate redeemed humanity in the new heavens and the new earth, where God will be all in all. The substance remains ever the same although the mode of its administration has changed. The same God makes the same eternal demands on man. He does so on the grounds of his divine and eternal sovereignty and his desire that all that exists will suit his perfect will. Even he cannot excuse man from those obligations. As long as God is God, he will demand holiness from his rational creatures.

That is the Law that Jesus satisfied for us by his perfect life and his glorious death. That is *the righteousness of the law*, which his Spirit fulfils in and through us (Rom. 8:4). That is the *righteousness of which our regeneration by the grace of God has made us slaves* (Rom. 6:1-19).

Holiness of life is the product of a work of the Spirit of God in man, wrought by the Spirit through regeneration by grace. It consists of inner conformity to the righteousness of the Law (because the image of God is reflected in the Law) and is expressed in deeds worthy of God and his Messiah. The Law inaugurates the gospel, and is accomplished through the gospel. The Law sets the standards of God's holiness before man and says, *do this and live:*

I must now work my soul to save
for that the Lord commands be done.
I must work like any slave –
If not, I am undone!

This leads us to recognition of our guilt as well as of our inability, evoking in us a craving that nothing except the grace of God can meet. The gospel is the message of God's grace in making up for our lack of Law-keeping and in remaking us into God's perfect image (Col. 3:10) as reflected in the Law, so that grace now says, 'live and do this'. In this way the Torah leads to the gospel, and the gospel to fulfilment of the Law and to glorifying God. As C. T. Studd once quaintly put it,

> I would not work my soul to save
> for that my Lord has done.
> But I will work like any slave
> for love of his dear Son.

What we have, therefore, is not a new Law but the old one under a new form. The covenant of Moses no longer binds us with its rituals and civil forms, while its moral aspects remain in force.

The Mosaic Law in its moral aspects has lost none of its commanding authority. The moral aspects of the covenant are now the rule of life for all those who live by grace. That is one of the reasons why the English Puritans and the Scottish Covenanters identified so warmly with our forefathers. While they longed and prayed for the salvation of our people and our restoration to grace, they knew themselves to be bound to our destiny by the common duties they shared with us as promulgated in the Mosaic Law.

Messiah and the Law

Of course, the ritual aspects of the Law, its symbols, hopes and expectations, all find fulfilment in Jesus. Having been fulfilled, they no longer have the religious value they had in the past yet, for us Jewish Christians, they form part of our national culture. The shadows have passed to give room for the reality, and it is not right for us to insist upon those shadows as if they were still in force. The Mosaic religious institutions, including the sacrifices; the feasts; the specific form of the Sabbath duties; and the restrictions and requirements in terms of dress codes, beards and the such like, are no longer binding. Nor may we exercise our liberty by living as if they were binding. It is our glad and happy duty to demonstrate by our lives, our worship and our communal behaviour that Messiah has come.

The ritual aspects of the Law, particularly the sacrifices, intimated God's method of salvation, but salvation itself was never provided by it except as it reflected the sacrifice of Messiah. It was *not possible* that the *blood of bulls and of goats* could provide a sufficient sacrifice (Heb. 10:4). The promise of forgiveness made in the Torah was dependent on the sacrifice of Messiah and derived its strength from that ultimate sacrifice.

To act now as if Messiah came but did not affect our relation to the Law is – as I said before – to deny with our lives what our mouths profess. To think that the coming of Messiah did not alter the Mosaic Law's relation to us is to ignore the biblical message, which declares that *the Law was given through Moses, grace and truth were realised through Jesus the Messiah* (John 1:17). Whatever else we may want to say about this passage, there is no doubt that it contrasts two periods – that of the Mosaic Law with that of Jesus, the Messiah.

Leo Baeck (*Judaism and Christianity*, Harper Torchbooks, 1958, NY, NY) was right. In a section titled 'The Faith of Paul' he states that in Paul's writings,

'the knowledge of God ... is different from what is meant in Judaism. By proclaiming the risen Christ he proclaimed the presence of God's kingdom: Now the righteousness of God without the Law is manifested' (pp. 160-161).

On the same page he summarises Paul's teaching by saying, 'If the days of Messiah have come, those of the Torah have come to their close'. To prove his point, Baeck refers his readers to Jewish sources which arrive at the same conclusion concerning the relation between the coming of Messiah and the Mosaic Law, such as

Walkout Isaiah 26:2, Midday 61b and Peachy 50a.

Of course, the early church did not at first realise the fuller implications of the teachings of Jesus. The first followers of Jesus never thought of proclaiming the gospel to Gentiles, and when it was proclaimed, they were of the opinion that the Gentiles who believed should assume the yoke of the Mosaic and rabbinic traditions in order to join the community of Israel.

Such a misunderstanding was to be expected. Israel had been taught for many years to think of herself as the sole object of God's saving kindness. The Law of God, with the temple sacrifices, the sacred calendar of celebrations, commemorations and its list of forbidden foods – these had all become part and parcel of their thinking about serving God according to his Word. It was extremely difficult for them to think in any other terms.

Understanding the wider, fuller import of Messiah's accomplishments came only gradually, as the number of Gentile believers in Jesus increased, the issues came to a head and the Holy Spirit enlightened the church. As long as the community of faith consisted almost exclusively of Jews living among their own people, the implications of the teaching of Jesus with regard to the Law and the traditions did not need to be worked out. When they were, difficulties arose and differences of opinion gave rise to tensions in the early church.

THE MESSAGE OF COLOSSIANS

In Colossi there were those who, like the mistaken brethren in Galatia, claimed to have found the way to achieve a higher level of spirituality – what they chose to describe as fullness (Col. 2:10), as putting off the sinful nature (v. 11) or as obtaining a kind of spiritual insight (vv. 2-3). They claimed that the way to higher spirituality is through a combination of rituals and acts of obedience, such as circumcision (vv. 11, 13), avoiding certain foods (v. 21), observing religious festivals, celebrating the appearance of New Moons, the keeping of Sabbath days (v. 16) and various other kinds of regulations. They were also fascinated with angels and forms of self-humiliation (v. 18).

Apparently, mystical concepts (that had became quite common in that period of the Roman Empire and for which Colossi was a notorious outlet), combined with some aspects of Judaism, had influenced the young church in the west of what is now Turkey.

Paul was deeply concerned by these trends, no less than he was when he wrote so forcefully to the Galatians. He warned the Colossian Christians not to be deceived *by fine-sounding arguments* (v. 4) and called upon them to see to it *that no one takes [them] captive through hollow and deceptive philosophy, which depends on human tradition and the basic principles of this world rather than on Christ* (v. 8). Note, the source of such views of the way to ultimate spirituality is human tradition. This tradition is described by Paul as the product of 'the basic principles of this world'. To embrace them is to let go of Christ – nothing less! Paul makes this doubly clear in verse 19, where he says that whoever follows such a course *has lost connection with the Head*, that is, Christ, on which connection the health and growth of the body depends.

What does Paul mean by *the basic principles of this world*? It is worth reminding ourselves that a similar term appears in his letter to the Galatians. Perhaps the discussion there will help us identify those *principles*. As you will remember, the problem in Galatia arose due to the fact that some believers who had arrived from Jerusalem taught that faith in Jesus was wonderful, but not quite enough. Circumcision and the keeping of the Mosaic Law were required in order to achieve what they described as 'righteousness', the Jewish version of 'fullness'.

Paul had asked the Galatian Christians, *Did you receive the Spirit by observing the Law or by believing what you had heard? Are you so foolish? After beginning with the Spirit, are you now trying to obtain your goal by human effort?* (Gal. 3:2-3). He then made his point by saying, *When we were children, we were in slavery under the basic principles of the world* (4:3), that is to say, under the Mosaic Law. *But when the time had fully come, God sent his Son, born under Law, to redeem those under the Law that we might receive the full rights as sons* (4:3-5). Then he asked, *Now that you know God – or rather are known by God – how is it that you are turning back to those weak and miserable principles. Do you wish to be enslaved by them all over again?* (v. 9). And he explained in the verse immediately following: *You observe days and months and seasons and years* (v. 10), concluding his argument with an expression of concern: *I fear for you, that somehow I wasted my efforts on you ... (v. 11).*

So, the *basic principles of this world* are any teachings that attribute spiritual progress to human effort rather than to divine grace, and that interprets human effort as a keeping of the Mosaic Law or any other form of religious ritual.

What, then, is the right way to spiritual fullness? Paul's reply is immediate: The way to be *perfect in Christ* is to focus on Jesus rather than the Law: *We proclaim him* (Col. 1:28), declared the Apostle. In him are to be found all the treasures of wisdom and knowledge (Col. 2:3). We are to continue living *in Christ* on the basis of grace, just as we initially received him by grace, and are rooted and built up in him (v. 6); because in him dwells *all the fullness of the Deity in bodily form* and we have been given fullness in him.

In this way, rather than in glorying in a circumcision performed by human hands, ours is a circumcision that is truly spiritual, of the heart, executed by God himself (v. 11). Of course, Paul is here referring to the promise and call God gave Israel through the prophets (Deut. 30:6; Jer. 4:4; see also Jer. 31:31; Ezek. 11:19). God has removed our sinful nature through the grace that caused us to participate in the death, burial and resurrection of Jesus, as typified in baptism (Col. 2:11-12).

When we were dead in our sins, God made us alive in him, that is, in Christ. He then disarmed the evil powers arrayed against us and *cancelled the written code, with its regulations, that was against us and that stood opposed to us, nailing it to his cross* (2:13-14). The Mosaic covenant has, therefore, no further claim upon us. Having died with Christ to *the basic principles of the world*, we ought not live as if we are still subject to them (v. 20). We are not to submit to their authority, or to that of any tradition. These indeed have an appearance of wisdom, with their self-imposed worship, false humility and harsh treatment of the body, but they lack any real value in restraining sensual indulgence (vv. 22-23). That is something that only grace can do, and grace is to be found in Christ, not in the keeping of Mosaic stipulations or those of any human invention.

Instead of the Law, then, in whole or in part, we should be taken up with Jesus. He achieved for us and accomplishes in us what nothing else can ever hope to achieve. Our hearts should be set on things above, where Jesus sits at the right hand of God (3:1). We are dead, and our life is now hid with Christ in God. Whatever others might tell us, ultimate glory is not to be experienced here and now. But *when Christ, who is [our] life appears. Then [we] will also appear with him in glory* (3:3-4).

Meanwhile, what we need to do is struggle against our love for and habits of sin, relying on grace rather than on our efforts (3:4 and the verses following). That is the way to true spirituality. There is nothing distinctly Jewish about it, but it is certainly altogether biblical. We Jews have no advantage over Gentiles with regard to spirituality because we are all sinners in the very same sense and to the very same degree as are they. The church is one in this respect as in any other, and to deny it is to make Gentiles second-degree citizens of the kingdom, or less. True spirituality is to be found in focusing on him, not on the Torah or on human effort of any kind.

ACTS 10–11, 15:
NO DISTINCTION

The early apostolic church did not, at first, understand the unity of the church in sin and in grace. That is why Peter had to defend his right and that of the brethren that were with him to preach the gospel to the Gentiles and to fellowship with them freely. Remember? They had spent some days in Caesarea, at Cornelius' house – not a home likely to observe the dietary laws of Israel. The charge against Peter and his companions was that they had gone *to uncircumcised men and ate with them* (Acts 11:3). In other words, Peter and those with him had not observed the national traditions. They had eaten non-kosher food as a consequence to the faith Cornelius, his family and friends exhibited.

Peter's defence refers only to the issue of preaching the gospel, and when the brethren in Jerusalem heard that God had given the uncircumcised Gentiles the Holy Spirit just as he had previously done to the Jews

(Acts 11:1), that he had not made any difference between them and the Jewish Christians although Cornelius had not kept the Law, the issue was settled – at least for a time. If the Gentiles could be converted without observing Judaism, Jews could break away from Judaistic custom to express and maintain the unity of believers in Messiah.

The same issue arose when Peter, Barnabas and Paul were in Antioch. Some emissaries from James in Jerusalem demanded that the Gentiles follow through on their faith in Jesus by being circumcised. We have already looked at the letter to the Galatians, but it is worth reminding ourselves that Peter and Barnabas erred in withdrawing from unrestricted fellowship with the Gentile believers. Paul openly challenged them, and the two were apparently convinced of their error, mended their ways and joined Paul in his controversy with the Jerusalemites who had caused such a stir.

Finally, Paul, Barnabas *and certain others* (Acts 15:2) were sent to Jerusalem to have the matters discussed and determined by the elders and apostles there, with Peter apparently joining them at his own initiative (Acts 15:7). The question to be answered was: are the Gentiles in any way obliged to the Mosaic covenant or to other Jewish traditions? Peter's argument was as passionate as it was logical: God sent me to preach to the Gentiles. God bore witness to them, *making no distinction between us and them, cleansing their hearts by faith.* Why, then, put God to the test by considering the imposition of a yoke on the necks of the Gentiles *which neither our fathers nor we have been able to bear?!* (Acts 15:7-11).

The decision carried no recommendations concerning spiritual advantages purportedly attached to keeping the Torah, or the wonderful insights into the teachings of Messiah that the Gentiles could have if they but kept the traditions. Instead, they were declared free from such traditions, except to the point of treating their fellow believers from among the Jews with a respect that will lead them to abstain from certain foods and patterns of behaviour. Please note: this is the only restriction imposed beyond the moral obligations to which all mankind is bound.

ACTS 21:
HOW ABOUT PAUL?

The believers in the early church at Jerusalem had yet to digest the implications of the death and resurrection of Messiah, but it already understood that there was no spiritual advantage in keeping the Law. That was the first step. Once they understood that the Law was not necessary to the service of God, all the rest would fall into place in the course of time. The church concluded, as has Paul Liberman in *The Fig Tree Blossoms* (p. 36): that keeping the ritual and civil aspects of the Mosaic Law is 'no longer required'. It took time for the church in Jerusalem to understand the further implications of that view, and the Apostle was wise enough to accommodate himself to the inability of his much-respected brethren in Jerusalem.

Paul was not engaged in a war against the traditions. He did not spend his time calling upon *all the Jews who live among the Gentiles to forsake Moses, telling them not to circumcise their children nor to walk according to the customs* (Acts 21:21). He had better things to do. He was a preacher of the gospel. Whence had this false rumour risen? It arose from the simple fact that at least some among the Jews who were converted under the message Paul preached in fact forsook the traditions, and Paul did not castigate them for doing so. They now *lived like Gentiles,* as did Peter and Barnabas in Galatia. Delighted with their freedom in Messiah, they had gone to the other extreme of shaking off anything distinctly Jewish although Paul had specifically addressed that issue when he wrote to the Corinthians, insisting that Jews should remain Jews and Gentiles should remain Gentiles because each of these was a *'calling'* (1 Cor. 7:17-20, 23).

Of course he was willing to help keep the peace of the church and participate in the traditional vows (Acts 21:23-26)! Seeing him *walk orderly, keeping the Law* (v. 24) would make it clear to all who were open to learn that there was nothing in the charges raised against him. Rather than embarking on a campaign against the Law, here he was, keeping it. Why not? He had already formulated in his mind the understanding that circumcision – that most sacred of all the symbols of Jewishness – and uncircumcision – that symbol of being outside the pale of the promises to Israel – were unimportant (*nothing,* 1 Cor. 7:19). He would yield for the sake of peace.

Now, you may disagree with my construction of the events just described. But surely, you will acknowledge that this construction is at least possible in the light of the text. The customary Messianic way of interpreting Paul's action as described in Acts 21 is at least open to question. I invite my readers to compare these two views with everything else Paul wrote and said. By participating in a traditional custom from which he knew himself to be free, Paul was yielding to the weakness of his brethren in Jerusalem. The Messianic Movement presents its subservience to the Torah as a strength. In this, they are mistaken. Law-keeping is not a means to spiritual progress or to sanctification.

After all, were it up to us, none of us would ever be sanctified. Our salvation, and our sanctification, is the fruit of God's work for and in us. We are saved and sanctified by grace. Does grace need to be supplemented by works? If our reply is in the affirmative, then grace is not grace because its fulfilment is dependent on human effort. The grace that saves and sanctifies us is the same grace that secures our ultimate glorification, *for nothing can separate us from the love of God, which is in Messiah Jesus our Lord* (Rom. 8:38-39). There is absolutely no room for any human boasting. No flesh can claim the right to glory in God's presence or to attribute even the smallest iota of accomplishment to itself. *By his doing you are in Messiah Jesus, who became to us wisdom from God, and righteousness, and sanctification, and redemption* (1 Cor. 1:30).

Jesus, not the Torah, is the *way, the truth and the life*. Nowhere does he say, 'Follow the Torah' or 'Maintain your traditions'. He says, 'Follow me' – and we remember that he frequently demonstrated his opposition to the traditions and incurred the anger of the Pharisees for doing so. We are to love him more than anything else in the world: more than our nation, our spouses, our siblings, our parents or our own selves, otherwise we cannot be his disciples. He demands a devotion that can be shared with none other. The way to love God is to esteem his Son, our Messiah, above all else, so much that we refrain from attributing spiritual advantage to anything but his grace.

We have not understood the gospel properly until we have understood that absolutely *every good gift comes from above* (Jas. 1:17) and is a gift of God's grace through Messiah. That is what biblical faith is all about. It focuses on God in Messiah and rests entirely on him. John Calvin put it well in his commentary on

Galatians 1:21: the gospel 'rules out anything that man might add' (Gal. 1:11).

We are free and no Law can condemn us, trouble our consciences or demand our attention. Our eyes are on Jesus, the glorious originator and completer of our faith. The Law brings wrath but we have peace with God through our Lord Jesus the Messiah (Rom. 5:1). In spite of our repeated failures, we *delight in the law of God in our inward man* and live, not by the Law but by the Son of God who loved us and gave himself up for us. *Dead to the Law by the dictates of the Law* (Gal. 2:19), we now live to Messiah, rejecting all glorying save that which is in the cross of Messiah Jesus our Lord. By this cross we have died to the world, its mockings, its promises and its pressures, even when they originate with our beloved nation or its vaunted religious leaders.

Hallelujah!

2. RABBINIC CUSTOMS

Lifestyle

Messianic Judaism is united in its insistence upon the necessity of maintaining at least a semblance of adherence to rabbinic custom. The motives quoted for such adherence differ: some insist that Jews in Messiah should follow rabbinic custom simply as a means of national identification. I have little argument with them, so long as our adherence to custom is subject to adherence to Messiah in more than just words, and so long as the custom to which they adhere forms part of the national consensus. If we follow national customs without attaching to them religious significance beyond the facts of history that they celebrate, we are simply acting as Jews in terms of our culture. But the national consensus that unites and identifies all Jews does not include, for example, the lighting of candles on Sabbath, keeping kosher, wearing a yarmulke or a tallit katan, or putting on phylacteries.

Menachem Ben Chaim is a much-loved and deservedly respected brother in Christ, living in Israel. He served faithfully for many years as the Israel Secretary for the International Hebrew Christian Alliance, and then the International Messianic Jewish Alliance, as it came to be called. He is absolutely right when he quotes Hudson Taylor (*King of Kings News*, Vol. 98, January 1998). Referring to the Chinese scene, Taylor wrote: 'the chief objection that people have against Christianity is that it is a foreign religion, and that its tendencies are to approximate the believers to foreign nations ... but why should a foreign aspect be given to Christianity?' Ben Chaim goes on to conclude: 'Messianic Judaism must become truly New Covenant Judaism and call for a dynamic challenge ... for a transformed Jewish life. We may adopt some aspects of normative Jewish life, and we can still learn from our Gentile brothers and sisters in Messiah. Yet we must remain open to the Spirit in the outworking of the New Covenant within Israel for renewed Jewish and Messianic life'.

In spite of his assertions, Menachem has not succumbed to the modern fad of affecting a Jewish lifestyle by acting as if he was still Orthodox except for his faith in Jesus. He is one of the very few supporters of the Messianic Movement who has come from a truly Orthodox background, and yet he lives, clothes himself and acts in life like any other fellow Christian. In traditionally Jewish terms, he lives like a Gentile. Of course, he celebrates the traditional feasts, but he does not wear a yarmulke, and he worships in a congregation in Israel that conducts a mode of worship free from most of the trappings of the synagogue. In other words, in the text quoted, Menachem is calling for a sincere cultural attachment on the part of Jewish people to what he describes as 'normative Jewish life' and what I have chosen to describe as the cultural consensus. Menachem's own lifestyle does not exceed that mark.

Yet even Menachem has said too much. It may be true that one of the main objections 'that [Jewish] people have against Christianity is that it is a foreign religion'. But that is merely an excuse Jewish people like to employ. The real reason why the Jewish people refuse to acknowledge Jesus has to do with a factor that Jews share with all humanity: sin, translated into rebellion against God. That more substantial obstacle cannot be removed by cultural adaptations, however thorough. It requires a work of the Holy Spirit. Menachem needs to recognise that, so long as sin reigns in Jewish (or Gentile) hearts, nothing we can do will save them.

In defending the right of Jewish Christians to adhere to their national identity through their national traditions, Menachem has correctly put that privilege alongside the right of other nations to do likewise. I assume that Menachem did not intend to draw this conclusion, but it derives directly from his argument: Jewish Christians have the same right to do what the Hottentots, the Inuit and the Magyars may do – no more and no less.

We need to take great care that our attachment to national customs is sincere, and that it does not spill over into religious observance. Former Shintoists ought not attach Christian meanings to their national customs, and Muslims who are converted to Christ ought not attach Christian significance to their religious traditions. The rabbis knew and know God to no greater extent than a Shinto priest and Muslim Kadis, and their traditions have no more religious force. Our practice of Jewish traditions is a matter of national custom – no more – and extends to the limit of the national cultural consensus – no further.

Regretfully, my dear friend Menachem has not been as careful in this matter as he should have been. He is increasingly more stringent in his insistence that Jewish Christians should adhere to the national customs. More disconcerting is the fact that the grounds of his insistence are increasingly those against which I warn in this book: confusing freedoms with duties and national culture with religious obligation.

I mentioned the disparity between Menachem's lifestyle and his theory. He is not alone in this respect. Most – no, all – of the Messianic leaders that I know personally, fall short in the same manner. I take comfort in the thought that their practice is better than their theory. I have yet to meet a Messianic Jew who really and truly follows rabbinic traditions. In spite of the vociferous insistence made by some regarding the duty of Jews in Messiah to maintain rabbinic traditions, I know of none who regularly pray at the stipulated times for prayer (Shacharit, Mincha and Ma'ariv), none who avoid tearing toilet paper on the Sabbath and none who avoid walking more than the stipulated three steps without a head covering. As Rausch puts it, 'it is not practical' (*Roots*, p. 227).

It is disconcerting to note that the overwhelming majority of those who adhere to the Messianic Movement do not measure up to the standard of sincerely identifying with their national customs. The greater part of the Messianic Movement is made up of Gentiles who have no business embracing Jewish national customs in the first place. Most of the Jewish people in the movement had no interest in these customs prior to their conversion. They were assimilated Jews. Theirs is not a case of preserving previously precious cultural norms, but of embracing as a part of their newfound religion, customs that they must now learn and apply. But why should the faith of Jesus lead anyone to national custom? Jeff Wasserman (p. 157) is right when he describes much of what goes on in Messianic congregations as an 'affectation of Judaism' and notes that 'an observant Jew from any of the three major American Jewish traditions would find much of what passes of Messianic Jewish worship to be aberrant at worst and unfamiliar at best'. He cites examples (p. 157): in true Jewish tradition, the tallit is not worn on Fridays whereas many Messianic congregations wear it on all occasions of worship. The wearing of the tallit and a kippa by Gentiles is an offence.

Something is wrong here. Jewish national traditions should be adhered to out of intelligent respect, not as a gimmick or a thing to play with. If we empty Jewish tradition of its original meanings and pour into them distinctly Christian content, to which content none of our nation subscribes, we are hardly treating our tradition with respect. Indeed, to what extent can we say that we are really following Jewish tradition? Yet Dan Juster would have us believe that 'Jewish observances point to Yeshua' (*Roots*, p. 131), that Jesus 'lived out the true meaning of Judaism' (*Jewishness and Jesus, 1977*, IVP, Downers Grove IL, p. 28) and that 'it is of spiritual value to mark off the day (Saturday) from other days by a special Friday evening meal, the lighting of candles and prayer' (*Roots*, p. 214). He does not hesitate to declare in the presence of God, 'as [thy people] place the prayer shawl upon themselves, they return to their first love' (*Roots*, p. 214).

Paul Liberman makes similar statements when he says that 'ritual and tradition were previously obligatory. They now take on a higher meaning. They are seen as the foreshadowing of God's overall plan' (*Liberman*, p. 2; see below his amazing statements concerning the Messiah, hidden in the rabbinic traditions of the Passover Seder [see footnote below[1]]). Viewing such an adulteration of its traditions, Judaism

1. *The Fig Tree Blossoms* by Paul Liberman/ The Higher Meaning of Jewish Holidays: Passover (pp. 90-93). People often forget the word 'holiday' is derived from 'holy day'. In many ways these solemn assembles have lost much of their original meaning. By celebrating these holy convocations, Messianic synagogues not only can observe them in the traditional sense, but the new covenant also gives them a higher meaning. Thus, otherwise meaningless ritual can be seen as a foreshadowing of future events. (cont.)

rightly considers itself betrayed by Messianics. How can we persuade our people of the sincerity of our attachment to traditions we emasculate in such a manner by attaching to them new and foreign meanings?

All too many in the Messianic Movement have not done as well as they should have in ensuring that their attachment to Jewish national custom does not spill over into religious observance. One of my correspondents wrote, 'Most of the believers who adopt Jewish practices do so because it is drawing them personally closer to God, because they are finding richness in practising some of the things that are considered (Jewish) Orthodoxy.' Here we are at the crux of the matter. If lighting incense, praying before

---

Much of the ceremony of these occasions was proscribed in the old covenant. However, over the centuries the rabbis have added embellishments. Messianic Judaism believes the biblical ordinances of such convocations should be observed and rabbinical additions de-emphasised. God said these feats 'shall be a statute forever throughout your generations'.

Passover. Exodus 12 gives a full description of the first Passover and its observance as commanded in Leviticus 23:5-7. According to these instructions, the first and last days of this seven day convocation were to be considered holy. Unleavened bread was to be eaten during this period. Traditionally, this was to commemorate the exodus of Israelites from Egypt. They were so rushed they were unable to wait for the yeast to rise in the bread they were baking. Today, bread eaten on this holiday must be unleavened (matsah).

In the New Covenant, the Messiah compared Himself with this bread when He celebrated the Passover. The parallels are worth noting. Yeast is a symbol of sin. It swells, ferments and decays. The Messiah was not puffed up; neither was the matsah. Both have holes from having been pierced. The stripes on the matsah are reminders of the stripes on the Messiah's back from the whipping he suffered. During the Passover Seder (supper), three pieces of matsah were placed in a cloth. The middle piece was broken, as was the Messiah's body. Half of the matsah is hidden and awaits discovery. Isn't this how it is with the Messiah? Anyone truly seeking him will find him. The middle piece is called the afikoman. Afikomenos in Greek means 'I have come'. It also means 'I will return' (the italics are mine – BM).

an icon or gesticulating 'draws me personally closer to God', am I entitled to practise these pagan customs? Remember how much God hated the introduction of any such means of 'drawing closer' to him in the Old Testament, and how he punished our forefathers for the adoption of such measures.[2]

We are not allowed to introduce into the worship of God anything but what he has commanded. No human invention is permitted however effective we might deem it to be in drawing us nearer to God. Paul expressly states that a man praying with his head covered dishonours God – how dare we pray with a yarmulke? Dare we not only add to Scripture but also subtract from it?

It needs to be asked: how do we know that this or another practice draws us closer to God? Feelings? They can be terribly deceptive. The only reliable measuring rod we have is the Bible, and the Bible does not justify the use of Jewish cultural customs in order to draw near to the Almighty. God has shown us his own way to draw near to him: prayer, disciplined holiness, a cultivated spirituality that expresses itself in loving obedience, sincerity guided by the Word of God, self abnegation and an acknowledged dependency upon God, above all, trusting in Christ. These are the means by which we draw near to him. Kissing a Torah scroll, celebrating Purim or eating *matsah* (unleavened bread) during Passover will bring us not one millimetre closer to him who is a consuming fire. They may accord us a genuine emotional experience, but not all emotional experiences are of God.

To insist that Jews in Messiah are required by God to follow rabbinic injunction is to play into the hands of those who oppose the gospel by every means at their disposal, and to accord them a level of religious

---

2. When Aaron presented the golden calf, he said, 'Here is your God, O Israel, who brought you out of Egypt.' The calf was meant to help the people draw near to God.

authority to which only God has the right. Only he may oblige man's conscience.

To assume that the rabbis have such authority is to concede to their claim to the exclusive right to determine the content and confines of Judaism. It is to accept their claim that Judaism as a religion and Jewishness as a national entity are identical, and that their theory of Judaism is the right one. In other words, it is to give credence to their denial of Jesus and to the bondage under which they have placed our people for 2,000 years of darkness and despair. Why should we make such concessions?

Daniel Juster wishes to call us back to what he describes as a 'biblically consistent Judaism' (*Jewishness & Jesus*, p. 34). There simply is no such thing. Judaism is not Jewish; it is in many instances a direct contradiction of biblical teaching. The truth is that the rabbis hijacked Jewish national identity some 2,000 years ago, when the Temple was destroyed. Under the leadership of Rabbi Yochanan Ben Zakkai, they had the foresight others lacked and thereby became, by a fluke of history, the exclusive and recognised guardians of Jewishness. Since then they have held Jewishness captive, distorting her image and threatening to destroy every vestige of her original nature. No, Judaism is definitely not Jewish.

Hengel states that 'more and more the former pluralism (which existed within Judaism prior to the destruction of the Temple – BM) gave way to the pursuit of unity, to a period of consolidation, which began with quick success, was interrupted by the Bar Kochba revolt, and ended with the redaction of the Mishna at the beginning of the third century; this affected a deep change in Judaism that has stamped its further history up until the reforms of the nineteenth century and even until today' (p. 34).

BLIND GUIDES

Even before these rabbinic misconceptions were adopted we heard Jesus describing the rabbis as *blind guides of the blind* (Matt. 15:14). Paul does not hesitate to tell us that the minds and hearts of our people, rabbis included, have been *hardened* (2 Cor. 3:14) *for until this very day at the reading of the Old Covenant the same veil* (described in the preceding verses of Paul's letter) *remains unlifted because it is removed in Messiah. But to this day, whenever Moses is read, a veil lies over their heart; but whenever a man turns to the Lord, the veil is taken away* (2 Cor. 3:14-16).

Is this a coincidence? Is it an afterthought on God's part? Not at all. Apart from those within Israel whom God *reserved for himself* (Rom. 11:2-10), the people of our nation have been blinded and their ears stopped by God himself *lest they see with their eyes, hear with their ears, understand with their hearts, and return and be healed* (Isa. 6:10; compare Rom. 11:8-10). That is exactly what God said he would do. In Isa. 29:13-14 he warns the people: *Because this people draw near with their words and honour me with their lip service, but they remove their hearts far from me and their reverence for me consists of tradition learned by rote, therefore, behold, I will once again deal marvellously with this people, wondrously marvellous; and the wisdom of their wise men shall perish, and the discernment of their discerning men shall be concealed.*

Earlier he said (Isa. 29:9-12), *Be delayed and wait, blind yourselves and be blind. They become drunk, but not with wine; they stagger, but not with strong drink. For the Lord has poured over you a spirit of deep sleep, he has shut your eyes, the prophets; and he has covered your heads, the seers. And the entire vision shall be to you like the words of a sealed book, which when they give it to the one who is literate, saying, 'Please read this,' he will say, 'I cannot, for it is sealed.' Then the book will be given to one who is illiterate, saying, 'Please read this.' And he will say, 'I cannot read'.*

Happily, this is not all Isaiah had to say to Israel in the name of the Lord. God had revealed to him that the day would come when the veil will be removed. *And on that day the deaf shall hear words of a book, and out of their gloom and darkness the eyes of blind shall see and those who err in mind will know the truth, and those who criticise will accept instruction* (29:18, 24). Paul spoke of this too, when he spoke of *the veil* being removed in *Messiah*, when our people *turn to the Lord* (2 Cor. 3:14, 16). This has not yet happened, and the typical rabbinic attitude toward Jesus testifies to their total blindness. Our Lord's assessment of them remains true. Rather than being reliable guides to an understanding of the Torah and in spite of their great learning, their Jewish background and every other advantage they might have, they are blind leaders of the blind. As such, they should not be accorded the high status that Messianic Judaism accords them.

Off With the Shackles!
It is time for our nation to throw off the distorting shackles of rabbinic tradition. Rather than affirming

rabbinicism, we Jewish Christians should challenge it by presenting the only viable alternative: the gospel. Rather than submitting to rabbinicism, we should deny and disprove its claim to be the true interpreter of God's will for our nation. We should reject the tyranny of the rabbis, who seek to impose their religious customs on all who would describe themselves as Jewish.

It is our joy and duty to proclaim that Jesus is the essence of true Jewishness, not rabbinic teachings. Moses, King David, Isaiah and any of the prophets would feel completely out of place in a typical Jewish neighbourhood. They would certainly not find their way through the maze of rabbinic traditions or be comfortable with what now passes as Judaism.

The rabbis have been heartless in their attitude to other Jews who did not accommodate themselves to their standards. Jewish Christians were relentlessly persecuted in the early years. Their persecution was stepped up following the destruction of the Temple. During the Bar Kochba revolt (132-135), Jewish Christians were hounded, hunted and slain because they refused to fight under the banner of that false Messiah, who enjoyed the support of prominent rabbis. That misguided support led to one of the most terrible catastrophes in the history of our nation, yet, rabbinic folklore glories in the error of those days. Throughout the Middle Ages, Jewish Christians were thrust out of the nation into the arms of a waiting church – and then accused of losing their Jewish identity. This reminds me of the young man who murdered his parents, and then asked the judge for clemency because he was an orphan.

In the 1960s, when a large number of (non-Christian) Jews from India arrived in Israel, the rabbis questioned their millennia of devoted sacrifice and demanded that they undergo a 'minor conversion' before they could be recognised as fully Jewish. When the Ethiopian Jews arrived, they were likewise treated, although their traditions had clear biblical foundations and had served to preserve their Jewish identity for over 2,500 years, since the destruction of the first Temple. Both communities were faced with the choice of either being declared non-Jewish or accepting the yoke of rabbinic injunction that is far removed from the biblical sources to which these two ancient communities more faithfully adhered.

Rabbinicism today threatens the free nature of Israeli society by cynically utilising the democratic process in order to undermine it. The Orthodox refuse to recognise the legitimacy of any form of Judaism other than that which they can control, setting themselves up as sole representatives of true Judaism.

Rabbinic totalitarianism has been repeatedly challenged among Jews since the European Emancipation in the 19th century. Reform and Conservative Judaism in Israel and abroad is challenging it. We Jewish Christians ought to challenge it even more specifically: 'Your tradition has contributed greatly to the preservation of Jewish existence. In that respect, we owe you sincere thanks. However, as interpreters of God's word you have failed dismally, and you are consequently guilty of distorting Jewish identity.

'You denied and rejected the Messiah, you institutionalised hypocrisy, you have focused on rites and neglected internal devotion, and you have cultivated a religion of human pride and self-achievement in the very face of contrary biblical testimony. You have been a cause of our continual misery, opposing the rejuvenation of Jewish national life, opposing the founding of the modern state of Israel and now are seeking to draw it back to the dark ages. Repent and believe the Gospel!'

We need to recognise the truth of Jocz's statement, that Judaism 'exists by virtue of its negation of the Christian Faith – [the] affirmation of Christianity would have meant the dissolution of rabbinic Judaism' (*Auschwitz*, pp. 145-146). The infamous Birkat HaMinim – a malediction upon sectarians, inserted into the Eighteen Daily Benedictions shortly after the destruction of the Temple, when Jewish Christians were many and the gospel was spreading all over the world – requests: 'For apostates let there be no hope, and uproot the kingdom of insolence spreading in our days. Cause the Christians (Notsrim) and the heretics (Minim, an inclusive term which had as its focus the Jewish believers in Jesus) to perish in a moment. Blot them out of the Book of Life and write them not among the righteous. You are blessed, O, Lord, who humbles the insolent' (*Jewish Christians: In Controversy* by W. Horbury, T & T Clark, Edinburgh, 1998, p. 67. See also Jocz, *The Jewish People and Jesus Christ*, S.P.C.K. 1962, pp. 51-57).

Judaism Rejects Jesus
Paul Liberman rightly reminds us: 'The New Covenant tells of conflicts (between Jesus and the Pharisees) centering on such things as the various traditions. Messiah's opposition to Pharisaism led to (the Pharisee's) rejection of him and, ultimately, to his crucifixion' (*The Fig Tree Blossoms*, p. 35). Judaism as it is now is a concerted, conscious, determined denial of the message of the gospel, a rejection of Jesus and all that he is, taught and did. There is no way that faithful disciples of Jesus can accommodate their faith to such a negation. There is no way that we can appear Jewish to our people so long as we believe in Jesus, until we successfully challenge rabbinicism's hold on our people by insisting time and again that Judaism is not Jewish. It is a denial of the most fundamental convictions of a truly biblical Judaism.

Juster wrongly describes Messianic Judaism as a movement 'created by a people who responded to the Abrahamic Covenant by faith and were [spiritually] connected to Yeshua' (*Roots*, p. 175). One of my correspondents insisted: '... Overall, the movement is striving to express a Judaism and faith in Jesus the Messiah which is entirely biblical, not rabbinic'.

Messianic Jews are sincerely seeking to do what they believe is right, and they insist that 'right', in this case, means 'biblical'. However, in spite of their best intentions, the results are somewhat different. What most distinguishes Messianic Jews from their fellow believers who are not Jewish is rabbinic practice, adhered to on the wrong grounds, not biblical custom. Kippot, Sabbath candles, Yiddish phrases, prayer shawls, the synagogue readings and other such paraphernalia are all rabbinic, not Jewish, because they have no basis in the Bible.

The Messianic Movement wrongly insists that the only way to be Jewish is to incorporate into our religious practice elements of rabbinic precept. Ariel Berkowitz is mistaken when he fails to distinguish between rabbinic Judaism and the biblical Jewishness of the patriarchs by claiming that 'Judaism began with Abraham when God entered into a covenant [with him]' (*Berkowitz*, p. 66).

Dr Richard C. Nichol, a well-educated and mild defendant of Messianic Judaism, puts it succinctly. Replying to the question posed by the title of his article, *Messianic Judaism – So What Exactly Is It* (*Messianic Life*, Vol. LXXII No. 3, July–Sept. 1999), he says that Messianic Judaism has to do with maintaining Jewish identity 'through rabbinic traditions'. But this practice is fundamentally wrong. James Parkes, a lifelong (non-evangelical) Christian friend of the Jewish people was surely right when he said 'Judaism is no more the religion of the Old Testament, than Catholicism is the religion of the New'.

Rabbinic Traditions
God never commanded many of the traditional rabbinic practices. He never commanded Jewish people to adorn phylacteries or place mezuzahs on their

doorposts. These customs are the convoluted interpretations of the rabbis. Where phylacteries and mezuzot are supposedly mentioned in the Bible, Israel was commanded to place the Law on its heart and as a frontlet between the eyes, to tie the commandments of God on their hands, post them on the doorposts of their homes, and talk about them as they come in and go out (Deut. 6:6-9). These are simply homely ways of saying that the people of God should always be preoccupied with God's Word, and that the Scriptures should guide their every step. In no way can we even begin to satisfy such a commandment by placing a box with a handwritten text that nobody reads on the doorposts of our homes or on our foreheads, any more than we are required to quote a text each time we leave our homes or return to them. Dan Juster is, therefore, mistaken when he describes the use of phylacteries as 'a meaningful way of worship' (*Roots*, p. 215).

In other words, traditional rabbinic interpretations of these instructions from the Mosaic covenant completely miss the point. They are untrue to the meaning of the text, which has nothing to do with boxes, but calls us to be engaged with and live according to the Word of God at all times. This is one of many examples that could be given of the way traditional Judaism is simply not Jewish and why Jewish believers in Jesus should not accept the yoke of that tradition as any part of their obedience to God.

Rabbinic legalism has destroyed the spirit of the Law and rendered it ineffective. Instead of being recognised as the spiritual reality it is, teaching man about God's perfect holiness, his righteousness and truth, Judaism has transformed it into a means through which man in his pride seeks to satisfy the holiness of God. Instead of revealing to man his sinful weakness and teaching him to cast himself on the mercies of God, Judaism has persuaded its adherents that they have the ability to storm the walls of their sinful inclination and overcome it by the power of religious devotion.

The Law is viewed by Judaism by way of legalistic literalism, which takes it out of the realm of morality and into the realm of a commercial transaction: if I do this and that, you will do this and that for me. Judaism has also terribly lowered the moral standards of the Law of God, thus giving man a false sense of security when he should be fleeing for refuge to Messiah.

For example, God forbade our forefathers to glean fallen sheaves, reap what had been forgotten in the field or harvest the fringes of the fields. The rabbis, who believe they have both the right and the duty to legislate everything, faced a problem: how much of a field is its fringe? Instead of allowing each individual to contend with his own heart before God, as do the Scriptures, the rabbis defined the width of a fringe. Now, without a shred of moral reflection, a Jewish farmer may harvest his field up to the very extremities of the rabbinic fringe without a shred of consideration for the needs of his fellow humans. So long as he has not exceeded the bounds determined by the rabbis, his conscience is free and he may exult in his fine religious accomplishment.

But what if the needs of his neighbours exceed the amount he has left in his field? Tough luck. Our devout farmer has fulfilled his obligation to God and, unless his heart is kinder than is his legalistic mind, he is free to go his happy way without a thought for those around him. He can attend synagogue and pray, *'God, I thank you that I am not like other people*, swindlers, unjust, adulterers. I fast twice a week, I pay tithes of all that I get and have left the required, rabbinically defined fringes of my field for the needy. Surely I am worthy of your blessings.' In the hands of the rabbis, the Law has been transformed into an instigator of human pride and self-satisfaction. It has been robbed of its ability to educate toward a sensitive, heartfelt morality that truly fears God and loves one's fellow human.

Rabbinicism Is Not Jewish
Measured by what the Bible teaches, rabbinicism cannot be considered truly biblical. Some have said that the only substantial difference between Judaism and the gospel has to do with whether or not Messiah has already come. This is grossly incorrect. The differences are wider by far than the sole but important question of the Messiahship of Jesus.

It might surprise some of my readers to note that rabbinic Judaism is much closer to Roman Catholicism than it is to the message of the Bible. Its views of the role of the saints, the authority of tradition, the place of the Scriptures in a believer's life and the right of private interpretation, its view of sin, salvation, grace, the value of human effort and of religious ritual, are all contrary to what the Bible teaches and largely identical to those of Catholicism.

The prophets frequently challenged the people's adherence to the letter of the Law instead of to its spirit (Isa. ch. 1, for example). It ultimately served to bring the judgement of God upon our nation. In these and in many other important areas, rabbinic Judaism and its traditions constitute a massive, illegitimate intrusion into the relations between God and man. It is human opinion enthroned above the very Word of God.

As we have seen, some speak of 'returning to the roots of the Faith' by returning to Judaism or an observance of its traditions. An example from the Finnish 'Shorashim Fellowship' is characteristic: 'Shorashim is the Hebrew word for roots. The name describes a new effort in Helsinki to gather together believers who wish to *grow deeper in their Hebraic-Jewish roots*. Our purpose is ... to increase Christians' realisation of the richness of our Hebraic-Jewish *Roots* and how *this may deepen our relationship with God.* The goal is *to win the prize offered by God's upward calling in the Messiah Yeshua* (Phil. 3:14). Specific objectives of this fellowship are ... home meetings on Friday evenings (Erev Shabat) for food, fellowship, fun in song and dance, focus on Messiah and God's teachings (Torah) and meeting family needs' (Shorashim, Liusketie 16 L 67, 00710 Helsinki, Finland – emphases added).

The faith of Jesus is rooted in the Scriptures, not in rabbinic tradition. This is true theologically, and as a fact of history. The apostles and the disciples of the rabbis strongly disagreed as to how the Old Testament was to be understood. They were not united in their views of rabbinic tradition. What is more, Judaism was wholly transformed shortly after the Temple was destroyed. The Jewish Christian challenge to the authority of the rabbis then took on national dimensions. Judaism before that time was multi-formed, free, largely focused on the Torah and the Temple, and engaged in a struggle against idolatrous polytheism. The Judaism of the second century became increasingly monolithic, focused on ritual and tradition, and engaged in a conscious struggle against the gospel.

Rabbinic Judaism constitutes a conscious, determined denial of the claims of Jesus. Evidence of this may be found in Appendix F, which summarises Talmudic teaching on the person of Jesus. To accord that form of Judaism even a modicum of religious authority in the lives of those who profess faith in Jesus as Messiah and Lord is to accord it a place that our Lord clearly denied it.

It is not biblical to say, 'let's prove our Jewishness by submitting to the injunctions of the rabbis'. However vocal may be their claims to the contrary, the rabbis have no right to define what makes Jews Jewish. Messianic Judaism errs by making its central message the very opposite of that which we Jews in Messiah should be affirming. Faith in Jesus is an alternative

– the right alternative, the only true one – to rabbinic Judaism, not its ally.

Some Messianic Jews defend their observance of rabbinic tradition as a matter of religious obligation or as a means to increased spirituality, by claiming that Jesus himself adhered to that tradition. True, but Jesus also ate with his fingers (the use of forks and knives is a relatively modern convention), travelled on a donkey and wore what we would call today a 'dress'.

Of course he kept the traditions! He lived among a people that had not yet been enlightened by the gospel and at a time when the gospel was not yet fully made known. He also openly transgressed those traditions by healing on the Sabbath and defending the disciples' right to pluck grain, peel and eat it on the Sabbath – contrary to tradition – and to eat without the ritual washing of hands. He castigated the Pharisees for their customs because those customs transgressed the Word of God (Mark 7:6-13). When challenged as to why he and his disciples did not observe the pharisaic tradition of fasting on Mondays and Thursdays, he replied by saying that he had not come to improve on rabbinic tradition or to mend whatever was wrong with it. He came to present something completely new (Matt. 9:14-16). The new wine of life that Jesus imparts cannot be contained in the old wineskins of rabbinic tradition. It needs a completely new framework (Matt. 9:17). If Jesus said so, dare we disbelieve?

MATTHEW 23:
RABBINIC JUDAISM IN JESUS' DAY

It is worth looking here at the words of our Lord in Matthew chapter 23, where Jesus gives the most extensive treatment of rabbinic Judaism in the New Testament. He did so long before it unanimously rejected him. As we will see, already at this relatively early stage, rabbinicism had hardened into a system that was in direct conflict with the fundamental principles of God's revelation. Some seek to soften the harshness of our Lord's words by insisting that he was not speaking of Phariseeism as such, but only of those among the Pharisees who were guilty of the charges he raises. They fortify their view by references to similar passages in Jewish writings of the time.

This is incorrect on two accounts. First, the words of Jesus make general reference to the Pharisees as a group and not to those among them who were hypocritical. He describes them all in one sense as *hypocrites* (vv. 13, 15, 23, 25, 27, 29 – not those among the scribes and Pharisees who are hypocrites but *scribes and Pharisees, hypocrites*), and states in verses 3-4 that their demands of the people exceed their demands of themselves. He speaks of those who *have seated themselves in the chair of Moses* (v. 2), thus pointing out that the Pharisees had arrogated to themselves the right to legislate for Israel.

Now, of course, there are exceptions to the general rule. Some rabbinic leaders demanded as much of themselves as they did of their disciples. But the general trend of their religious views still bred and breeds hypocrisy because of its emphasis on the symbolic and external aspects of religion rather than on the issues of spiritual motivation and morality. In Matthew 23 Jesus challenged the general trend of Phariseeism as a whole, not its more extreme or erroneous examples.

The second grounds on which we must reject the view that Jesus is speaking in Matthew 23 only of some among the Pharisees has to do with the nature of the criticisms he raises. As anyone who is acquainted with Judaism knows, these were and are true of rabbinic Judaism as a whole, not just of its fringes.

An emphasis on the symbolic and the external brings men to put on airs, to seek to appear to be devout even if they are not. Large phylacteries, long tassels on the *tsitsit*, are the order of the day, much as devout Jews today will insist on public prayer wherever they may be, demonstratively drawing attention to their devotion by conducting prayers in the presence of others, or walking to the synagogue on Sabbath with their prayer shawls over their heads or shoulders, all *to be seen of men* (Matt. 23:3-5).

In verses 6-12 Jesus speaks out against the abomination of honouring man in a way that should be reserved for God alone. It is disconcerting to see how the hands of famous rabbis are kissed today, their clothing deemed sacred, their presence viewed as the very presence of God. Verses 13-15 make Jesus' view of Phariseeism very clear: instead of opening the doors to spiritual reality, rabbinic Judaism shuts the door to the kingdom of God. It transforms converts into what Jesus calls *sons of hell.*

Why? How? Why such stark language? Because Phariseeism is a total worldview that shuts out the light of the gospel by inculcating concepts that run directly contrary to those of the gospel. The gospel says that no man can meet God's just and perfect requirements. Judaism says that a man's good deeds can outweigh his evil ones. The gospel says that God is independent of human initiative. Judaism says that God would bring Messiah if only Israel kept the Torah and aspects of rabbinic tradition. The gospel declares God to be a gracious, merciful One to whom all men may turn in faith and repentance and be brought into a personal, spiritual relationship with him. Judaism knows of no such grace and of no such relationship.

Jesus calls the Pharisees *blind guides* (v. 16) and shows in verses 15-24 how their sense of priorities is altogether mistaken precisely because they put an emphasis on the visible, the symbolic and the ritualistic. Phariseeism attaches too much attention to measurable incidentals while neglecting the *weightier provisions of the Torah: justice and mercy and faithfulness.* It is a fact of history that Orthodox Judaism has done nothing to promote these qualities in Israeli or Jewish society. Only to the extent that Jews have thrown off the burden of Orthodoxy have they become moral activists, joining forces with others of like heart and mind to labour against the immorality of their respective societies. Orthodoxy tends to cloister itself in small, walled communities in which there are few gardens, little attention given to beauty and the streets are far from clean.

Jesus goes on to say (vv. 25-28) that the rabbinical emphasis on externals leads to a surreptitious but determined immorality in which individuals are thoroughly cleansed on the outside, *but inside they are full of robbery and self-indulgence,* much like the whitewashed graves still to be seen in Israel, *which on the outside appear beautiful, but inside they are full of dead men's bones.* With such a stringent insistence upon the need to obey the Torah, one would expect Jewish religious Orthodoxy to excel in moral achievements. The truth is that a sinful corruption underlies Orthodoxy no less than it underlies all human effort.

In verses 29-36 Jesus charges Phariseeism with the death of the prophets and prophesies that rabbinicism will undergo no change in this respect. *I am sending you prophets and wise men and scribes. Some of them you will kill and crucify, some of them you will scourge in your synagogues and persecute from city to city* (Matt. 23:34). Our people are eminently adept at castigating the Gentiles for their (unquestionably shameful) treatment of our people over the centuries. But rabbinicism has treated the disciples of Jesus with equally consistent hatred. Jewish Christians were forced out of the nation, cursed in the synagogues, refused the rites of marriage and burial, and, where opportunity permitted, physically persecuted. During the Holocaust, Jewish authorities refused to save or succour Jewish Christians, leaving them to the wrath of their persecutors. I would dread to think what would happen in Israel today if the rabbis were free to act according to their convictions. The present infrequent violent activities of semi-official organisations in the country against Jewish Christians, fully supported by the religious establishment, would become commonplace, everyday occurrences.

Jesus brought a revolution in respect to the traditions of Judaism. On the one hand, he deepened and widened our comprehension of the demands of the Law. On the other, he challenged Orthodox tradition as a human imposition. We cannot, we ought not and we dare not act as if the tradition Jesus opposed still has the right to rule over us. Certainly we should not follow that Judaism which chose to reject him almost as firmly as he rejected it.

There seems no room for doubt that Jesus rejected Phariseeism's claim to be a faithful representative of biblical traditions. However sincere may have been the rabbis' efforts to faithfully interpret the commandments of God in the light of the greatly altered situation that prevailed after the destruction of the Temple, that effort failed. Their interpretations created a distance between the believing heart and Scripture, forcing those who would serve God to depend on their traditions. Custom replaced truth and tradition supplanted serious study of the biblical text.

Rabbinic interpretations are described as 'a hedge to the Torah', devised in order to safeguard Jews from ever coming near to transgressing the Laws of God. But by creating such a hedge, the rabbis have created a barrier between believers and their God. Instead of obeying him heartily, directly and sincerely, we are now told that we must place the rabbis and their traditions between God and ourselves.

No! A thousand times no! In no way can human inventions cultivate a truly spiritual love for God. Only God can do that by his Spirit and through the means he has placed at our disposal in his powerful, living, life-transforming Word. None but the Holy Spirit can draw us closer to God, and none but God himself can tell us how to worship him in spirit and in truth. Everything else is a human intrusion into realms where the hand of man is not to be seen.

Did the Apostles Keep Jewish Traditions?
Some insist that the apostles continued to keep rabbinic tradition. Juster states 'It was assumed (*by the early church – B.M.*) that Jewish Christians will maintain their heritage in a biblically consistent way as Jews' (p. 74; see also p. 82), that is to say, in accordance with the traditions.

There is no biblical evidence to support such a statement. All we can say on the basis of biblical data is that there were some within the early church who continued to think in rabbinic terms. This group never succeeded in persuading the apostles or prominent others in the early church of their opinion.

We cannot even say that James supported them, although some who came in his name to Galatia were of the opinion that both the Torah and the traditions should apply to Gentile believers as well as to Jews. There is not a single statement attributed to the apostles that says that Jewish believers are obliged to maintain the traditions. The early church never discussed whether or not Jewish Christians were obliged to maintain the national religious custom. The only issue had to do with the Mosaic Law.

Some continued to observe tradition and were to be borne in loving patience by the rest, until the light of the gospel would impact their thinking and they would be freed from their error. Paul instructed: *Accept the one who is weak in faith, but not for the purpose of passing judgement on his opinions ... who are you to judge the servant of another? To his own master he stands or falls. Why do you ... regard your brother with contempt? Each one of us shall give account of himself to God ... for the kingdom of God is not eating [kosher foods] and drinking [kosher drinks] but righteousness and peace and joy in the Holy Spirit* (Rom. 14:1-17).

We who are strong ought to bear the weaknesses of those without strength and not just please ourselves ... wherefore, accept one another just as Messiah also accepted us to the glory of God (see Romans chapters 14:16–15:13).

Paul addresses Gentiles in these chapters, calling on them to bear with the weaknesses of those among their Jewish brethren who still had qualms about certain aspects of Jewish tradition. He does not describe such qualms as the evidence of spiritual strength but as a weakness (14:1; 15:1). As for himself, he declares, *I know and am convinced in the Lord Jesus that nothing is unclean in itself* (Rom. 14:14).

Everything is kosher, everything is acceptable to be received and eaten with thanks to God, the gracious Provider (see 1 Tim. 4:4). The dietary restrictions imposed upon Israel by the commandment of God and as an integral part of the Mosaic covenant are no longer binding (see also Mark 7:14-19). Whoever thinks something to be unclean, it is unclean in his own mind (not in and of itself, Rom. 14:14). So, do not wound the oversensitive and misinformed conscience of your brother by demonstratively partaking of foods that offend his conscience (14:15).

The fact that Paul was eager to be in Jerusalem to celebrate the feast (Acts 18:20-21) cannot be used to argue that he was an avid follower of the traditions, because he spent many a year without going to the feast. In fact, he did not arrive in time for Passover – the main feast – only for Pentecost.

Upon arriving in Jerusalem, Paul was requested by James to demonstrate that he did not oppose the traditions as such, by participating in a traditional ritual. The reason James gives for his request is very instructive. Note how James speaks of a certain party in the Jerusalem church (among whom he does not number himself): *You see, brother, how many thousands there are among the Jews who have believed, and they* (not 'we') *are all zealous for the Torah...* (Acts 21:20).

Paul was requested to show that, by following the national tradition, he was not in opposition to the Torah and that he could also freely keep its commandments (Acts 21:24). In this way, it was hoped, Paul could put an end to the rumour that he had embarked on an anti-Torah campaign, *teaching all the Jews who are among the Gentiles to forsake Moses, telling them not to circumcise their children, nor to walk according to the customs* (Acts 21:21).

Paul preached the gospel to *all the Jews who are among the Gentiles.* His efforts caused them to be driven out of the synagogues. Their faith brought them into close and constant fellowship with their Gentile fellow believers. In other words, as a result of his efforts, Jewish Christians in fact forsook the traditional customs. But Paul was not engaged in an all-out campaign against those customs. His concern was for the gospel.

Of course, the apostles continued to make their way to the temple (Acts 3:1; 5:25). They did so at the times of public prayer (Acts 3:1). But this in no way proves that they participated in the temple worship. Worship in the temple focused on public sacrifice, not public prayer, and there is a very good reason why the New Testament never once portrays the apostles offering sacrifice. Every time they visited the temple, the apostles proclaimed the gospel. There was no better place and no better time to do so, just as Paul could find a better place to preach than at the local synagogue or market-place (Acts 9:20; 13:5, 14-17ff.; 14:1, etc.).

The council in Jerusalem (Acts 15) set no bars to fellowship between Jews and Gentiles in Messiah. It did not call upon the Gentiles to maintain Jewish religious tradition because 'there is a glorious and beneficial dimension to some of the traditions of Judaism', as many modern-day Messianic Jews insist. Paul circumcised Timothy because his mother was Jewish (Acts 16:1-3) and *because of the Jews who were in those parts* (v. 3), not for any religious or spiritual purpose.

Messianic congregations should not adhere to rabbinic traditions in the way that they do. Distinctions between the duties of Messianic Jews and those of their Gentile brethren in Messiah in matters relating to obedience to God inevitably become barriers to unqualified and open fellowship. If I am required to do anything beyond believing in Jesus and obeying him to be accepted as an equal, I am being obliged to meet a condition that restricts my fellowship to the extent of my obedience.

Paul has some interesting things to say about his day's Judaism in terms of its knowledge of God. Remember, he wrote before Judaism had crystallised into the concerted and consistent rejection of the Messiahship of Jesus it now is. In chapter three of his second letter to the Corinthians, Paul contrasts the divinely inspired religion of Moses with the equally divinely inspired religion of Jesus, but goes on to reflect briefly on rabbinic Judaism. He describes the faith taught through Moses in terms of *the ministry of death ... engraved on stones* (v. 7) and as *the ministry of condemnation* (v. 9) whose glory fades away (v. 11) under which there is now *a hardening* of minds (v. 14) and hearts (v. 15). In consequence, as Moses is now regularly read in the course of the synagogue ritual and according to Jewish custom, instead of spiritual insight there is *blindness:* a veil has been spread over the minds and hearts of the readers. That veil can only be removed in Christ (vv. 14-16). So, rather than spiritual insight, Judaism suffers according to Paul from a judicial blindness. How is progress in spiritual things obtained? Paul tells us that it is not through the Torah but by *turning to the Lord*, who sends his Spirit to remove the veil. Then, *beholding the glory of the Lord* revealed in the Torah as in a mirror, we are steadily *transformed into that same image* by the powerful workings of the Spirit, *from glory to glory* (vv. 16-18).

Rabbinicism and National Custom
Some Messianic Jews are delighted to see Gentile fellow believers aping Jewish custom (it is a matter of considerable embarrassment to note that the overwhelming majority in Messianic congregations throughout the Diaspora is, in fact, non-Jewish, including a sizeable part of its local leadership). Fellowship on such grounds is not true Christian fellowship. Fellowship in Messiah connotes unconditional equality, not the superiority of Jewish (or any other) custom. That is precisely Paul's

argument against Peter's behaviour in Galatia (Gal. 2:12). If we cannot walk into the home of a non-Jewish believer and eat freely whatever he serves, our fellowship is compromised. If we do eat freely, our professed obedience to the covenant is compromised. If we insist on our duty to keep the traditions, we cannot eat freely because our professed obedience to the covenant would be compromised. It is not possible to have one's cake and eat it. Either we are under the commandments of the covenant or we are not. Either the body of Messiah is one, or it is divided.

We do acknowledge that rabbinic traditions form a large part of the culture of the Jewish nation and, as such, are the means by which Jews express and identify themselves as Jews. They form the consensus of cultural symbols by which Jews identify themselves as Jews throughout the world. Such traditions determine which holidays Jews celebrate and, to a great extent, how they celebrate them. Jewish national holidays have become one of the few distinctive national features, along with a theoretical nod toward other aspects of rabbinic custom (some of which are remotely related to biblical injunctions) such as not eating pork – at least at home – and attaching some slight importance to a seventh-day Sabbath rather than to Sunday. To this we might add the traditional festive meal on Sabbath eve, when the family meets together at the table. In other words, rabbinic customs play a large role in the formation of that tradition which constitutes the national cultural consensus among Jewish people, and which distinguishes them as such.

Of course, much of that tradition has pagan roots. One example of this is the traditional belief that, in the period between Rosh HaShanah and Yom Kippur, God determines the fate of each individual for the coming year.

The roots of some other features in Jewish tradition are unknown. No one knows, for example, when or why male Jews began covering their heads. No one knows the reasons for some aspects of the Passover Seder. It may be surprising to those who have never thought about it to observe how much of their own national traditions, Jewish and Gentile, have religious – even pagan – roots: the lighted Christmas tree in some Christian traditions and Hanukkah lights in the Jewish tradition both have roots in pagan custom, as daylight became increasingly shorter and the night encroached on simple folks' confidence and joy.

Most of these distinctly pagan religious overtones have been supplanted, blurred or, to some extent, lost. Christians who celebrate Christmas do so in commemoration of the birth of Jesus. Jews who celebrate Hanukkah are commemorating the Maccabean victory over the impositions of Antiochus Epiphanes. The pagan overtones are long forgotten. When practised as a matter of national culture, not as a religious duty or to gain some purported spiritual advantage, there is nothing wrong with such traditions. That is the way national and religious groups identify themselves both to outsiders and to those within.

Jewish rabbinic custom can serve Jewish Christians in the same manner, just as it does the rest of the nation. However, any such practice must be subject to careful scrutiny so as not to allow it to conflict with the gospel, or permit any part of its message to be less than crystal clear. This is where the book now in your hands controverts Messianic Jewish practice. Although Messianic Jews make much of quoting the Bible, Messianic Judaism is in fact not guided by truly biblical standards in its attitude to Jewish tradition. The extent to which I have succeeded in proving this is the extent to which Messianic Judaism should be rejected.

For example, Paul teaches that a man who prays to God with a head covering *dishonours his head*, that is, Messiah (1 Cor. 11:4). The adoption of any form of headgear (such as kippot) in worship is a deviation from the biblical norm. The practice of some Messianic congregations to accord the Torah prominence over other portions of Scripture (by placing a Torah scroll in the sanctuary, by celebrating Simchat Torah, kissing the Torah scroll and the such like) is a tacit acceptance of rabbinic religious norms that fly in the face of Scripture (Heb. 8). A further example is the now popular attribution of Christian symbolism to purely rabbinic custom, such as certain features in the Passover Seder. The rabbis who invented the afikoman,[1] for example, were not inspired by the Spirit when they did so and Messiah is not hidden in the afikoman.

Rabbinic custom has no religious authority over those who are in Messiah and should not be accorded tacit legitimatisation by having Christian spiritual significance attached to it. Besides these relatively minor contradictions, Judaism clashes with the message of the Bible on every crucial point imaginable. God, man, salvation, righteousness, the person of Messiah and many other fundamental issues as seen by Judaism are the exact opposite of what evangelical, biblical Christianity holds to be true. I need not elaborate because we have discussed these issues earlier.

David Stern's unbelievable insistence that 'many scholars believe that these customs were started by Messianic Jews and invested with the meanings we have noted here, but somehow the customs were absorbed into non-Messianic Judaism' (*Manifesto*, p. 171)

---

1. The afikoman is the middle of three layers of unleavened bread that serve in the Passover meal. The afikoman is hidden at the beginning of the festive meal and must be found (usually by one of the children) before the festive meal can formally end. Whoever finds it can have it redeemed from him by way of a gift from the leader of the Passover meal. Some have taken to identifying the afikoman with Messiah, the second of the three persons of the Godhead, smitten and pierced for Israel and now hidden from the people. Those who 'find' him are rewarded with the gift of salvation.

is wholly contrary to fact. There are no such scholars and there are no grounds for such an assertion except wishful thinking and a certain (welcome) discomfort with the attribution of Christological intimations to a central Jewish tradition.

A no less unhappy example of Messianic efforts to find biblical grounds for rabbinic tradition is to be found in the words of Russel Reskin in his article *Torah for Today*, published in the March-April 1999 issue of *The Messianic Jewish Life*: 'The sages ask, "where is there an allusion to the book of Esther in the Torah?"'(Chullin 159b). They answer with a reference to the warning of exile in Deuteronomy 31:18, "and I will certainly hide my face". In Hebrew this reads, "anochi haster astir lanai". Astir – hide – sounds like the name Esther. The term *haster panim*, to hide the face, describes ... conditions that dominate the story of Esther. Rashi (a well-known rabbinical commentator – *BM*) wrote, "in the days of Esther there will be hester panim, hiding of the divine countenance..."' This is not biblical interpretation but playing fast and loose with Scripture to make it say what we want it to say.

Again, Barney Kasdan writes in *Passover and the Feast of Unleavened Bread, 1993* that there are 'spiritual lessons' to be found in the rabbinic traditions surrounding the Passover feast. 'These customs may seem strange to the uninitiated but the deep spiritual truth will be evident to discerning believers in Yeshua.' (*Messianic Jewish Life*, Vol. LXXII, No. 2, p. 6). Discerning believers and Orthodox Jews alike know this not to be true.

It is important to understand that consistent religious observance of rabbinic custom cannot be limited to a merely outward symbolism. Rabbinicism was designed to affect the totality of life and indeed does so. It encompasses all of an individual's life: what he eats, what is the first thing he does in the morning, what kind of toilet paper he buys, when he can get into his car and travel – there is no end to rabbinic injunction. In this way, rabbinicism becomes a trap. If consistently followed as a matter of religious obligation, no area of life can remain unaffected.

Still further, if the authority of the rabbis is recognised as representing the will of God for the Jewish people, why not submit to their authority when they deny biblical truth and join in the one affirmation that has united rabbis everywhere for two millennia who declared that 'Jesus is not the Messiah'? Dan Juster goes so far as to say, 'At no time can we biblically draw a line and say, "from this time forward, if a Jew hasn't accepted Yeshua, he is lost".' Jews can be saved from the wrath of God 'through natural revelation or the Abrahamic Covenant... We cannot preclude the possibility of Jews responding in faith to God's revelation in the Tanach even if they reject and deny Jesus the honour that is due him as Lord, Saviour and Messiah' (*Roots,* p. 17ff., 172). What is this if not a denial of the necessity of the atoning death of Messiah and the regenerating work of the Holy Spirit, giving faith and repentance?! Or have we bought into the modernistic, liberal view that speaks of an 'unconscious faith'. As if Jews can believe in Jesus by the force of 'God's revelation in the Old Testament', without knowing it is him in whom they believe.

If Jews can be saved by virtue of such a faith, why can Gentiles not be saved in the same way? Indeed – why did Jesus come to suffer in the first place? In rejecting the uniqueness of Jesus as the way to salvation, Messianic Judaism is in danger of losing its grip on Jesus altogether. Such statements give rise to the concern that Messianic Judaism is losing its grip on the gospel and is on the way of becoming just another cult.

So, then, we Jews in Christ do not cease to be Jewish by virtue of our faith in Jesus, nor ought we. If believing in Jesus amounted to a termination of our Jewish identity, it would also amount to a denial of the Old Testament and thereby to Jesus' claim to be the

Messiah of Israel. The difference between Jews in Messiah and their Gentile brethren is not one of religion or of religious duty. It may only be one of national culture.

Jewish Christians are Jews and most of us wish to remain Jews. We identify with our people: we celebrate the biblical feasts, we delight in the existence of our State, honour the Israeli flag and maintain those aspects of our national traditions that form part of the national consensus that serves as a means of self-identification with fellow Jews the world over. But we are free from the Mosaic Law and from rabbinic authority, and we refuse to submit again to that yoke of bondage. Messiah is our sufficiency. We freely confess,

> 'Nothing in my hand I bring
> Simply to thy cross I cling.'

In so doing, we find life.

EVANGELISM AND CONGREGATIONAL LIFE

How to Become More Effective

One of the main justifications that supporters of the Messianic Movement raise for Messianic Judaism is the hope and desire that the Movement will be more effective in promoting faith in Jesus among the Jewish people. David Stern explains that Messianic Judaism is designed for 'sparking the salvation of the Jews and the fulfilment of the church's great commission' (*Manifesto*, p. 10). He insists: 'Messianic Judaism will not make significant inroads in the Jewish community without interacting seriously with the Judaism that exists today' (*Manifesto*, p. 174).

Paul Liberman states, 'for nearly two thousand years the Christian church has missed chances to fulfil its mission to bring the good news of the coming of the Messiah to the world's Jewish population. A time for change has come.' The change called for is then described: 'by becoming better Jews ... Traditional

Judaism no longer can justify the claim that acceptance of the New Testament is an attempt ... to assimilate' (*Liberman*, p. 2). 'This adds credibility to Jewish believers in the New Testament... Thus, the existence of completed Jews forces the fair-minded traditional Jews to examine his criteria for determining what a Jew is' (p. 6). He concludes, 'If you want fewer Jews to accept the Messiah, make the faith less Jewish. If you want more Jews to accept him, then reinforce the Jewishness of the faith' (p. 70).

We already noted that the Messianic Movement has attracted many more Gentiles than it has Jews, and that it has failed both in promoting the gospel among the Jewish people and finding acceptance within the Jewish community. These facts should move every sincere lover of God in the Movement to reconsider his position.

The Messianic Movement is right: it is indeed best 'that Jews are able to hear [the gospel] message from Jewish lips in a Jewish idiom' (*Jocz, Auschwitz*, p. 215). But the Jewish people need to hear the gospel, not a confused, unintelligible message, or one that focuses on some form of Jewishness and on the Messiahship of Jesus instead of the essentials. The crux of the gospel is man's sinfulness and God's grace in Jesus – nothing less. It is the gospel that is God's power to save, not the purported wisdom of how we present it. That is where a good part of the statements by David and Paul and quoted above fall short.

"Sparking the salvation of the Jews and the fulfilment of the church's great commission' is something that God has promised to do – by the power of the gospel. It is a work he has reserved exclusively for himself because only he can do it. *Faith comes by hearing and hearing by the word of Christ* (Rom. 10:17). It is our duty to preach the gospel. But our main responsibility is to preach it faithfully, not effectively. The human heart is so infected with and so enslaved to sin that no amount of human persuasion can convince it to turn from it to God. God must work to free our people from the shackles that bind every man on earth, and only then will they look upon him they have pierced and turn to the Lord in repentance.

In the things that pertain to God, there is no such thing as a 'fair-minded' traditional Jew, any more than there can be a fair-minded Gentile. Our minds, wills and emotions are affected by sin to the extent that we are inherently prejudiced to the point of hostility (Col. 1:21) against the true message of the gospel. There is nothing we can do to change that. The Jewish people need to be born again, from above, by an act of God. Until then traditional Judaism will continue to raise determined objections to the gospel, including the charge that Jews who believe in Jesus have apostatised, gone over to the enemy, forsaken their people and turned their backs to their culture.

We do not need to become better Jews, but far better Christians. It is the holiness of our lives, the measure of our Christ-likeness that will count, far more than a self-defeating effort to persuade an unwilling Jewry that we are still Jewish by making some Jewish customs part of our Christian obedience. We should be declaring the gospel to our people with complete confidence in the power of God, who stopped Paul dead in his tracks and transformed him into a preacher of the very gospel he opposed, and he can do it again. It was not anyone's Jewishness that persuaded Paul of the grace of God in Christ, but the power of God. Conversion always is an act of divine power.

We need to preach to our people much more than the simple message that Jesus is the Messiah and that the gospel is Jewish. We need to preach about *sin, righteousness and the judgement* to come. We need to call our people to repent of their sin, of their self-reliance and their determined rejection of Jesus. They must learn to acknowledge him to be God our Saviour, the only sufficient atonement for our sins. Instead of looking for more effective ways to win the hearts of our people, we should have more confidence in the Spirit of God and in his ability to change the heart of all and any. God is the Saviour. We are merely heralds of his mighty Word.

Authentic Judaism?
Messianic Judaism has sought to justify many of its distinctive congregational practices by reference to the purported evangelistic appeal of those practices. There is an important difference between evangelism and congregational life, often overlooked in discussions of the Messianic Movement.

While, as we have seen from 1 Cor. 9:20 (see also Acts 17), Paul accommodated himself to his respective national audiences when presenting the gospel, there is no biblical evidence of nationally based congregations, or of congregations that focused on culture or ethnic identity. Quite to the contrary. We learn from the books of Acts that congregations were nationally mixed (13:43, 48; 14:1, etc.). The apostolic epistles also evidence congregations that were made up of Jews and Gentiles (Rom 2:17 and 11:13; Gal. 2:11-12, for example). In other words, there is no biblical example of ethnic or cultural distinctives as the grounds for congregational life.

Naturally, congregations will take on the cultural baggage of their respective surroundings and of the majority of their congregants. Culture is, after all, a language of sorts and people are expected to speak their own language. There is no need to learn Hebrew, Latin or Esperanto in order to worship God if those are not the languages of the nation or people we seek to address. Nor is there need to take on a 'universal culture', if there is such a thing. Jews in Messiah remain Jews, and Gentiles in Messiah remain Dutch or Chinese, French or Hottentot Gentiles. They identify themselves as such by their culture, including the culture of their worship. Where a congregation is largely made up of Greek or Hindu speakers, the language of worship will inevitably be Greek or Hindu. But Messiah must be the focus, not culture or national identity. Jesus must have the glory, the prominence, the praise and the attentive obedience of the people, none other. This is an area in which consistent Messianic Judaism has failed dismally.

The modern-day emphasis on ethnic backgrounds, epitomised in the Messianic Movement, is an expression of a contemporary individualism that is less biblical than we might think. Of course the individual has worth – Messiah died for individuals. He also died to make both Jew and Gentile into *one new man* (Eph. 2:15) in which our oneness is far more important than our individuality.

The Messianic Movement is an expression of Jewish Christian insecurity, and a desire to find and to assert a sense of worth. For the many Gentiles in the Movement, Messianism provides a sense of being 'in', of belonging to an elite of some kind. I was flabbergasted to find, during my visit to Namibia in 2001, a 'Messianic Jewish' group wholly made up of Gentiles. Imagine: smack in the middle of nowhere, with the African sun beating down on their heads and the Namibian desert all around, a group of Gentiles had found a shortcut to God! As someone enthusiastically described the practice of one of the group: 'It's wonderful. She sits there, lights the candles, and just enjoys the presence of God.'

No individual, no group of individuals, is void of legitimate worth. True worth comes from God in Messiah. We find ourselves by losing ourselves, not through self-assertion. We are granted life when we fall into the ground and die rather than when we develop our respective identities and promote our personal or group agendas. Being Jewish will not get us very far in the kingdom of God. It is Christ we should be seeking, not our own identity.

In an effort to be different, Messianic Judaism has created liturgical practices that can in no case be recognised as Jewish, although a large and still-growing Gentile populace seems to think that they are. Most of so-called 'Messianic music' has nothing distinctly Jewish about it. It is simply modern-day charismatic chorus singing, often in truncated Hebrew ('Arkhamcha Adonai') or with a heap of garbled Hebrew words that make no semantic sense ('Baruch Hashem Adonai Yeshua'). Messianic Judaism does not identify with Judaism as such, but with those cultural forms of Judaism that developed in Eastern Europe [chicken noodle soup on Sabbath eve, corn beef sandwiches and Jewish delicatessen foods] or in Israel [dancing the Hora, eating tehina and humus, singing Hava Nagila]. As to 'Davidic dancing' – I invite any of my readers to try and perform such a dance in a synagogue service, or allow women carrying banners to prance about in the aisles.

Is there truly any spiritual value in singing in Hebrew (much in vogue nowadays) when no one can understand what he or she is singing? Ought we not sing with the understanding as well as with our hearts? Why not, then, have our sermons in Hebrew and conduct prayer in that language, much as did the Catholic Church when it restricted its worship to the so-called holy language of Latin?

Congregational Practice
What has happened to the church of God? Have we forgotten the Reformation? Have we forgotten the Reformers' call to do away with empty ritual that could not address the mind, and to ensure that the people are addressed and invited to worship in a language they can understand rather than in the mumbo-jumbo of a foreign language? Or is that mumbo-jumbo transformed into a spiritual exercise simply because it is Hebrew? Can true worship be found where we do not understand what the people nearby are saying?

God is a Spirit and, as such, must be *worshipped in spirit and in truth*. 'Spirit' in biblical terms is not equal to emotion. It is a heartfelt response to truth that has been understood, imbibed, loved and experienced. As we hear or sing of the majesty of God and of his unfathomable love, our spirits are stirred to worship him. The more we discover his awful, glorious holiness and our abject sinful nature, the more we discover our inability to please him, make atonement for our sins or in any other way be acceptable to him. The more we discover of the wonder of his grace in Messiah, our hearts will be moved to true biblical worship. 'Spirit' is always linked to 'truth'.

Paul Liberman asks, 'Isn't it much more reasonable ... to speak Hebrew when talking to a Hebrew?' (Liberman, p. 5). Of course! It is always right to present the gospel in the language of the people we address, taking into account their sensitivities, their prejudices and their fundamental concepts. But why speak or sing in Hebrew when no one understands, or can understand better in English, French or Russian?

Richard Gibson writes from England: 'Give thanks to God for a young Israeli man who recently made a profession of faith in Jesus as his Messiah. He has faced much opposition and misunderstanding from family and the local community. In recent days his faith has taken a real battering from the enemy. We do all of our studies in Hebrew, so there is no problem with English church culture and confusing terminology. (Hebrew is his mother tongue.) When he did come along to church he found it very difficult, not just because most of the imagery and language represented what, for most of his life, was "the enemy". Please do not underestimate just how genuinely difficult this is for him. He has no such problems when he attends Leeds Messianic Fellowship as it is his culture that is the context for our presentation of the Gospel and not one that is, in his experience, anti-Semitic' (*Richard and Rita Gibson Newsletter*, August 1999. See also Appendix A).

Churches should do a great deal more than has

been done to rid themselves of the remnants of anti-Semitism that crept into their thinking over the centuries. More effort needs to be invested by churches so that Jewish and other minorities can discover that they are sincerely welcome, that they have not 'gone over to the enemy' by embracing their fellow believers in Messiah.

I ask again: is it right to make ethnicity the focus around which a congregation gathers? Is it right to establish congregations whose sole distinction is cultural, especially when the majority of those living in the given area do not share that culture? In other words, is it biblically justifiable to form congregations on national bases? I believe not. I see no such justification for such practice in Scripture. Paul spent most of his Christian life opposing such a tendency, because it threatens the delicate fabric of unity in Messiah. Worse: it displaces the Lord of Glory and gives his rightful place to national culture. Brothers and sisters, that is something we should never do. Jesus must always have the pre-eminence.

Why should a Sikh Christian imbibe Hindu cultural mores when he is living among his own Sikh people? Is Hindu culture more akin to the gospel than Sikh? Why should a Gentile Christian take on Jewish cultural trappings in order to worship in a congregation that has chosen to describe itself as Messianic? Rabbinic Judaism is not more inherently spiritual than, say, Norwegian Lutheran culture. It is certainly not more biblical, even if it makes endless references to biblical passages. Norwegian Lutheran culture does so almost as much. Why should a Gentile Christian forsake his own culture? Did not Paul insist upon Jews remaining Jews and Gentiles remaining Gentiles (1 Cor. 7:18 again)? There is no doubt in my mind that, if Paul were with us today, he would strenuously oppose the Messianic Movement.

A CHURCH AMONG JEWS:
SOME THEOLOGICAL REFLECTIONS

God Over All

This is God's world. For this reason, everything that purports to be godly, wise or just should be guided by his written Word (Isa. 8:20). God is wise, just and gracious beyond human comprehension. He is the adored object of the angels' eternal praise. Human wisdom is not sufficient for the management of this world, nor is it truly wise in comparison with the wisdom of him who made the worlds (Isa. 55:8-9).

Everything that purports to be biblical should have Jesus, his glory, his deeds, his teaching and his accomplishments as both its ground and its focus (Col. 1:16). No other name, no other authority, no other interest may be allowed to intrude into the centre of our activities or the focus of our lives. This is true because God's Word has Jesus as its object (Luke 24:27, 44-47), and the glory of God – through and in Jesus – as its eternal goal. All Scripture speaks of and leads to him.

These principles should be doubly clear when we reflect on our theme, 'A Church Among the Jewish People'. Our task as theologians differs in no essential way from our task as disciples of Messiah: not to seek out the most cost-effective or socially acceptable means to promote the message committed to us, but to engage the society into which we have been sent with the message of Messiah, and to do so in the most biblically faithful manner God puts within our reach. If this means calling upon those who hear us to bear the price of discipleship by going outside the camp, where the lepers and the unclean are sent, so be it. We have neither right nor inclination to try to improve on what God has done or said. Our primary duty is also our greatest delight – to obey.

The Biblical Data

Ephesians Chapter Two
The text that follows is the second chapter in Paul's letter to the Ephesians:

> *You were dead in your trespasses and sins, in which you formerly walked according to the course of this world, according to the prince of the power of the air, of the spirit that is now working in the sons of disobedience.*
>
> *Among them we too all formerly lived in the lusts of our flesh, indulging the desires of the flesh and of the mind, and were by nature children of wrath, even as the rest.*
>
> *But God, being rich in mercy, because of His great love with which He loved us, even when we were dead in our transgressions, made us alive together with Christ (by grace you have been saved), and raised us up with Him, and seated us with Him in the heavenly places in Christ Jesus, in order that in the ages to come He might show the surpassing riches of his grace in kindness toward us in Christ Jesus.*
>
> *For by grace you have been saved through faith, and that not of yourselves; it is the gift of God.*
>
> *Not as a result of works, that no one should boast.*
>
> *For we are His workmanship, created in Christ Jesus*

for good works which God prepared beforehand that we should walk in them.

Therefore remember, that formerly you, the Gentiles in the flesh – who are called 'Uncircumcision' by the so-called 'Circumcision' which is performed in the flesh by human hands – remember that you were at that time separate from Christ, excluded from the commonwealth of Israel and strangers to the covenants of promise, having no hope and without God in the world.

But now, in Christ Jesus, you who formerly were 'far off' have been 'brought near' by the blood of Christ.

For He Himself is our peace, who made both groups into one and broke down the barrier of the dividing wall by abolishing in His flesh the enmity, which is the Law of commandments contained in ordinances, that in Himself He might make the two into one new man, thus establishing peace, and might reconcile them both in one body to God through the cross, by it having put to death the enmity.

And He came and preached peace to you who were 'far away' and peace to those who were 'near'.

For through Him we both have our access in one Spirit to the Father.

So then, you are no longer strangers and aliens but you are fellow citizens with the saints and are of God's household, having been built upon the foundation of the apostles and prophets – Christ Jesus Himself being the cornerstone in whom the whole building, being fitted together, is growing into a holy temple in the Lord, in whom you also are being built together into a dwelling of God in the Spirit.

Gentiles and Jews – Past and Present

In chapter one of his letter to the Ephesians, Paul focused on the centrality of Christ in the history of the world in terms of salvation and, most importantly, in the eternal purposes of God, who has determined to *sum all things up in Christ – things in the heavens and also things upon earth* (v. 10). The salvation of man is not an end in itself, but part of a glorious plan, presented in the remainder of this letter.

In chapter two Paul goes on to describe how God has worked towards the accomplishment of that eternal goal. In verses 1-2 Paul speaks of the Gentiles, *you,* formerly dead in trespasses and sins and captive to the devil. In verse 3 he speaks of the Jews, *we,* who were in no better a state: in spite of the repository of divine trust granted to them, they were *by nature children of wrath* just like anyone else.

Why does he speak of the two groups? In order to indicate the new unity in Christ that God has created, thereby incorporating *all things* – in this case, all nations – in Christ:

But, he says, with regard to the sad state in which both groups were to be found, God has reversed their condition: *being rich in mercy because of his great love with which he has loved us* ('us' in this case refers to both Jews and Gentiles)*, even when we were dead in our transgressions, [God] made us alive together in Christ ... and raised us up with him, and seated us with him in the heavenlies in Christ Jesus, in order that in the ages to come he might show the surpassing riches of his grace in kindness toward us in Christ Jesus* (vv. 4-7).

Note that Paul has repeatedly used the term *in Christ.* This often serves no grammatical purpose, but it is a means to revert to his statement in 1:10, namely God's eternal determination to *sum all things up in Christ.*

In spite of external dissimilarities, Gentiles and Jews essentially differed very little from each other with regard to God, and they now differ to no greater degree in Christ. Both groups are *'alive together* in Christ'. That togetherness forms the substance of God's dealings with both Israel and the nations.

In verses 11-12 Paul reminds his non-Jewish readers of their former state, as being *Gentiles in the flesh,* rejected by Israel because of their uncircumcision as being outside of the covenants of grace, *separate from Christ, excluded from the commonwealth of Israel and strangers to the covenants of promise, having no hope and without God in the world.*

But (v. 13), once again, God has reversed the situation. *'But now', since Christ has come, died, risen and ascended on high, 'in Christ Jesus'* – a familiar theme by the time we have come to this stage of our study – *you, who were formerly afar off, have been brought near by the blood of Christ. For he himself is our peace, who has made both into one and broke down the barrier of the dividing wall.* In Christ, there are no longer two groups. God has made of both one. He has broken down the wall that formerly divided them.

As commentators well know, Paul is referring here to the wall in the Temple that divided the court of the Gentiles from that which only Jews were allowed to enter. Any infraction of this restriction was punishable by death. Paul is saying that, whatever social and other differences might remain, there is in Christ no difference of any kind between Jews and Gentiles. Whatever differences existed until then and outside of Christ have been broken down in Christ by God.

The Means
Paul describes in the next sentence how God achieved this incorporation of Gentiles and Jews in Christ: *By abolishing in his flesh,* that is, by his sacrifice, *the enmity, which is the law of commandments contained in ordinances* (v. 15).

There, Paul is discussing the former role of the Torah in drawing a distinction between Israel and the nations. That very distinction created an enmity because Israel looked upon herself as the exclusively chosen one and held herself not merely apart but also aloof from the rest of the nations. Had God not shown the people of Israel his favour, given them his Law and granted them his presence through the years? Had they not received the covenants of promise, including the promise of a Messiah and been given reason for hope in God? Were the Gentiles not strangers to all this? No longer. *But now,* says Paul. Now, things are different. Those formerly *afar off* have *been brought near by the blood of Christ.* The dividing Law of ordinances given to Israel has found its fulfilment in Christ and, by this means, has been *abolished* – that is to say – set aside as accomplished.

Because the meaning of the Greek word translated as *abolished* is hotly contested, it is worth our while spending just a few short minutes in clarifying the meaning of the term, κατργεω. W. Bauer (*A Greek-English Lexicon of the New Testament and Other Early Christian Literature,* University of Chicago Press, 1957, Translated by Arndt and Gingrich) informs us that κατργεω means to *make ineffective, powerless, idle, nullify, abolish, wipe out* or to *set aside.* In Romans 7:2 he gives the meaning as to *be released from an association, have nothing more to do with.* These are strong words, can they be justified by Paul's use of the term?

The apostle uses κατργεω extensively in his letter to the Romans. Following are but some examples: he tells us that the faithlessness of Israel cannot abolish (κατργησει, 3:3) God's faithfulness; that faith is rendered ineffective (κατργηται, 4:14) if salvation may be obtained by the Law (cf. Gal. 3:17); that the death of a woman's spouse releases her from any obligation toward her dead husband (κατργηται, 7:2) and that this is precisely what the death of Christ has accomplished on behalf of the redeemed with regard to the Law (κατργηθημεν, 7:6). In other words, what the Law could not do to faith, faith has done to the Law – the Law has now been 'abolished, nullified, set aside' as to its authority to regulate the relationships between God and man, or between men.

It is important, though not for our present purposes, to note that Paul is discussing the role of the Law in connection with the unity of the body of Christ. He is not speaking of the Law in general. It is the firm conviction of the present writer that the Law, rightly understood, leads to grace because it leads to Christ, and that grace brings about a true fulfilment of God's Law through the loving obedience of those redeemed by Christ.

Why has God done this? *That in himself he might make the two into one new man, establishing peace* between Israel and the nations by dealing with *the enmity* between them (v. 15 again). Further, God has so worked that he *might reconcile them both in one body to God through the cross by having put to death the enmity* which constituted both the *children of wrath* (v. 3). Therefore, Gentiles and Jews are reconciled to God by the cross as well as to each other, and both enmities are set aside by the sacrifice of Christ. *And he came and preached peace to you [Gentiles] who were far away and peace to those [Jews] who were near, for through him we both [Gentiles and Jews] have our access in one Spirit to the Father* (vv. 15-18), which mutual access is possible because *the barrier of the dividing wall* in the Temple (v. 14) has been *broken down* (ibid.).

The Centrality of Christ

It is well known that, from the moment Jesus revealed himself to Paul on the road to Damascus (Acts 9), Paul's preoccupation was with Jesus. His most earnest longing was to know him and to be found in him (Phil. 3:9-10), even at the expense of his Jewishness.

When Luke describes Paul's preaching he tells us that he 'preached Jesus' (Acts 9:20). This is also Paul's summary of his message: 'We preach Christ' (1 Cor. 1:23; see also Phil 1:15). This is also Luke's summary of the apostolic message (Acts 5:42): Jesus sent by God for the salvation of the world – crucified, risen, reigning in glory and coming again – filled the whole scope of Paul's message and that of all the apostles. So much so that Paul counts all other things, however precious in themselves, as *dung* (Phil. 3:8).

Paul perceived Jesus to be the sum of all God's gifts. Those redeemed by his blood and granted a true faith in him are also *complete in him* (Col. 2:10), *in whom the whole fullness of the godhead dwells* (Col. 1:19; 2:9), of whose fullness we have received (John 1:16) and into whose fullness we should grow (Eph. 4:13). It is not, therefore, surprising to discover that Paul summarised the whole of the Christian life as an ongoing reality *in Christ*. Christians believe in Christ (Eph. 1:1, 13), are blessed in Christ (ibid. v. 3), chosen in him (v. 4), redeemed and forgiven in him (v. 7). The whole creation is to be summed up in him (v. 10), in whom Christians – both Jewish and Gentile – obtain an eternal inheritance (vv. 11, 13), for which they hope in him (v. 12) and are sealed in him (v. 13).

Paul wrote to the Ephesians concerning the Church, but Jesus fills the whole of his vision because God has subjected everything to Jesus, made him to be the head of the church and established the church as Jesus' body, the fullness of him who totally fills everything (1:22).

This latter statement is worthy of contemplation. Paul, who was in no way blind to the weaknesses and failings of the church (after all, problems in individual churches were the cause of most of his letters and the primary source of his sorrows), does not hesitate to describe the church as Christ's fullness – *the fullness of him who fills all in all* (Eph. 1:23)! So, in the church, Jesus should be the focus. His amazing personality should be expressed, his sweet glory manifested, the wonder of his deeds professed and exemplified, his teachings taught and adhered to, his purposes primary, and his name loved, revered and promulgated on every occasion. The focus must be on Christ and nowhere else.

Unity in Christ
That is why Paul worked so hard for the unity of the body of Christ. Truly Christian unity gives expression to the supremacy of Christ over all other considerations precisely because it renders all other considerations

relatively peripheral. I repeatedly find this to be true as our congregation in Israel, which refuses to be defined as Messianic, incorporates Jews and Arabs together, worshipping and serving God in Christ.

Paul's concern for such a unity is expressed time and again by his many statements, as well as by his life's work. Examples abound: in the letter to the Ephesians Paul exhorts his readers to conduct themselves in a manner worthy of their calling which, he explains, means that they should be *diligent to preserve the unity of the spirit in the bond of peace* (4:1-3). He then goes on to remind them that there is but *one body* (v. 4), as he had earlier insisted that Christ died to undo distinctions within mankind and *to create one new man* (2:15). In Romans chapters 12-16, he cries out against those who would disturb the unity of the church by contending over secondary matters or focusing on their differences or abilities. He stringently reminds his readers: *just as we have many members in one body, and all members do not have the same function, so we – who are many – are one body in Christ, and individually members one of another* (Rom. 12:4-5).

In his first letter to the Corinthians Paul is distressed to hear of contentions in the church over the respective qualities of various leading teachers (1 Cor. 1:10-17), showing how such a tendency runs contrary to the spirit of the gospel (1 Cor. 1:11-29). He returns to the theme of unity in Christ later on in this same letter when discussing the Lord's Table. *For by one Spirit are we all baptized into one body, whether we be Jews or Gentiles, whether we be bond or free; and have been all made to drink into one Spirit* (1 Cor. 12:13; see also 1 Cor. 10:17 and chapter 12). He discusses this theme again in Colossians 3:11, stating that 'there is neither Greek nor Jew, circumcision nor uncircumcision, Barbarian, Scythian, bond nor free: but Christ is all, and in all'.

Surprising as it may seem at first glance, the letter

to the Galatians is likewise taken up with the unity of the body of Christ, in which there is no difference between duties incumbent on Jews and those to which Gentiles are bound, or in the blessings they respectively receive (Gal. 3:28), for they are *all sons of God through faith in Jesus Christ* (ibid. 26). He calls upon the Philippians not to be taken up with earthly distinctions. His own Jewishness is not something he takes into account and he invites his readers to follow his example, because their real sense of belonging has to do with heaven, from whence they await the reappearance of Messiah (Phil 2:1-20). Because of this, they should not succumb to the call to be circumcised (see the beginning of the chapter just quoted).

A CHURCH AMONG THE JEWS

The Centrality of Christ

Jesus, the Son of God, the glorious Maker and Sustainer of heaven and earth, our Redeemer and one and only Saviour from the guilt and from the power of sin, should be the focal point of congregational life, of any congregation among any people. Whatever may be true about a church among the Jewish people, this must be the main feature; otherwise, such a congregation is not a congregation of Messiah.

The question of the validity of distinctly Jewish Christian congregations, even among the Jewish people, immediately rises. As we have seen in the short history of the Messianic Movement and of the somewhat similar efforts that preceded that Movement, such congregations can only be maintained if both their practice and their theory focus on Jewish identity, Jewish custom, Jewish history, and present-day Jewish hopes, aspirations and conflicts.

These foci, it must be admitted, are more than enough to occupy the minds and hearts of any body of people. Jewish tradition is so rich, Jewish identity so all-encompassing, that making Jewishness an important feature of congregational life must ultimately engage the whole of that body's attention, leaving insufficient room for him who should be the fundamental heartbeat of Christian congregations and therefore the crux of all congregational life.

That is where our theological evaluation must come in. There are no biblical and therefore no theological grounds for ethnically focused congregations. Blacks and whites, rich and the poor, highly educated and those without an education, Jews and Gentiles, men and women, slaves and freemen – all are equal members of the one body of Christ. This truth must have maximal practical expression in the life of every congregation among any people, including the Jewish people. If we are to think theologically about a church among the Jews, we must begin with the biblical data and derive our theological thinking thence – and there is no biblical evidence of an ethnically pure congregation, or of a congregation in which one ethnic identity was allowed to be paramount to any other.

If 'among the Jews' means in an area (such as Israel), where the majority is Jewish, then it is to be assumed that the majority of those owning the name of Christ will also be Jewish. It will be their glad and holy duty to maintain a congregational life that will enable every redeemed member of the body of Christ to be at home, without having to act as if he were Jewish, educated, male or rich, Gentile, influential, female or cultured. That is the point of the letters to the Galatians and to the Ephesians. There is, therefore, no room for Jewish Christian congregations. A church among the Jews must be first and foremost Christian, and to be such it must never make ethnic identity or culture a test of fellowship or the grounds of co-operation.

This is not an easy task, but if it means anything at all, it must mean that Jesus and everything to do with him is to be the focus of the congregational life, not ethnic identity, the level of social or economic achievement the majority has achieved, or whether they are black or white. The church is not to reflect the world but to reflect Christ in the world, thereby calling the world to forsake its divisive, mistaken and evil ways in order to join the victorious train of King Jesus, who reigns over all, and will reign until his Father makes his enemies his footstool and he delivers the kingdom up to the Father. The church may not, therefore, be supremely preoccupied with anything but Jesus.

Unity in Christ

Of course, distinctions remain: slaves remain slaves (Philem. 12) and the rich remain rich (1 Tim 6:17). Jews in Christ remain Jews and Gentiles remain Gentiles (1 Cor. 7:18). The uneducated do not suddenly obtain an education and the educated do not, by virtue of their conversion, forget all they have learnt. Jews and Palestinians do not lose their national identities or become inured to their respective views of the Israel-Palestinian conflict. But all these differences are to be left at the doorstep of the church, be it among the Jews or among the Palestinians. Woe betides a church that has allowed itself to be enlisted for the promotion of a national or sectional political programme.

In fact, the very mixture that should pertain in a local church – in just about every church – should help safeguard that church from the dangers of serving the world instead of the Lord Christ. It is a statement to the world that our ultimate citizenship is in heaven and that, insofar as we are Christians, we no longer regard men *after the flesh* (2 Cor. 5:16) but after the Spirit, and that the concerns of the kingdom override those of the kingdoms of this world, even those national kingdoms which our beloved fellow Jews or Palestinians hold so dear.

Some might ask, 'What, then, can be the appeal of

such churches?' My answer is ready: their appeal is Christ. God forbid that we should boast in anything apart from Christ – and him crucified. There is no need to beautify the gospel or to render it more attractive. We cannot improve on what God has done. Nor can we make the gospel more appealing to sinful man. If men and women come to the kingdom, it is because they have been brought in by the power of God – and the naked gospel is that power (Rom. 1:16), first in relation to the Jew and also to the Gentile.

Ethnicity, secondary issues of doctrine that do not reflect on the glory of Christ, respective cultures and human interests must not be allowed to define congregations. To transgress this standard is to give in to a man-centred gospel, which is inevitably defective. It is a form of anthropocentrism (a substitute for the much clearer but supposedly less theologically impressive term, selfishness). It is to place various human interests and conflicts at the centre instead of Jesus. It is to forsake the biblical theocentrism (a focus on God) that should characterise every body of people who seek to serve God in Christ.

Tradition ... Tradition!

A church among the Jews, in which the Jewish people are the majority, will naturally partake to a large extent of the culture of the majority. Rightly so. You would not expect a church among the French to conduct its services and have its sermons delivered in any language other than French (Ooh la la! No! Not by any means!). A church among the Korean will naturally use the Korean language. Language is but one of many aspects of culture, all of which are integral to the people concerned. So, too, are ways in which the congregation shows respect for the Scriptures, worships in song and so on. There is no such thing as a cultureless church or cultureless worship. So I am not here calling for congregational life that is the colour of water. What I am saying is that we learn from the Bible that no culture may be exalted above another, not even Jewish culture.

All cultures have a measure of truth, and all are, to a meaningful extent, sinful. They also differ from each other with respect to the gospel in comparative relevancy and in their ability to faithfully communicate the content of the gospel to and by the worshippers. But they should never be adhered to so as to render even a sizeable minority of the worshippers or of the surrounding people incapable of meaningful participation or understanding.

It is worth noting in this context that Judaism is, with respect to the gospel, the most directly reactive religion than can be found anywhere on the face of the globe. It is therefore historically incorrect and theologically unsound to claim that Judaism represents the roots of Christianity or to find Christ in rabbinic tradition where that tradition deviates from or adds to the Bible. The roots of the Christian faith are not Jewish. They are biblical.

The various members of the various cultures in any one congregation may cherish, maintain and cultivate their respective cultures outside the framework of the church. They may well invite others who do not belong to their cultures to share in their cultural activities. But they should never claim divine authority for their cultures, or consider them superior ways to obey and to worship God.

The Essentials
In other words, a congregation among the Jews should be recognisably Christian. It should hold, with all other true churches of Christ, to the five Reformation Solas:

Sola **Scriptura**
Sola **Fide**
Sola **Christus**
Sola **Gratia**
Sola **Deo Gloria**.

The Scriptures should exclusively govern all aspects of its life and activity. There is no room for interpreting Scripture through the authoritative grid of tradition – not even rabbinic tradition. Nor is there room to introduce into the worship of God anything but what he has explicitly commanded. This rules out incense, prayer shawls, candles, kippot, distinctly clerical garb, Torah scrolls and other traditionally Jewish or Christian paraphernalia, no less than it rules out icons, idols, gesticulations, drama or dancing. God is to be worshipped and served 'in spirit and in truth', not by the traditions taught by men. Truth is only available in Scripture. Our fear of God must be the result of a personal encounter with him as he is revealed in Scripture. Such an encounter is only possible by the workings of the Holy Spirit, who moves in full and exclusive accordance with the written Word of God.

Christian traditions that insist upon the freedom to introduce into the worship of God anything not explicitly forbidden in Scripture are particularly exposed to error in the matter of its mode and content of worship. This is, of course, a bone of theological contention between Lutherans and Calvinists ever since the Reformation and here is not the place to discuss it. But it is an issue that requires re-examination in light of the challenges of the day.

Faith, as defined by the Scriptures, should be the exclusive grounds on which members are accepted into the church. If their faith is truly evangelical, however imperfect, they are heirs and joint heirs with Christ, children of our father Abraham. There is no room for any form of elitism in the church. No works, no keeping of the Torah, no adherence to traditions can advance one in the matters of the kingdom nor add to his spirituality.

Christ, as revealed in the Scriptures, should be the only focus of the church. His teachings should be reflected upon and imbibed, his example studied and followed, his honour defended, and his will done without reserve. We can know God only in Christ and we can serve him only in Christ. There is no room for anything alongside him, for he fills the whole expanse of a faithful church's vision and is the sum of a faithful Christian's passion: to know him and the power of his resurrection, to be conformed to his death, and to love him more than father, mother, brother or our national brethren. These count as less than nothing compared to the excellency of loving, serving and knowing him. If we choose to live by any other standard, we cannot be his disciples.

Grace, as defined in the Scriptures, should be the only ground of our labour and our hope. It should characterise our every human relationship. Even our faith is a gift of grace, leaving no possibility for human boasting (Eph. 2:8-9). Grace encompasses the whole of our life and constitutes the fundamental fibre of the fabric of our faith, labour and hope. We can add nothing to what God has done. Sanctification, spirituality, the nearness of God – yes – our very endeavours in the kingdom, are the fruit of God's grace working in us and recreating us back into his glorious image.

God alone, as described in the Scriptures, should be recognised as sovereign and his inscripturated will and kingdom esteemed above all. He must be recognised as the author of all, the overseeing master and the source of our salvation. We chose him because he first chose us. He must be the ultimate goal of our worship and devotion.

Conclusions

So then, you [Gentiles] are no longer strangers and aliens, but you are fellow citizens with the saints and are of God's household, having been built on the foundation of the apostles and prophets, Christ Jesus himself being the chief cornerstone, in whom the whole building, being fitted together, is growing into a holy temple in the Lord.

Note again the centrality of Jesus. The cornerstone is not only that part of the building on which the whole structure rests, but that according to which the whole was to be built. Note further the repeated use of the word *together*. The church is to grow into 'a holy temple' in the Lord only as it is *fitted together* – Gentiles and Jews worshipping and serving God as one new man.

Paul concludes this address to the Gentiles by assuring them that, *in the Lord*, they are *being built together [with the Jews] into a dwelling of God in the Spirit*.

That is the whole point of his plea in 4:1-3, that his readers conduct themselves *with all humility and gentleness, with patience showing forbearance of one another in love, being diligent to preserve the unity of the Spirit in the bond of peace*. True spiritual growth will only occur when Christ is accorded his rightful place as the centre and heart of congregational life, and when Gentiles and Jews live out the fruits of God's accomplishments in Christ by maintaining a unity that obviates any form of elitism or distinction in Christ between the two.

How should culture be treated in the context of church life? More specifically, how should Jewish culture be treated in the context of congregational life? Culture is an important aspect of human life and has been so under the direction of God ever since creation. Part of mankind's calling is to develop cultures that will rule the earth and subdue it to God. But that is precisely the point: our cultures, too, must be part of our obedience to God, our Maker and Redeemer. To the extent that they are so, they will serve to give many possible forms of expression to the gospel. To the extent that any culture gives such an expression, it is a valid means by which mankind may worship God.

But since all men are tainted with sin, their cultures are also tainted and therefore limited in their ability to express the gospel faithfully. God did not inspire any one human culture except those religious duties ordained for Israel, and that naturally impacted Israelite culture over the years. Rabbinicism is not divinely inspired culture and should not be allowed to lay claim to such authority. Moreover, the religious authority of those duties imposed by God has been done away with by God himself through the arrival of Messiah.

As cultural norms, Jewish traditional practices still convey a religious message and (with the exception of the sacrifices, the temple worship and the Day of Atonement) may be practised as such. But this is true also of customs in other cultures, because mankind has ever been engaged both in a search for and a flight from God, which search and flight have found expression in its many and fascinating cultures. Mosaic religious ritual, including the calendar, are no longer matters of obedience to God and may be allowed only a very limited role in the formulation of a nation's worship – no more than that accorded other cultures – and never as in any way spiritually advantageous or superior.

It is an interesting fact that we do not find in the New Testament, particularly in Paul's writings, any discussion of culture as such. One would expect that Paul, having needed to encounter various cultures in the course of his missionary endeavours, would have been forced to seek the mind of the Lord on this matter and thence to frame a coherent policy.

It seems to me that the following, however, may be gleaned from the pages of the New Testament:

1. Obviously, all cultures are impacted by their religious contexts and are more often than not the bearers of religious messages. In spite of this fact and of the significant differences in culture between Israel and the Gentiles, between relatively primitive Phrygian Galatians and cultured Athenians, sophisticated dwellers of Rome and the often crass Corinthians, the only instances when culture was

allowed to overtly intrude into Paul's dealings with the churches is when culture directly addressed religious issues. In such instances Paul took a firm, uncompromising stance.

In Galatia, for example, where custom was presented in terms of religious duty, Paul took strong issue with it and forbade it to be introduced into the life of the church. In no case did he teach or encourage adherence to Jewish religious custom. Nor did he call upon his converts to eschew their own national cultures and languages.

2. By determining to be *as a Jew to the Jews and as a Gentile to the Gentiles*, Paul demonstrated a freedom from cultural obligations of all kinds. In his letters to the Romans (ch. 14) and the Corinthians (1 Cor. 8), in the course of discussing the rights and wrongs of eating meat bought in the market-place, he completely ignores the fact that most of such meat had been previously offered to idols. Idols are nothing and there is no God but one (1 Cor. 8:4). No religious overtones are to be attached to the eating of such meat (Rom. 14:20 – *all things are pure*) until the unbeliever or the weak Christian makes such an attachment. Then the meat is not to be eaten because of the message such wrongly informed individuals (1 Cor. 8:10) are liable to receive from the exercise of Christian liberty.

The issue is never religious because neither eating nor abstaining commends us to God (1 Cor. 8:13). It is one of loving consideration of another's weak conscience. None are to be destroyed by our enjoyment of liberty (Rom. 14:15-17, 20). The evil resides in *eating and causing offence* rather than in the meat itself. The virtue is to be found in our attitude to our brethren (1 Cor. 8: 13).

That is precisely why Paul was so adamantly against the circumcision of Gentile believers. The issue is neither circumcision nor uncircumcision

(Gal. 5:6) in and of itself. But circumcision is not a purely cultural matter; it connotes extensive theological and therefore religious implications. For this reason, and for this reason alone, for a Gentile to agree to be circumcised is equal to falling from grace (Gal. 5:4), rendering Christ *of no effect* (Gal. 5:2, 4).

3. From the above we conclude that none has the right to criticise, look down upon or boast in comparison to another of his national culture or tradition (Col. 2:16). Dietary laws, holy days and the like are at best mere shadows, which find their substance in Christ (Col. 2:17; cf. Heb. 8:5; 10:1). This much is clear:

• There is no biblical call to forsake one's culture, except in isolated points where that culture may conflict with the gospel. Converted Jews may remain Jews by practising those aspects of their national cultures that do not conflict with the gospel.
• In the New Testament, no one culture is treated as superior to another and should not therefore be so treated in the church. There is no room for any form of cultural elitism in the church.
• There is no room to draw national or cultural distinctions within the church. The church should express its unity in all aspects of its life and witness, regardless of differences of national background, social standing or gender. Social, cultural or other differences that may be found to legitimately exist among Christians should not form the basis for church fellowship, and may find expression outside of formal church life.
• In relation to our discussions, Jewish Christians may choose to form Jewish Christian fellowships outside of yet perhaps alongside their respective congregations, where they celebrate their feasts,

give expression to their shared Jewishness and reach out to their own people. But such fellowships should never be allowed to supplant the role of the church in their lives.

• It is forbidden to introduce into the worship of God any cultural forms that are considered binding or spiritually advantageous to the worshippers.

'A church' among the Jews, therefore, should partake of all of these traits in order to be a faithful church. It should 'be among the Jews' in the sense that it will address issues relating to life among the Jews, in the sense that the main cultural language used will naturally be Jewish, and in the sense that it will consciously engage the Jewish people with the gospel.

But such a church ought not to prefer the Jews or buy into Jewish self-interest or traditional error. It should exercise a truly prophetic role among the Jewish people by calling the nation to repentance and by daring to criticise and challenge sinful ways adopted by the Jewish people in pursuit of their national interests. It should at all times be a reflection of the gospel, a proclaimer of righteousness, an example of what God in Christ does in the life of a community, and how he calls and brings men from all nations to the obedience of faith.

Even among the Jews, we should consciously labour for multi-ethnic congregations that will proclaim to be Christ pre-eminent, by both word and deed. Such a church will naturally partake of the majority culture but constantly subject it to careful scrutiny and reformation in accordance with the spirit of the gospel.

May God forgive us our many errors!

MAKING CHURCHES MORE COMFORTABLE FOR JEWISH CHRISTIANS

The Beloved Comfort Zone

We tend to seek our maximal comfort zone, where nothing surprises, disturbs or challenges us. This kind of attitude lies behind a significant part of the modern search for 'balance'.

Our forefathers knew little of such a search. They were anxious for truth, at any cost, and paid high costs in order to discover and maintain it. It would be right to say that they sought, not balance, but a truly biblical tension between all the wonderful facets of truth.

The search for balance has often led to the affirmation of one truth at the expense of another, simply because we humans are unable to see far enough into eternity, where parallel lines inevitably meet. We are anxious to have everything within reach of our understanding, our grasp, and our control – for knowledge is a kind of control. So, if we cannot explain how God can be sovereign over the free acts of man and yet man be truly free, we choose to redefine either God's sovereignty or man's freedom in terms that will relieve us of the tension. If we cannot understand how God could still be in covenant with Israel and, at the same time, in covenant with the church, we deny or qualify either of the covenants.

All evangelicals affirm the unity of the church. But we tend to evade the kind of tensions that such a unity would create if we really lived it out. We have different churches for different language groups, cultures, races and people. There are few blacks in white churches in the West, few Koreans in Chinese churches, few Pakistanis in the average British church and few poor people in the congregations of the rich. Is it not a common thing to hear younger people explaining why they choose one congregation over against another by the age groups of those attending, rather than by more biblical considerations? Seeking the comfort zone, we seek to evade the tensions that a multi-cultured, multi-national, multi-language, multi-layered church would create.

We act as if it were not worth the effort to preserve the unity of the church in the bond of peace. We redefine the unity of the body of Christ as if it were meant to refer only to communion between churches, formal or otherwise.

Why do we not, then, have churches for males and females? That seems to be the only remaining, universally recognised restriction on 'felt-need based churches'. After all, many of our churches are divided by the social strata shared by the majority of the members of the congregation. We have also been gifted in recent years by congregations for Jews and those who choose to act like Jews, and all the rest. Such a view of the church constitutes a denial of the biblical affirmation that, 'in Christ there is neither Jew or Gentile, male or female, slave or free man'.[1]

This book is written with a passion: a passion to see the church united, virile, ever changing in form, and ever growing in her intellectual and experiential knowledge of God, his Word and his ways. It is written with a longing to see the church challenge the world rather than becoming more like it by adopting the increasing divisiveness that prevails where Christ is neither known nor loved – for to know him truly is to inevitably love him. It is written with the conviction that the unity of the church is an important manifestation of the glory of God in the gospel and of the gospel's power to save and transform.

It cannot be denied that some Jews have left churches because they felt – or were made to feel – uncomfortable there. The following is written in the hope that it will serve in some small way to help both churches and Jewish Christians find a way to serve Christ by the way they serve each other in the context of a biblical church life, so that the world might know that the Father sent the Son to be the Saviour of the world.[2]

What the Bible Has to Say

In the section which precedes Ephesians 2:11–22, Paul has praised God for the wonder of his free, and absolute grace. He has also prayed that his readers would be enabled to comprehend that grace in its full, boundless expression and power, by which God is glorified in Christ and by which individual sinners, dead in their sins, are made alive.

Paul then exulted in a particular aspect of the gospel – the way it undoes the differences within mankind, uniting members from all parts of the human race into one.

Verses 11-12

'Therefore', says Paul, in light of the glorious grace of God in Christ to both Gentiles and Jews, 'remember'. The church has generally chosen to forget what Paul here calls upon it to remember, because the church was largely taken over by Gentiles who chose to arrogate to themselves privileges which carried all too few responsibilities, and to attribute to themselves superior qualities over against the despised and persecuted Jews. While it is true that Jewish pride is no more commendable, Gentiles in Christ should have known better.

Remember that formerly you, the Gentiles in the flesh, who are called 'Uncircumcision' by the so-called 'Circumcision' which is performed in the flesh by human hands. The Jewish people divide the world of mankind into two major groups: 'them' and 'us' – Gentiles and Jews. Paul rejects this division. His mind has been transformed by Christ. He makes light of the traditionally Jewish division of the world. The Gentiles are only *called* Uncircumcision. They are not such any longer for they have been circumcised at heart. They are called the Uncircumcision by those who are only the so-called Circumcision and who have nothing more than a circumcision which is *performed in the flesh by human hands.* Instead of despising others, the 'so-called circumcision' should have sought the circumcision of the heart.

Paul calls upon his Gentile readers to remember their former state in its fullest religious and spiritual meaning: *Remember that you were at that time without a Messiah, excluded from the commonwealth of Israel and strangers to the covenants of promise, having no hope and without God in the world.* These words are expressive of the New Testament view of man without Christ. Those who did not, or do not at present, belong to the commonwealth of Israel are without hope, without a Messiah and without God in the world, regardless of the originality of their thought, the beauty of their ethics, the finality of their sacrifice or the sincerity of their convictions.

According to the Old Testament order of things as commanded by God, the world was divided into two parts: the people of the covenant, and the rest. Israel, in covenant with God, had the promises of his presence, protection and guidance, the wisdom of his commandments, the privileges of his worship and the assured hope of the Messiah. Others had none of these, and the only way they could enjoy them was to become part of the nation of Israel. In New Testament times, this division had become so much a part of Jewish thinking that religiously faithful Jews did not sit at the table with Gentiles, let alone worship alongside them. The division was epitomised by an inscription placed at the entrance of the court of the Temple, on the wall that divided the court of the Gentiles from the court of Israel. The inscription read: 'No Gentile may enter within the wall which surrounds the sanctuary and its enclosure. Anyone caught doing so will be guilty of his own ensuing death'. The partition was firm and final.

Verse 13
Paul goes on to say, *Remember ... But now in Messiah Jesus, you who were formerly afar off have been brought near by the blood of Messiah.* Contrary to the expectations of the Jewish people, who believed that Messiah would come and enthrone Israel above the nations, Paul insists that Messiah undid the ancient separation that existed with regard to spiritual privileges between Jew and Gentile. He shed his blood equally for both. He brought them both *near.*

Paul is thoroughly true to his Old Testament faith. His terminology is taken from one of the divine promises to Israel, found in Isaiah 57:16-19. There, after describing the sin of Israel and its punished state (afar off), God promised to work savingly for the people (due to be brought near by grace). Their purported righteousness will be to no avail (v. 12). Like the Gentiles, Israel has become idolatrous (v. 13a). But, God promised, *he who takes refuge in me shall inherit the land and shall possess my holy mountain* (v. 13b).

In other words, since Israel apostatised from God, it has become like any nation in terms of rights and privileges – it is now *far*, as far as any Gentile nation could be – but God is ever true to his grace. He will bring them back by a unilateral act of mercy. Those in the past *afar off* will be *brought near*. So too spoke Hosea in the name of God, at one moment declaring Israel to be *not my people* (Hos. 1:9) and in another promising *where it is said to them, 'You are not my people' it will be said to them, 'You are the sons of the living God'* (Hos. 1:10; cf. 2:23).

What Paul is saying is that, just as both Gentiles and Jews were *formerly, by nature, children of wrath* (Eph. 2:1-3), with no difference between them, so too has God now not made a difference between them. He has brought both *near by the blood of Messiah*. Jesus levels all mankind. Jew and Gentile, male and female, bond and free are all equal before him and by virtue of his sacrifice.

Verses 14-18

For he himself is our peace, who made both into one and broke down the barrier of the dividing wall by abolishing in his flesh the enmity, the Law of commandments in ordinances, that in himself he might make the two into one new man, establishing peace, and might reconcile them both in one body to God through the cross, by it having put to death the enmity. 'And he came and preached peace to you who were far away and peace to those who were near', for through him we both have our access in one Spirit to the Father.

The peace of which Paul speaks is of two kinds. The first has to do with the enmity created by what Paul describes as *the Law of commandments in ordinances* (14-15). This Law served as a dividing wall between Israelites, sons of the covenant, and those who were strangers to the covenants of promise, that is to say, between Jews and Gentiles. It served in the same way as did the inscription we described, placed on the wall dividing Jews from Gentiles in the Temple court. The Law itself was not meant to create enmity, but it did. Human pride is always xenophobic: it always resents and rejects those who differ. The Jews, exulting in their Law, considered the Gentiles to be 'dogs', soulless pagans. The Greeks and Romans despised the Jews for their strange dietary traditions, their eschewing of sports and their other national habits. That enmity has now been dealt with because God *broke down the barrier of the dividing wall* (v. 14). He has abolished *through his flesh the enmity* (v. 15). There is but one atoning sacrifice for both Jews and Gentiles, by which both are now *brought near* (v. 13) to God and thereby also to each other. There is but one Spirit, by whom they both now have access (v. 18), and there is but one body of the redeemed (v. 16). God has taken Jews and Gentiles, formerly separated, and made them 'one' (v. 14), 'one new man' (v. 15) – *thus establishing peace* between them (v. 15).

The other kind of peace is more fundamental, having to do with the enmity between God and man, which created a situation in which even the sons of the covenant were distant from God because they disobeyed his commandments and rejected his Son. That enmity has also now been *put to death* through the cross (vv. 15-16). Sinners are *reconciled* in the eyes of God (v. 16), peace is now preached to them (v. 17), and they have access to the Father (v. 18). But, important as the atonement is in terms of its restoration of the relationship between God and man, Paul is emphasising another aspect of the atonement. He is stating in stark, clear terms that the atonement has restored the relationship between members of mankind, undone the terrible effects of sin and the inevitable consequences of pride. Man, in rebellion against God, hated his fellow man. Man in Christ is relieved of that disgusting burden and united with all mankind by a recognition of his own burden of sin and, by a reality of saving grace shared with all the redeemed, made into one body into which the redeemed are united. They share in the benefits of the one sacrifice that is sufficient to atone for a universally shared sinful state, in the one Spirit of God and in access to the one and selfsame Father – these all relegate the remaining minor differences between mankind to the realm of the relatively unimportant.

Verses 19-22

So then, you (Gentiles) *are no longer strangers and aliens, but you are fellow citizens with the saints and are of God's household* (v. 19). In all matters relating to spiritual privileges, God has done away with the distinction between Jews and Gentiles. The cross has made them equal. In the past, the Gentiles were *strangers to the covenants of promise, having no hope and without God in the world* (v. 12). Now they are *no longer strangers.* In the past they were *without a Messiah, excluded from the commonwealth* (πολιτέιάς) *of Israel.* Now they are citizens (συνπολιται) – no, fellow citizens. Now they are a full part of the household of God, just like those among the Jews who are redeemed.

Having been built upon the foundation of the apostles and prophets, Messiah Jesus himself being the cornerstone (v. 20). In addition to all the other wonderful things they share, Jews and Gentiles in Christ are both established on one foundation. No longer are Jews founded on the Word of God while Gentiles are left to their respective traditions. The revelation is now shared, as is whatever tradition may develop from it. Jews and Gentiles now have a common foundation in the apostles and prophets, with Messiah himself serving as the cornerstone according to which the building is constructed. We need not enter the ancient discussion as to whether the prophets referred to here are those whose words have been enshrined in the Old Testament or if the reference is to New Testament prophets. Whatever be the case, Jews and Gentiles in Christ share that one foundation – a fact that once again emphasises the erasure of any difference between them in all matters relating to the Christian faith and to Christian experience.

But that is not all. A glorious process is taking place. In Jesus the Messiah, God is still at work. He is drawing Jews and Gentiles to his Son, freeing them in a single blow from the tyranny of sin and weaning them from the habits sin has inculcated in them. Slowly but ever steadily, Jews and Gentiles are being remade into the image of Messiah both individually and as a body. *The whole building* (v. 21) is undergoing continual change, *being fitted together* and thereby *growing into a holy temple in the Lord.* God would dwell among men. But he would do so among men united in Christ, made one in him, divested of the jaundiced intolerance and of the ignorant enmity that presently divides mankind. *Being fitted together* the body is *growing into a holy temple in the Lord.* Paul stretches the limits of imagination by using mixed metaphors – a habit against which my fine composition teacher warned me repeatedly. From the metaphor of a building being assembled he goes on to speak of the building as a living thing, steadily growing, for the temple of the Lord is alive with human life that has been sanctified by the blood of Christ, and with the workings of the Holy Spirit through and in those lives.

Returning to his original metaphor, Paul concludes both this passage and our study by a closing statement: *in whom* (v. 22), that is to say, in Messiah, *you also* Jews and Gentiles, are being *built together into a dwelling of God through the Spirit.* God is the builder, and individual Christians from every nation are the building blocks.

Paul would have his readers aspire to great and glorious things. He would have them yearn to become *a dwelling of God through the Spirit,* where God is to be found, known, loved, adored and served, where mankind, torn by continual conflict, can learn to live together united by the gospel. But they can only achieve this together, as one body. Jews and Gentiles in Christ united by an eternal band that nothing can ever break.

This is Paul's inspired view of the church. It is not a mere conglomerate of humans, united to some limited extent by their shared sorrows, conflicts or interests. It is not another human pressure group. It is not primarily a sanctuary where human wounds are healed and the bones of bruised individuals find rest. It is a temple, indwelt by God, where *he* is the focal point and everything else is secondary – and such a wonder cannot come about as long as we are occupied by the differences between Jews and Gentiles in Christ. The church is one and so should we be.

God dwells in the sanctified unity that has been established by the one sacrifice of his Son, not in the man-centred unity of the ecumenical movement, but in that unity which is truly focused on him and which is grounded in the saving work of Christ on the cross and in the consequent regenerating and transforming work of the Holy Spirit.

Why Can't You Be Like Everyone Else?

What do you mean when you say that the church should do more to accommodate Jewish Christians? All too many think that no real problem exists, but it does.

Most Jewish people have grown up in non-Jewish environments. They speak the common language, dress as does the majority, live in similar homes and send their children to the same kind of schools. They are, therefore, expected to be like everyone else in every sense. We Jewish Christians are the same, only different in many respects.

Cultural distinctions often become a stumbling block to human relations because it is human nature to be suspicious of anything different. Note how the only redhead in class draws negative comments, as if there is anything wrong with the colour of his hair. Jewish Christians are repeatedly asked, 'Why can't you be like everyone else?!' Quite simply, because we are not like everyone else. Nor is anyone else. Who on earth is 'Mr Everyone Else'? Is he black or coloured, tall or short? Does he sing heartily like the Welsh, the Germans or the Latin Americans? How does he dress in church? What is his social status? His way to express himself? His most loved form of music or the way he expresses adoration?

We're not like everyone else. We're not anyone else. We're Jewish. We're not even like most Jews, because we're Christians. We have a warm attachment to the State of Israel, eat knishes, kneidlach and kreplach (those of us who come from the western Diaspora), our mannerisms are Jewish, and we are sensitive to jokes that begin with 'A Jew, an American and a Frenchman meet on a bus. The Jew says...' Wouldn't you be sensitive, if your people had borne the brunt of persecution for over 2,000 years?

Of course, Jews are not only Jews. We're British, Dutch, Swedish or American – some of us are even Chinese, Ethiopian or Latino. We have a real sense of loyalty to our adoptive countries. Most Jews were born outside of Israel. All are sincerely patriotic when it comes to the communities and countries in which they live. But this does not lessen their strong attachment to Israel, nor can it reduce their concern for the fellow Jews wherever they may be. All too many non-Jewish believers assume that, since their Jewish Christian friends are so much a part of the general run of things, their Jewish identity has been relegated to the distant past. Not so, Jews are usually very Jewish – and very sensitive to their Jewishness. Many cringe when introduced as coming 'from a Jewish background'. Would you not feel uncomfortable if you were introduced as 'someone from a French (or British, of Scotch background)' – as if you had no identity of your own and your Christian faith wiped out your national identity?

One of my correspondents related how she was introduced to a fellow believer who, upon hearing that she was Jewish, reached out to touch her arm, exclaiming, 'Wow! I've touched a Jew!' Others are put on the spot when, upon being introduced, are informed, 'I really love your people!' as if one was saying, 'I really like ice cream'. The best of intentions are simply not enough to make Jewish Christians comfortable in churches. We need to stop being treated as museum pieces.

Another young Christian whom I met, who has very little knowledge of the Scriptures, was asked to teach in her church simply because she is Jewish – as if that can make up for the lack of solid, careful Bible knowledge. Another was asked to teach the Old Testament 'from a Jewish point of view'. Why on earth would a church want to have that point of view, when that was the view that led to the rejection of Jesus? Would you have a 'Muslims Studies Group' in your church? Would you ask a former Buddhist to teach your congregation the tenets of Buddhism? Are fellow believers from among the Gentiles aware of the fact that the Judaism of today is in many significant respects very different from the Judaism of Jesus' day, and that even the Judaism of that day was a departure from biblical truth? An ignorant fascination with things Jewish is a poor substitute for simple human friendliness.

Yeah, But What Does It Mean to Be Jewish?
Jews in Christ remain Jews. We have our own culture, our own festivals and our own ways of doing things. We also bear the scars of a specific history. Our brethren in Christ ought not be put off by the fact that we love our heritage and wish to preserve it. Nor should they be surprised when we are offended by insensitivity. Being Jewish does not constitute us an authority on anything but our own culture. Nor does it, as such, justify the fear that we may be Judaising. Churches should encourage Jewish Christians to be active parts of the fellowship of the church, at the same time encouraging the establishment of inner and intra-congregational fellowships, where Jews in Christ can meet and address their special needs. After all, this is done for youth, men, women and the Golden

Age. Of course, it is important that all such fellowships be conducted under the supervision of an understanding elder or another trusted individual in the church. But a warm welcome and a sincere measure of goodwill surely require an awareness of the specific needs of the whole church in its various parts and portions.

Jewishness often has to do, as another of my correspondents put it, with nature rather than nurture. The sense of estrangement that Jewish Christians may feel in a church is likely to accompany us into secular life. The strong sense of community, the drive (some call it pushiness) that many Jews put into their business life, the kind of humour in which we engage, our delight in reading between the lines, taking note of legal gaps and identifying legalistic opportunities – these are some national traits that the forces of a painful and very lengthy history have developed in us as an instrument of survival. We just can't help being what we are – and many of you, my Gentile readers, have helped to make us that!

Our non-Jewish fellow believers are sometimes irritated or amused by such traits, at times portrayed in the worse possible light. True, the gospel modifies behaviour and alters even deeply bedded national traits. But are all those who criticise Jewish Christians for their behaviour free from their national characteristics, including their own national weaknesses? Let him who is perfect in this matter cast the first stone.

Is the Bible Anti-Semitic?

All too many sermons from the Old Testament completely divorce the passages expounded from any relation to the Jewish people, except as that body of people who were once the objects of God's mercy and are now of his wrath. Promises explicitly made to Israel are spiritualised into promises to the church, while warnings and curses hurled against Israel manage, by some form of spiritual alchemy, to remain the sole domain of the Jewish people. How would *you* feel if you were Jewish and that is how the Scriptures were dealt with, day in and day out?

This is especially true when so much of the language of the church is unintentionally but thoroughly offensive to Jewish Christians, who often find themselves writhing under sermons innocently delivered in churches around the world. This because the term, 'the Jews', is often used perjoratively, when describing negative behaviour recorded in the Old or New Testaments. The more oblique, 'God's people', is reserved for those who believed and lived according to their faith. As if to say that all 'the Jews' are bad, unbelieving, unfaithful to God, while there are no Jews among 'God's people'.

Whence the contrast between 'the Jews' and 'the Apostles' or 'the early church'? Were the apostles not Jewish? Was there not a majority of Jewish believers in the early church? Why is the land of Israel today called 'Palestine', when that term is a politically loaded one, often used to deny the legitimacy of a Jewish homeland in the Middle East? How can a Jewish person, who loves his people and numbers himself among them, feel comfortable when he and his people are castigated so often in the name of the gospel?

The fact of the matter is that the only way most Jewish Christians can feel comfortable in a church today is by following one of two options: either by absconding from their Jewishness and forgoing their Jewish identity, or by agreeing to become 'token Jews'. Neither option best serves the cause of the gospel. Nor does either of them address what it means when we say that the church is truly one.

Don't ignore us, but don't make too much of us either. Just let us be what God has made us to be, and let us make our own contribution to the manifold aspects of the beauty of the one body of Christ.

KEEPING TORAH

The focus of congregations in Messiah should not be national distinctives but devotion to God in Messiah, obedience to his Word and worship of this glory. The Bible speaks of the one body of Messiah, in which Jews and Gentiles, men and women, slaves and free persons may worship him on equal grounds, with no impositions and without the intrusion of human requirements or innovations. Everything else tends to eclipse the glory of Messiah and to establish a competing value.

One Messianic ministry actively teaches Gentiles to keep 'Torah', and claims a biblical basis for doing so. The editor of *Bikurei Tziyon,* published by First Fruits of Zion, writes:

'Gentiles drew closer to the God of Israel before the days of Messiah, (eg. Ruth, Rahab) and eventually united completely with Israel in submitting to Torah. FFOZ (First Fruits of Zion – BM) teaches that believers from the nations have that same privilege today – "one Torah shall be to him that is home born (Israeli), and unto the stranger that sojourns among you ..." (Exod. 12:39; Num. 15:14). The prophet Isaiah also mentions those "that join themselves to the LORD ... to be his servants, every one that keeps the Sabbath from polluting it, and takes hold of my Covenant ..." (Isa. 56:6). Yeshua's words cannot be clearer when he said "...whosoever shall do and teach them (the Torah), the same shall be called great in the kingdom ..." (Matt 5:19). His instruction to his talmidim was exactly this, that they should teach the nations to observe all these things (Matt. 28:20). This is the message of the kingdom of God to those who were "born without God and without hope", to "take hold of his covenant" ... Examples of ordinances of Torah that don't apply to those in the nations are to do with the Land of Israel ... which even Jews outside of Israel can't observe... Or those for Kohanim (priests – BM) ... which even Jews who are not kohanim can't observe' (*Bikurei Tziyon,* May/June 2000, p. 9).

A long-standing member of a Messianic congregation wrote to Dr Nichol:

'I am married to a Jewish believer and we have been attending services together for the past 20 years. Although I have been a part of the congregation for so many years I have never really felt like a member. If it were an Orthodox Jewish congregation I could convert and be accepted as a Jew. I know there are others who feel the same way. If God has called us to be a part of the body, why should we be separate?'
Signed: Feeling Excluded.

Nichol's response is indicative of the tendency to exclusivism amongst many adherents of the Messianic Movement:

'Your experience is not uncommon and actually touches on one of the most complex challenges facing Messianic Judaism... In Scripture the basic human categories are Jew and Gentile. Contrary to popular opinion among many believers, these categories were not erased with the coming of the Messiah.'

He goes on to say that

'if Jewishness is still important to God ... then our Messianic Jewish congregations must seek to have a majority of Jews present. We must protect the "boundaries" so that over the long haul, the congregations will maintain their Jewish character... If significant numbers of Gentiles buy in, how can the Messianic Jewish congregation ensure its Jewish make-up and character among future generations? And how can the larger Jewish community take Messianic Judaism seriously if significant numbers of non-Jews dominate the membership rolls? ...Such questions form a subtext in your congregation's interactions, which may lie behind your sense of low-grade rejection... Messianic Jews, the remnant of Israel must protect themselves from dilution through the incursion of large numbers of Gentile believers who may or may not have as deep and abiding a commitment as your own' ('Ask the Rabbi', *Messianic Jewish Life vol. LXXII no. 2*, pp. 27-28).

Dr Nichol further states that because the New Testament has not adequately addressed the issue of Jewishness amongst Jewish believers, we are 'left holding the bag of an unresolved theological tension that touches the very nature of our Messianic Judaism'. The solution is 'found' in undergoing a 'conversion' to Messianic Judaism, though again, Mr Nichols warns that even in traditional Jewish communities the converts are often not fully accepted on an emotional/relational level. In conclusion, he urges his correspondent to 'try to view your participation in a Messianic Jewish synagogue as a kind of sacrifice for the sake of the Jewish people ... you may be suffering a bit, but it may be very redemptive suffering'.

How sad! How thoroughly unbiblical!

Of course, there are differences between Jews and Gentiles, as there are between women and men. But these distinctions have nothing to do with how one worships or serves God. The exaltation of Jewish religious tradition in a congregation of believers in Messiah tends to blur the difference between cultural mores and biblical norms, resulting in an attribution of religious authority to rabbinic tradition which, as we have seen, that tradition must never be accorded.

So, when we evangelise, we may freely use those cultural terms that will render our gospel more intelligible and more immediately relevant to those whom we are addressing. But we must not cloud the gospel by cultural accretions. Furthermore, we must respect the various cultures into which we speak the gospel by declining to attribute to them meanings that are not germane to those cultures.

True evangelism is an act of worship, and worship must always focus on him whom to know is life eternal.

Semantics

The above discussion brings us to the issue of semantics, a discussion of the language we use in speaking of the gospel. There is a tendency in the Messianic Jewish Movement to insist on a new, supposedly Jewish, terminology. Jesus is to be called Yeshua, the Old and New Testaments are to be described respectively as the Tanach (mistakenly pronounced by many, Tenach) and the Brit Chadasha, while the words 'Christ', 'Christian' and 'church' are to be substituted with suitable Hebrew terminology.

It is quite amusing to witness the convoluted efforts

of some who seek to avoid terms they consider unhelpful, while using them to translate terms they consider more acceptable but which simply do not mean anything to those who hear or read them. Messianic literature will carry reports such as the following: 'On Sabbath (Saturday) our Kehila (congregation) met in order to worship Yeshua (Jesus)'. What's the point?

There is more to the change in terminology than meets the eye. Messianic terminology is a semantics of disassociation: Christians are 'converted' but Messianic Jews are 'completed'. Gentile evangelicals are 'real Christians', while Jews who believe in Jesus are 'truly Messianic'. If 'real Christians' and 'Messianic Jews' share the same faith (a reality which many Messianics find embarrassing to admit in the presence of their own people), why should they not be united by a common terminology? When Messianic Jews say 'I am not a Christian' (Feher, p. 80, among many others), they are denying the link that exists between them and their fellow believers from among the Gentiles.

This is tantamount to taking a small but very significant step towards reconstructing the middle wall of partition that Messiah destroyed when he died on the cross for both Jew and Gentile. If we are fellow believers, then we are all Christians or we are all Messianic. The term used to describe one should be used to describe the other because the only difference between us is our respective national identities. We really and truly share the same faith, so let's admit it and have the courage to defend our common faith before the Jewish people.

Moishe Rosen tells the story of the Jewish lady who heard all about Yeshua and was fascinated with the beauty of his personality, the perfection of his teaching and the wonder of his sacrificial death. 'Of course I believe in him!' she declared. So she became an attendee of the little Messianic congregation – until she discovered that Yeshua is Jesus, and was seen no more.

We must sound the gospel loud and clear. We must insist on the essential ingredients of our faith, such as: the doctrine of the Trinity; the deity of Messiah; the corruption of human nature; the sinfulness of all mankind, including our beloved people; the lordship of God in all things; the inability of man to please God; and the identity, work and teachings of the Messiah, no matter where the chips may fly. Anything else is less than honest – and less than biblical.

Rabinowitz, a Jewish Christian pioneer in pre-Second World War Kishineff, attempted to create a Jewish Christian congregation. But his efforts collapsed immediately following his decease. The congregation scattered and all the property he accumulated fell into the hands of his unbelieving family precisely because he declined to be clear on some of the major issues that distinguish our faith from that of the rabbis. Instead of focusing his work on Jesus, he focused on Jewish identity. On the one hand he affirmed the deity of Jesus but never explained it in clear terms. On the other, he rejected the term 'Trinity', asking, 'Why should the Christian Church burden Israel with doctrines that were taught them by their fathers to keep them from false conceptions of the Godhead? ... We do not find anywhere in the Holy Scripture that the belief in "The Persons" is to form a necessary part of our confession' (Kjaer-Hansen, *Rabinowits*, 92-93).

The term 'Messianic' is preferred by some because it is meant to serve Jewish believers in Jesus as a means to distance themselves from the ills and evils of a history, during which the nominally Christian church persecuted the Jews in the name of the gospel and represented to the world a faith that had little to commend itself to the average thinking Jew. However, to the extent that 'the church' was indeed the church of God (and there were – and are – many sinners among the true followers of Messiah), then one should not seek to disassociate oneself from its failings by giving the impression that one does not belong to it.

One should certainly not use contradictory terminology when addressing different audiences. We Jewish believers in Jesus cannot deny our Christian faith in the presence of fellow Jews, and then affirm it when we seek the support and understanding of non-Jewish Christians. Honesty requires moral courage. We must dare to speak the truth even when it is not popular.

We are in danger of obscuring the gospel by avoiding clearly biblical terminology. Jews (and Gentiles) do not need to be completed. They need to be converted. Their whole mindset, the tendency of their hearts, the direction to which their life is set, must be radically altered. If some Messianic Jews have not been converted, they need to be.

Why has repentance all but disappeared from the language of the Messianic Movement? After all, the gospel is a message about God's holiness and man's extreme sinfulness, about God's grace to sinful man and about Jesus, the Messiah whom God had sent to save his people from their sins. Salvation has to do with sin and its forgiveness, with sin and its being forsaken, with sin and with man being released from its power by the death and resurrection of Messiah. Faith and repentance are both necessary for salvation. If we do not preach repentance, can we really claim to have preached the gospel?

An Interim Summary
Like all Christians, Jewish Christians are free from the Mosaic covenant, as we are from rabbinic tradition.

- We are free to maintain our national identity and should maintain it, if we wish to further the best interests of our people.
- The only way to do so is to maintain that cultural consensus by which the majority of contemporary

Jews express and maintain their Jewishness.

- But we must do so in a manner that is consistent with the Scriptures: the issues of the gospel may never be obscured.
- Nothing but God in Messiah and his finished work on Calvary may be the focal point of congregational life, worship or evangelism.
- The unity of the church should be maintained, and rabbinic tradition should never be accorded religious authority.
- God reigns among his redeemed by his Word.

May it be so with us.

Section B:

A
Practical
Assessment

A PRACTICAL ASSESSMENT

Standards

The Messianic Movement has created its own standards by its unequivocal statement of purpose. The Movement has repeatedly declared that it has formulated its practice in terms of specific goals:

1) Achieving acceptance as believers in Jesus within the Jewish nation.
2) Impacting the Jewish people as a whole with the message of the gospel. In other words, increasing the effectiveness of its evangelism.
3) Providing a distinctly Jewish spiritual home for Jewish believers in Jesus.

So far we have sought to examine the Messianic Movement by comparing it with the Scriptures. In this section of our study, we will evaluate the Movement by the measure of success it has had in achieving its declared goals. Some reference to these matters has been made in the previous section, but it is appropriate that we consider them separately.

Who Has Been Persuaded of What?

In an effort to convince doubting Jews of the Jewishness of faith in Jesus, Messianic Jews have chosen to express that Jewishness in terms of rabbinic custom in worship and, to a much lesser degree, in lifestyle. They are increasingly saying that this practice is a matter of religious obligation. In the Diaspora they meet in what are often described as Messianic synagogues. By such practices, the Movement has recognised rabbinic tradition as the rightful arbiter of Jewish life. It has done so at a time when the majority of the Jewish people in Israel and abroad prefer to express their Jewishness in terms of cultural rather than religious custom.

Instead of convincing the nation of our Jewishness (why on earth should we even concede to having it questioned?), our persistent emphasis upon our Jewishness is confirming doubts in the minds of those we want to reach. Was Shakespeare wrong when he said, 'Methinks the man protesteth overmuch'? The Jewish community doubts the sincerity of our claims because our protest betrays the insecurity that plagues so many among us.

Why should we care if the rabbis refuse to recognise our Jewishness? They are wrong, and nothing on earth can undo that. They can insist that, by virtue of our faith in Jesus, we have cut ourselves off from the nation, but we know better and so will the nation in due time. Meanwhile, we are willing to go outside the camp, bearing our Lord's reproach.

The doubts of our detractors are, however, well founded when there are so many Gentiles in Diaspora congregations, acting as if they were Jewish. Why should a congregation which is primarily Gentile be considered Jewish? What should we, what can we do to remedy this – cast the Gentiles out? Of course not. We recognise our unity with all who worship God in Messiah, and cherish the fellowship that such unity affords. If the Messianic Movement had the courage to opt for such an unbiblical option, the Movement would immediately collapse for lack of moral and financial support. It would be seen to be what it really is: a tiny fringe group of interesting individuals, united around a quaint but shared view.

Is it likely that our vague, sometimes not quite honest, stand will persuade anyone of our integrity? How can any among us bear the title 'rabbi' if we have not been ordained to the rabbinate, and then speak to our people of the holiness of God and our duty to truth? Some Gentile leaders in the Messianic Jewish Movement have taken to wearing a yarmulke and a prayer shawl, and to using a few Hebrew words. They then expect to be recognised as Messianic rabbis. Such practices do not carry the hallmark of sincerity, let alone of holiness. They alienate rather than attract truly observant Jews.

Has the Messianic Movement Found Acceptance Within the Jewish Nation?

It has not, nor will it ever so long as it insists upon the Messiahship of Jesus. Judaism is a religion of rejection. Over the last 2,000 years it has been formulated in conscious reaction to the gospel, however poorly that gospel has been represented. The boundaries of what is now known as Judaism have been defined in conflict with the message of Messiah. Jews can believe or deny almost anything without threat to their Jewishness. They can believe that a prominent, now deceased, rabbi from Brooklyn is the Messiah, and that his illness and death were redemptive. They can believe that he is now with his people by his spirit. They can believe that he will soon return to redeem Israel – but they must not attribute such characteristics to Jesus so long as they wish to be considered Jewish. That is how far Judaism has been removed from its biblical roots.

Even if Messianic Jews came to the place where they no longer acknowledged Jesus as God in any sense or measure (God forbid that this should ever happen!), even if we begin to perceive him merely as a human Messiah, divinely gifted by God and devoted to the Torah, we would not be recognised by Orthodox Judaism as legitimate members of the nation because rabbinicism rejects Jesus in every sense and form. The rabbis give no quarter here, and we should not yield an inch.

John Fischer makes it clear that one of the main purposes for which the Messianic Movement exists is to forward effective preaching of the gospel among the Jewish people. John says,

> 'The mainstream of the Jewish community is much more ready to come to the Messianic synagogues. Here they see recognizable Jewish things, yet can perceive a difference due to the life, reality and faith in Jesus. And they hear the New Testament as well as the Old. As a result, they are more willing to hear about Jesus and the atonement he provides. In effect, they go back in time to the first century biblical Jewish setting; they return to the way Jesus and the apostles worshipped. Messianic congregations have the potential for communicating God's message to entire Jewish families and neighbourhoods as never before' (John Fischer, *The Olive Tree Connection: Sharing Messiah with Israel*, InterVarsity Press, Downers Grove IL, 1983).

This being the case, measuring the extent to which the Movement has succeeded in achieving this major goal is an important measure of the Movement itself.

Messianic Judaism is very far from finding acceptance among their fellow Jews who do not believe in Jesus. This truth should give rise to serious thought about the viability and justification of the Movement. Shoshana Feher quotes prominent American rabbis. Their response is typical, although the response of rabbis in Israel tends to be more vitriolic. Rabbi Geller, a prominent member of the American Jewish Congress and a feminist rabbi, informs us, 'The gift of feminism is to teach us that the community of Israel includes everybody... Among that group of people are gay and lesbians ... all of the categories of Jews you know'. But 'the [Messianics] are not Jews. They are people who are trying to convert Jews ... I don't think they're really relatives. I think they are people who are pretending to be relatives and using their pretended relative status to trick the rest of my family' (Feher, pp. 29-30).

On pages 30-39 Feher catalogues a series of rabbinic responses to the claim of Messianic Jews to be accepted as such by the Jewish community. Some of the statements are unnerving. Just to take one, Rabbi Kravitz insists, 'even *no* relationship with God (emphasis his) is better than a Messianic relationship'.

Feher gives a perceptive explanation for this firm rejection by explaining, 'the one issue that increases group consciousness in the Jewish community is Christianity, which symbolises an external boundary and [thus] creates a strong corporate order. Those individuals who cross or straddle boundaries are particularly dangerous because they threaten the existing classification system in a fundamental way'.

Feher summarises this point on pages 41-42 of her work: 'The Jewish community gains more comfort from defining who is *not* a member of the community than from defining who *is*. The proverbial line in the sand is drawn at Jesus' feet. Atheists and agnostics, the so-called "fox-hole Jews", are welcome. Followers of Jesus, however, by whatever name they call themselves, Hebrew Christians, Messianic Jews or Jews for Jesus, in the eyes of the normative Jewish community are Christians all the same, "the worst of the *Goyim*". In other words, Messianic Jews gain nothing by straddling the two religious identities. Instead of being more winsome, they antagonise the very people they hope to reach.

'This exclusionary response of the Jewish

community has created problems for the self-definition of Messianic Jews, yet has simultaneously helped to shape that definition' (Feher, p. 42). How? By driving the Movement toward an ever increasing tendency to divest itself of essential biblical truth, shedding more and more of its new covenant roots and by seeking to become increasingly less distinguishable in terms of faith and practice from normative Judaism. That is one of the great dangers inherent in the Movement. It is so pre-occupied with being Jewish that it is in danger of becoming steadily less Christian, that is to say, less biblical. As Feher, an objective observer, noted (p. 51), 'many theological issues take a backseat to maintaining an emphasis on the Jewishness of the faith. No attempt is ever made to address them.'

Ask yourself in all sincerity whether or not this observation is painfully true.

In the course of my work as a pastor in Israel, I have met a large number who attended Messianic congregations in Leningrad, Moscow and throughout the former USSR, who were baptised and who consider themselves citizens of the kingdom of Heaven. Many of them have no inkling of the gospel, no idea of their inherent sinfulness, no understanding of the atoning death of Jesus and no knowledge of his deity. They were attracted by the affection of the evangelist, his flashy car, the emphasis on the legitimacy of Jewishness in a country where Jewishness served as an excuse for persecution and by the possibility of immigrating to Israel. Happily, this is not true of all Jewish converts from the former USSR, but it is true of far too many.

Jeff Wasserman (p. 76) reports that, among the congregations he surveyed, a mere 40 per cent are Jewish and that 'most couples are mixed marriages with one Jewish and one Gentile partner'. He asserts (pp. 103-105), 'American Messianic congregations are consistently unsuccessful in attracting Jewish converts'.

Schiffman's 1988 survey showed that 47 per cent of Messianic congregations saw themselves as only slightly effective or not effective in reaching Jewish family members. He notes that 'Jewish cultural elements in worship seem to have little value in outreach'. Data from the 1986–1991 Jews for Jesus 'Jewish Believer Survey' support this observation. Analysis of a sample of 300 of 5,000 surveys shows that only 4 per cent of believing Jews were evangelised by Messianic congregations. Schiffman's 1987 survey (Michael Schiffman, *Communicating Yeshua to the Jewish People: A Study of Variable Factors Which May Influence Growth in Messianic Jewish Congregations,* ONS, M. Div Thesis, Ashland Theological Seminary, 1988) indicated that only 2 per cent of American Messianic believers had come to faith as a result of Messianic congregational evangelistic activity. Respondents to my own surveys indicated a total of less than 300 Jewish converts as a direct result of evangelistic outreach of 62 congregations. Only half of these continued attending the congregations that evangelised them. Gentiles attracted to Messianic doctrine and worship style account for much of the membership growth of Messianic congregations. Later on (p. 106) he says, 'in my survey 98% of the Jewish members of Messianic congregations were brought to faith by Gentile Christians'.

Consequently, 'Some Messianic congregations presume that their simple existence is a significant element in establishing a witness to the Jewish community. Some respondents indicated a hope that eventually the Jewish community would take positive notice of faith in Yeshua as a viable option for Jews, a fourth or fifth branch of Judaism. Recent expressions of anti-Messianic Jewish sentiments by leaders of the Jewish Anti-Defamation League and "Jews for Judaism" make this recognition unlikely' (p. 104).

Has the Messianic Movement Been Evangelistically More Effective Among the Jewish People?

It has not, nor could it be, because its emphasis is misplaced. Following the initial stir the Movement created at its inception (especially among Christians), the Messianic Movement has hardly addressed the Jewish nation with the gospel at all. Nor is the Movement characterised by an evangelistic zeal. Most Messianic organisations in the Diaspora are engaged in dialogue with the church far more than with addressing their own people, and their Jewish membership is largely made up of individuals who were converted outside of the Movement and only then persuaded to join. The only exception to this is in the various countries of the former Soviet Union, as we have observed, where the level of true gospel understanding among many who profess to have been converted under Messianic leadership leaves much to be desired.

Feher confirms this information (p. 52): 'All but six of my interviewees were already "saved" when they came to Messianic Judaism'. In the footnote to this statement Feher quotes Carol A. Harris-Shapiro's 1992 Ph.D. dissertation, submitted to the Department of Religion at (the Jewish) Temple University, *Syncretism or Struggle: The Case of Messianic Judaism*, 'who also found that most Messianic adherents had been saved previously'.

There is an exceptionally high turnover of congregants in a large number of Messianic congregations, many of who remain but for a limited time. There is also a growing number of mixed marriages between Jewish and Gentile believers. This raises questions as to the ability of the Movement to build a significant body of Messianic Jews who will be able to address the nation with any integrity on the grounds of their Messianic Jewish identity.

Messianic Jews are persuaded that through their adherence to Judaism they will be more effective in witnessing to Jewish people. This is not likely for a number of reasons. Most important is the fact that no Messianic Jew is truly Orthodox. Messianic Jews pick and choose aspects of Judaism to which they will adhere.

For example, few if any really avoid travel or the use of any form of electric power on the Sabbath. Few if any avoid the wearing of mixed fibres (Sha'atnez, in Hebrew). Most do not regularly wear the fringes or the kippa that are prerequisites for truly Orthodox Jews. Few maintain a truly kosher kitchen. If they keep kosher, most keep what they describe as a 'biblical kashrut'.

In what sense can such practice be construed as traditional Judaism, which rejects such a version of kashrut and insists that only traditional Jewish practice – the Halacha – may determine what is to be eaten, when, and how. Feher is right (p. 83) when she says, 'They keep kosher in order to identify with Judaism, and yet, because they choose to keep biblical *kashrut* they end up by not belonging. Messianics' attempts to achieve balance creates a contradiction: in seeking to offend no one, they potentially offend everyone'.

Repeated efforts by Messianic Jews to force Christian meanings into Jewish traditions are as much an offence to Orthodox Jews as any one could imagine. It certainly does not convey a sense of honest loyalty to those traditions. This is a concern that will occupy us as we address the next important question.

Has the Messianic Movement Provided a Spiritual Haven for Jewish Believers in Jesus?

To some extent, it has, although we need to be reminded that an overwhelming majority of those who belong to Messianic congregations are actually Gentiles, and that most Jewish Christians are not part of the Movement. Much of the purported Jewish customs adopted in Messianic congregations is artificial. Many Messianic congregations meet on Friday night – the eve of the Jewish Sabbath – to light Sabbath candles and to worship together. But any one who knows something of Jewish custom can see through the facade: in Jewish custom, candles are lit at home – not in the synagogue. The mother of the house lights them, not a man, and before the Sabbath begins, not after. Furthermore, women never officiate in any part of public traditional Jewish services. So what is the point?

True, Reform Jewish synagogues follow a practice similar to that maintained by some Messianic Jews. But Reformed Judaism in no way represents the national cultural consensus and can hardly claim to be traditional when its practices are so recent. However large the Reformed Jewish Movement is in America, it represents a minority within Jewry as a whole, and enjoys no legal religious status in Israel. It is a moot question whether Reformed Judaism is not, in fact, a gateway to assimilation. Only time will tell.

In spite of protestations to the contrary, the largest number of Jewish Christians now in the Messianic Movement did not join the Movement out of a sense of need. They did not join because they longed to affirm their Jewish identity. Shoshana Feher's comment (p. 52) is true of the majority, who 'realised that they had Jewish backgrounds, or became identified with Judaism, only after they began attending services at a Messianic congregation'. Rather than addressing a need, the Movement has laboured to create one, and then support its claim to be able to meet it.

Messianic Judaism does appeal to Jewish Christians who are insecure about their Jewish identity. Such lack of confidence may be the result of their untraditional upbringing, the fact that one of their parents was not Jewish, or some other personal reason. They have been taught that one cannot be Jewish and believe in Jesus. By embracing rabbinic custom, they are now seeking to prove that they are Jewish in spite of their faith. But it is doubtful whether Messianic Judaism is really able to provide the grounds for a healthy confidence, since many of its leaders are themselves driven by a sense of insecurity. There is also room to ask if the confidence that some might obtain by this means is biblical.

Messianic Judaism provides those who have little or no knowledge of Jewish custom with the illusion that they are now manifestly Jewish. But, as we have seen, Jews who are acquainted with their national traditions are reinforced in their conviction that Messianic Jews have simply adopted a gimmick. Stern's words of warning here should be heeded, when he spoke out against 'using Jewish materials ignorantly' so as to create a 'parody of synagogue procedure'. David goes on to ask, 'What good can come of putting up a front... Only the congregations whose members are seriously trying to express the Jewishness that is in fact theirs will be able to weather ... criticism. They will weather it because they are doing something real, not acting a show' (*Manifesto*, p. 168 and following). A few Yiddish phrases, saying 'Yeshua' instead of 'Jesus', wearing Jewish religious paraphernalia and showing an affection for Jewish things, is simply not enough to make one Jewish.

How many Messianic congregations are able to profess a 'Jewishness that is in fact theirs'? Feher (p. 69) informs us, 'Messianics dig into the past to unearth a previously unknown familial connection with Judaism. In other cases, Messianic Gentiles have long been aware of some familial connection to Judaism that eventually creates or nurtures their curiosity in the Messianic Movement. Gentile recruits recreate their historical roots in order to identify with the desired Jewish ethnicity – or invent such roots in order to be fully accepted among Messianics'.

Hear Feher again as she summarises her chapter, *Meshuganeh for the Lord* (pp. 72-72):

'Other root seekers at the congregation claim Jewish descent based on a link that is many generations old. Thomas, an older man who brings his granddaughter to the services with him, met me one Sunday and told me his story. Born and raised a Roman Catholic, he did not "discover" that he was Jewish until relatively recently, when he read that, in 1492, when the Jews were expelled from the Iberian peninsula, there was not a single family in Spain without some Jewish blood. Although his family tree indicates that in the fifteenth century his family lived in Italy, they came from a part of Italy that was primarily Spanish.

'Growing up in this country, Thomas remembers that his grandmother did "Jewish things" such as following *kashrut*, or kosher ritual, when cooking. She always soaked chicken in saltwater for two or three hours before cooking it. She also boiled meat before cooking it, and butchered chickens according to rabbinic tradition, by cutting their throats rather than strangling them. Thomas' grandfather also made "those Italian biscotti" which are basically *kamish*, like the Sephardic Jews. These practices, along with his grandmother's maiden name Leonbruni (which he translates as "the Lion of Judah"), indicate to Thomas that his grandmother came from a family of crypto-Jews – Jews who converted to Catholicism in Spain during the Inquisition but secretly continued to practice Judaism.

'In their attempts to unearth a connection, other Gentiles also find links, however slight, to the Sephardic tradition. Liliana, in her mid sixties, told me that some ten years earlier she had spent time in Israel because she wanted to understand her Jewish background better. She was raised in the United States as a Catholic, both of her parents were Mexican, descended from the Spanish conquistadors. Their history, coupled with her mother's name (a name "similar to Cohen"), clearly indicated to her that her ancestors were also Jews, converted to Catholicism during the Inquisition.

'Even if all their ancestors are Gentiles, these respondents want to ensure that their children will be Jewish. One respondent felt strongly that her son (who was one and a half at the time) must marry a traditionally (matrilineally) Jewish woman so that their children in turn will be recognised as Jewish by the State of Israel and the family line will become Jewish. Likewise, another congregant wants to marry a matrilineally Jewish woman: "I feel like I want to get my name restored in Israel, because ... I'm not Jewish, according to rabbinic laws and stuff... And I would like to give my children that heritage."'

On the other hand, most Jewish Christians (at least 90 per cent by Jeff Wasserman's statistics)) still choose not to attach themselves to Messianic synagogues. This is particularly true of those few who have had an Orthodox Jewish upbringing. Most of them consider Messianic Judaism to be a distortion of what they know to be rabbinic custom, nor have they any desire to come again under the yoke of rabbinic bondage, however altered it might be.

The Messianic Movement's Achievements

The Messianic Movement has obviously awakened the church to a renewed awareness of the Jewishness of the gospel, no less than it has had its interest sparked afresh with regard to the Old Testament. Although the Movement has few competent scholars representing it, it has impacted many academics, who have published books relating to the Jewishness of the gospel, the Jewish background of the New Testament, issues of continuity and discontinuity between the Testaments, OT exegesis, and the such like.

A growing number of Christians all over the world

are fast adopting terminology framed and fashioned by the Messianic Movement. They increasingly attribute to Orthodox Judaism an inherent spirituality and a biblical integrity, both of which are, in some circles, no longer considered open to question. Jewish believers in Jesus are commonly described as anything but Jewish Christians. Terms such as 'conversion', 'church' and 'Christ' are being supplanted by Messianic terminology. Western style Charismatic tunes to Hebrew texts coming out of Israel are being sung the world over. There is a growing movement among evangelicals to identify the modern State of Israel with God's eschatological plans for the world.

The Messianic Movement has persuaded the church that faith in Jesus in no way constitutes a rejection of one's Jewishness, or a betrayal of one's nation. The people of Israel have yet to be convinced, but large and growing sections of the church have now accepted this true yet novel view of things.

'Novel' because, for 2,000 years, Jews who believed in Jesus were taught to think of themselves as no longer Jewish and were, within a generation or two, lost to the Jewish nation. They were expected to celebrate 'Christian' holidays and to eschew anything distinctly Jewish. The church's insistence that Jewish Christians distance themselves from anything Jewish has undermined the church's claim that the gospel is the fulfilment of OT promise. After all, if one had to cease being Jewish in order to follow Jesus, in what sense could Jesus be thought of as the Messiah promised in the Old Testament?

In a nutshell, the Messianic Movement has successfully forced the church to consider some important questions. It has waged an effective campaign on behalf of an important truth. In view of the fact that much of Messianic effort has not been internationally orchestrated, that the Movement has failed to secure meaningful unity between its various factions and that its resources are relatively few, these are remarkable achievements.

The Negative Impact of the Messianic Movement

When measured by biblical standards, the Messianic Movement has been more successful in raising the right questions than in providing the right answers.

The Messianic Movement has confused cultural mores with religious duties. It has insisted upon maintaining the Jewishness of its adherents by various degrees of obedience to rabbinic religious dictum. By this method, God's authority over the conscience has been replaced by that of human ingenuity – so much so that some in the Movement (Dan Juster and David Stern, for example) have called for the creation of a distinctly Messianic Halacha (Halacha is Hebrew for religious legislation).

Such a call embroils the Movement in impossibilities. For example, while discussing the problems associated with the creation of such a Halacha, David writes, 'whether the Spirit wants us to obey the rule or break it will be decided within a communal congregational framework in which our respected leaders and colleagues help us to determine the mind of the Messiah' (*Manifesto,* p. 54). Now, Halacha is a 'binding religious interpretative tradition'. You cannot have a binding tradition that does not bind. Moreover, to call for the creation of a Halacha is to call for the undoing of one of the most important accomplishments of the Reformation: an acknowledgement of the right of every man to study the Bible and to come himself to an understanding of its meaning. Boaz Michael, founder and director of First Fruits of Zion, a Messianic ministry approved by the UMJC, writes that 'we teach and obey Torah, the God-ordained thing to do as His redeemed people' (Bikurei Tziyon, May/June 2000 p. 3).

The Messianic Movement has accorded the rabbis a legitimacy to which they have no right. By attributing to the rabbis the authority to determine what constitutes Jewishness and what does not, Messianics have undermined their own denial of the rabbis' right to determine that faith of any kind in Jesus exceeds the boundaries of Jewishness.

By its insistence upon the central place of the Torah, of Jewishness and of Jewish custom in the lives of its adherents, the Messianic Movement has tended to minimise the fullness, the completeness, and the glory of the work of Messiah and of his person. Spiritual advantage is no longer considered to be a gift of grace, but the consequence of race.

There is a tendency among Messianic Jews to think of themselves as of a higher class of believers by virtue of their Jewishness and by virtue of their adherence to Jewish religious custom. The central place that Jesus had in the life of the apostolic church has thus been accorded to Jewish religious custom. Feher observes (p. 61), 'Messianic believers themselves create a hierarchy in which Messianic Jews are higher than Messianic Gentiles, and this often results in a search for Jewish *Roots* on the part of many Messianic Gentiles'.

Of course, this is not the conscious intention of most Messianic believers, who are sincere in their convictions that the body of Messiah is one, and all its members equal. But the emphasis on advantages derived from adherence to Jewish tradition and Jewish identity inevitably foments such an error. Note the struggle of one Jewish Christian who joined a Messianic congregation and to whom Feher accords (p. 64) the pseudonym 'Sara'. Sara was married to a Gentile Christian whom Feher names 'Gabe'. Gabe persuaded Sara to join a Messianic congregation. Having done so, she was repeatedly frustrated with the constant emphasis on Jewishness. 'Her focus was on her walk with the Lord, with her spirituality and not with her ethnicity.' Only now, after 'years of worshipping with Adat HaRuach' has she been able to settle in and feel comfortable.

Rich Nichol, active in the IMJA and leader of a

Messianic synagogue in Boston, writes of a customary ritual in his congregation before services begin. 'We (the men) pray in unison Hebrew and English prayers appropriate to the donning of the *tallit*. And then the sound of a "swoosh" fills the room as we almost in unison enwrap ourselves in the *talitot*. We then put our arms around one another's shoulders and pray that God would bless our service, one another, the women and children. We then file into the sanctuary, take our places and the service begins. The five-minute ceremony has its transcendent power. It embodies multiplied male energy directed to a holy purpose... the traditional male garment of prayer with its tactile and visual reality is an essential element in the ritual.' This Messianic leader concludes 'gathering for prayer without our *talitot* would just not work!' (*Messianic Jewish Life, April-June 2000 Vol. LXXIII No. 2,* pp. 24-25).

There have been unintended but strong tendencies in the Messianic Movement toward Judaistic legalism as well as an inability to distinguish between divinely given Laws and human inventions.

The semantics adopted by Messianic Jews have created more than a hairline crack in the unity of the church. This breech threatens to widen to the point of cleavage. The contention made by Messianic Jews, who insist, 'I am not a Christian', goes far beyond what is permitted by Scripture. Why are Gentiles 'converted' while Messianic Jews are only 'complete'? Are Jewish people not sinners? Is the humanity of Gentiles not brought to its fulfilment in Christ by the salvation he secured for those who believe? There is no room for religious distinctions between Jews and Gentiles in Messiah, just as there is no room to distinguish in these matters between males and females, black or white, or between individuals belonging to different social and economic strata.

A disconcerting illustration of this tendency is to be found in the fact that, in spite of the Messianics' professed unity with the wider Evangelical Christian church (a unity most Messianic Jews disavow when speaking to their own people), second generation Messianic Jews have been effectively cut off from the riches of the body of Messiah universal. Their Messianic upbringing has made many of them ignorant of the riches of Christian history, hymnody, theology and biblical interpretation.

Eve Fischer, the daughter of a Messianic rabbi, who left her hometown in order to study, writes:

'I'm expecting to spend the next few years of my life without a Messianic synagogue to call home. And I'm faced with the challenge of finding a surrogate home... I feel less tolerant of most Christian environments. Despite early exposure and an open mind – sometimes too open – I have problems with any spiritual environment different from my own Messianic Jewish *Roots*... I find myself uncomfortable in Christian settings.'

Fischer goes on to say:

'Even simple terminology turns me off. The name Jesus Christ strikes a discordant note in my ear: His name is Yeshua, and He's my Messiah. My father is not a pastor; he's a rabbi, and he leads a synagogue, not a church. I am not a Christian – and I'm certainly not converted – I'm a Believer. And I am a Jew.'

Fischer's solution is, perhaps, inevitable:

'what will I do when I find myself in Kalispell, Montana? I've been thinking and praying about this question over the last year or so. And I think I've found an answer: traditional Judaism ... given the choice between a conservative synagogue and a small Bible church, I think I'd prefer to wake up early on Saturday mornings, not Sundays ... my relationship with Yeshua is one of the most personal elements of my faith, I don't need anyone else to maintain that relationship. But the Judaic elements of my faith – the traditions, the holidays, the prayers – depend on a community ... it's a lot easier to lose track of Judaism in a church than it is to lose track of Yeshua in a synagogue' (*Messianic Jewish Life, Vol. LXXIII, No. 3, Sept. 2000, Youth Perspective,* pp. 18-19).

In spite of its best intentions, the Messianic Movement has tended to divide the body of Messiah into 'Messianic' and 'Gentile' segments. Most Messianic Jews act in consistency with their convictions by disavowing 'Gentile' church history, creedal achievements, hymnody and theologising. By so doing they tend to disenfranchise second generation Messianic Jews who belong to the Movement from the wealth of spiritual insight, gathered wisdom and practical experience that God by his grace has granted his imperfect church down through the centuries. This has greatly impoverished the Movement.

By way of example, individuals who have grown up in the Messianic Movement have no real idea who were John Bunyan, John Newton, Isaac Watts, Cotton Mather, Jonathan Edwards or William Carey. Nor do they attach any sense of value to the creedal declarations of the church. When they attend a run-of-the-mill evangelical service, many of them will not be familiar with the hymns, will expect a rousing sermon abut the importance of Israel and will be uncomfortable in a 'Gentile atmosphere'. In other words, national custom has been allowed to intrude to the point of division between Jewish and non-Jewish followers of Jesus. Fellowship is a wide, wonderful, glorious thing! It is never the paltry imitation of fellowship that most Messianic Jews profess to enjoy with their non-Jewish fellow believers, so long as Jewish traditions are respected.

Many in the Messianic Movement refuse to be formally associated with Jewish Christians who question or oppose Messianic Judaism. They accuse such Christians of 'no longer wishing to be Jewish' or of threatening the cause of the gospel among the Jewish people.

An elitism, that encourages Gentiles to convert to Judaism in order to become Jewish Christians, is evident within the Movement. Anything truly or supposedly Jewish is thought of as superior to 'Gentile Christian' things. Jews are presumed to be able to understand the Bible better than anyone else, and almost every Jewish custom is embraced with enthusiasm because it is assumed to have existed in the days of our Lord and therefore practised by him. In Israel, this is expressed in a form of unabashed discrimination against better-trained and better-experienced Gentile Christians who have come to serve, and who are expected to support Israeli leaders – unless they themselves have Jewish or Israeli spouses. If they do, they become an authority in and of themselves.

The Messianic Movement has been far too tolerant of deviant views on central doctrinal issues. In addition to those mentioned above, it is important to take note of the Unitarian tendency that finds acceptance among many non-Unitarian Messianics as expressed in a growing embarrassment with the Trinity and the deity of Christ.

The struggle for the right to maintain a Jewish identity in Messiah has tended to obscure the more important issues of the gospel, exposing Messianic Jews to a barrage of questionable teachings concerning the nature of the Godhead, the deity of Messiah, the absolute necessity of Jesus' atoning death for salvation and the perfection of his accomplishments by that redeeming death. Some Messianic Jews have even gone to the length of denying that faith in the atoning work of Messiah is necessary to salvation. Rich Nichol writes 'in our synagogues, Messiah Yeshua takes his rightful place as the jewel in the gold setting of our Jewishness' (*Messianic Jewish, Vol. LXXIII,* p. 25). Note, not as the centre because of his deity, or redeeming work in us, but as the jewel of our Jewishness.

In November 2001, *Israel Today* published the results of a survey among several Messianic Jews in Israel. Some of the answers give an indication of some of the trends in the Messianic Movement. One man, Nehemiah Fund Director Uri Marcus says, 'Yeshua is God's plan, but not God Himself... God is more than Yeshua.' Former Israel Secretary of the International Messianic Alliance, Menachem Ben Chaim, states, 'Yeshua is more than a messenger and Messiah, He is part of the Godhead. But we too, as human beings, were created in the image of the Godhead. But we too, as human beings, were created in the image and in the form of God... I see in Yeshua a wonderful man, pure and complete up to his death. And by means of his resurrection Yeshua has reconciled us to God.'

David (Victor) Bar David from Jerusalem says, 'Yeshua said of himself that he is not God, but rather his messenger ... Christianity has distorted Yeshua and his word, which is why the Jewish people no longer recognise their Messiah.' David Tel Tsur from Ma'ale Adumim, a leader of a former Messianic congregation, states, 'Yeshua Ha'Mashiach is not God, he is the Son of God and the Redeemer... The Trinity is completely pagan. On the cross Yeshua cried out, "Eli, Eli (My God), why have you forsaken me?" Does God turn to God? Can one nail a God to a cross? Millions of people were murdered because they were accused of killing God, and what were their last words? *"Hear O Israel, the Lord our God, the Lord is one."'*

Finally, Yosef Shullam, congregation leader in Jerusalem, in response to a purported misquote of his statement in this article, stated the following: 'I have never ... held or taught that Yeshua is not divine... The Tanach teaches that the Messiah is divine and is called "El Elyon" and "Aviad" and "JHWH, our Righteousness". The big question is the equality and hierarchy of this relationship and I believe that we need to use Jewish sources to understand this relationship rather than Christian creeds written by people who hated us and hated the Torah of God.' (Josef's terminology intimates that the Son is God not equally so with the Father. This implies a hierarchy of essence, which distinguishes the Father from the Son and them from the Spirit. 'Jewish sources' would attribute to Messiah an angelic nature, a kind of 'lesser godhood' – BM.)

The Messianic Movement tends to accord eschatology, and a very specific system of eschatological expectation at that, an inordinate role in its life, preaching and practice. There are more references to that system of eschatology than to the Trinity, to the glory of Messiah or to the regenerating work of the Holy Spirit. This inordinance indicates a lack of appreciation for the relative importance of the various parts of biblical revelation. It constitutes a deviation that is potentially very dangerous. I readily admit that a similar imbalance may be found in other contexts, notably among many of our fundamentalist brethren. But to err in good company is still to err.

There is a strong tendency among Messianic Jews to wed their eschatology to a particular political platform, and that to a test of true spirituality. To make such an assumption is to relegate those who think differently (among whom are many fine Arab Christians), to the level of the 'unenlightened'. It also reduces the prophetic message of the church to the pitiful level of end-times prediction and the provision of political support. This tends to 'flatten' moral and political thinking with regard to Israel, robbing it of depth, vigour and moral value.

Zionism may be a legitimate political platform (I believe it is). But to frame one's political views in such a way as to indicate that those who think otherwise are less spiritual or less biblical is to fail to distinguish between political aspirations and the promises of God in Scripture.

It is also to emasculate the prophetic message, which was far more than a Christian version of fortune-telling. The main burden of the prophetic message is spiritual and moral. Israel and Judah were called to conduct moral lives in the fear of God. They were also warned that, if they do not, God would punish them by sending them out of the land. Dealing with the prophets should strike fear in our hearts, not an exhilaration or a sense of control. It should drive us to call our people to repentance, rather than to write yet another book about the identity of the Antichrist.

The Future of the Messianic Movement

The Messianic Movement seems to have outlived its usefulness. It is likely that, as the number of Gentile Christians belonging to Messianic congregations continues to grow, Jewish believers in Jesus will face the same problems they had to face in regular churches.

On the other hand, as churches learn to accommodate Jewish Christians and to allow them their national, cultural distinctives while sharing a common spirituality, one faith and a common hope, the appeal that Messianic congregations have will weaken. The distinct purpose that such congregations presently serve would certainly be better served by inter-congregational fellowships, formal or otherwise, than by distinct congregations.

One major obstacle to the demise of the Messianic Movement are the personal and organisational interests created over the years by those in the forefront of the Movement. These will, most probably, peter out in the course of time. Organisations and movements void of a message do not tend to last very long in a highly critical-minded populace, and we Jews are certainly critical.

The second obstacle to the early demise of the

Messianic Movement is its relatively new impetus in Israel. American-born activists of the Messianic Movement in America have been working hard to strengthen Messianic Jewish consciousness in the country. Most probably, some years will pass before the Movement in Israel loses its initial vigour, the weakness of its positions are discovered and its inability to address the real issues facing Israeli Jewish believers in Israel is seen. Meanwhile, overseas leaders of the Movement will draw strength from this temporary rejuvenation.

The Messianic Movement, coupled with empty claims to having found access to a super-spirituality, now common among some Jewish Christian congregations in Israel, will ultimately collapse under the weight of reality. Until then, much damage will have been done to individuals and to the cause of the gospel. Messianic Judaism will never gain acceptance in Israeli society.

The Way Ahead – for the Church
In order to promote the gospel among the Jewish people and derive the benefit that could accrue from a growing Jewish presence within the body of Messiah, the church should dare review its assumptions with regard to Jewish evangelism.

A missiology based on the so-called 'people's movement' theory is not the product of mature biblical reflection but of the subservience of biblical considerations to modern scientific and sociological assumptions. The church will never be able to appeal to the Jewish people (nor to any people, for that matter) until it regains its confidence in the gospel. When the church learns to act with the courage of its biblical convictions, when it renews its commitment to declare the holiness of God in the ears of a hedonistic, opportunist and sensual society where morals are, at best, relative, then it will have an impact.

The church should reconsider its historic denial of the legitimacy of a continued Jewish existence within the body of Messiah, so long as that existence is based on cultural distinctions rather than theological ones and so long as those distinctions are at best secondary to the gospel, secondary to Messiah and secondary to any form of obedience to God.

The church should not adopt Messianic Jewish terminology, nor identify modern Judaism with the religion of the Bible. To the contrary, it should challenge both with a gracious courage that dares establish itself on the Word of God.

The church should cleanse itself of any form of racism, including an incipient anti-Semitism, evident in many of its commentaries and expressed from many of its pulpits. Instead, it should welcome Jewish believers and help them feel at home while maintaining their national and cultural identity.

The church should engage the Messianic Movement in a kind, mutually respectful theological dialogue. Both the Movement and the church at large can benefit immensely from such a dialogue. It should also muster the courage to question and, when necessary, criticise Jewish believers rather than accept anything that hides under the title 'Jewish'. I very much hope that the book you are holding in your hands will be a contribution to that end.

The church should deal with Messianic Jewish idiosyncrasies with a loving patience that is void of compromise, yet which sympathises in a spirit of gentle meekness with the pains, concerns and fears that have given rise to the Movement. The church must admit its own mistakes and work consciously to correct them.

The Messianic Movement should renew its commitment to Jesus as Lord and Saviour. Neither national nor cultural identity should be allowed to supplant the primary place God has accorded Messiah in both our personal and congregational life. The Movement should worshipfully accord him that primary place and reject any tendency to obscure the gospel of his grace.

The Messianic Movement should cleanse itself of the tendency to national or cultural pride. It should learn to walk humbly before both God and man. It should have the courage to distinguish between divine Law and human traditions, and to carry that distinction into practical effect. It should recognise and seek to maintain the freedom from the Torah that Messiah purchased for us, and learn to distinguish between religious obligation and cultural mores.

The Messianic Movement should reject any doubt concerning its confident faith in the Trinity, the full and absolute deity of Messiah, and the perfection of his completed work on the cross.

The Messianic Movement should recognise the glory of the unity that all the faithful in Messiah enjoy together. In consequence of that recognition, it should dissolve into the church at large by becoming a halfway house administrated, instructed and encouraged by the church for the purpose of primary contact with Jewish unbelievers and for fellowship among Jewish Christians. It should begin to rethink its theology, correct its methodology, and learn to distinguish between evangelistic outreach and congregational life.

The Messianic Movement should renew its acknowledgement of the fact that 'salvation is from the Lord' – from beginning to end. In ultimate terms, our goal is not to win many over to our position, nor to impact our nation. It is to glorify God and enjoy him forever. Such glorification and enjoyment are contingent upon and come as the result of God's gracious blessing upon our obedience. We need to seek God's face, to pray and fast, to cry out from the depths of our hearts for God to be glorified as he has promised, through the salvation of Israel.

May we have the grace to be obedient, and may our blessed, glorious Lord have all the glory in this world, in the world to come and forever, worlds without end.

Amen.

AN AFTERWORD

To the extent that there are, in this paper, any misrepresentations of the Messianic Movement, its views or its practices, they are unintended. I sincerely apologise. It is my sincere desire to present confirmable facts in an irenic manner in order to promote discussion, reconsideration and the growth of us all in the ways of God. I welcome criticism and corrections. I also welcome discussion of any of the issues raised or the facts referred to, and undertake to make, in future editions, any corrections that might be called for once an error has been proven. Our desire is not to win an argument, is it? We want to glorify God – together!

Many of the issues raised in this book question views that are very dear to a good number of my fellow Jewish disciples of Jesus. I kindly ask my good readers to consider what I have said in spite of the ire, hurt and consternation that it may have caused. Weigh my arguments by the Bible. Check for yourselves if my interpretations of texts are valid. If I am wrong, don't write me off; challenge me. If I am right, join me in seeking to correct what is wrong. In any case, seek with me God's kingdom and his righteousness.

Many of the leaders of the Messianic Movement are fine individuals with the best of intentions, a high level of dedication and a clear sense of direction. Many are sincere followers of Jesus who would be deeply troubled if they ever came to the conclusion that the course they have chosen is wrong. They are men and women who truly love God and long to serve him. They would be distressed beyond measure if they were convinced that their Movement has weakened and diluted the gospel rather than honed its redeeming message and its ability to promote the gospel among the Jewish people and in the world.

My earnest prayer to God is that fellow Jews will be convinced of the truth of these things, and that they will begin to perceive them in a new light. I implore them, as I did each of my readers, by the tender mercies of God in Messiah to be willing to consider the matters raised in this paper and to examine my arguments in the light of divine revelation in the Scriptures.

May it please the Lord to bless us in spite of our failings.

Amen.

APPENDIX A

An excellent example of what should be done in terms of non-congregational fellowships for Jewish believers in Jesus may be found in the 'Leeds Messianic Fellowship', established in Yorkshire, England. Below you will find that Fellowship's constitution:

Leeds Messianic Fellowship
Statement of Faith
Leeds Messianic Fellowship believes:

• **There is only one God**, the Maker, Preserver and Ruler of all things, having in and of himself all perfections, and being infinite in them all. To him all creatures owe the highest love, reverence and obedience. *Deuteronomy 6:4; 1 Corinthians 8:4, 6; 1 Thessalonians 1:9; Jeremiah 10:10; Job 11:7-9.*

• **There are three** distinct persons in the Godhead: the Father, the Son and the Holy Spirit. *Matthew 3:16-17; 28:19; 2 Corinthians 13:14; John 1:14, 18; 15:26; Galatians 4:6; Hebrews 1:2; Genesis 1:2.*

• **Adam and Eve**, through Satan's temptation, broke God's commandment, and fell from their original righteousness. All their descendants fell with them, and as a result have inherited a corrupt nature and are guilty before God. From this corrupt nature proceed all actual transgressions of the Law of God. By reason of this fall, men and women are unable of themselves to please God. *Genesis 2:17; 3:6-8, 13, 23; 6:5; Psalms 51:5; Romans 3:10-18, 23; 5:12; 7:14, 17-18; 8:7.*

• **Jesus, the Divine Messiah** is the only begotten Son of God and is the divinely appointed mediator between God and man. Having taken upon himself human nature, yet without sin, he perfectly fulfilled the Law (Torah), suffered and died upon the cross for the salvation of sinners. He was buried, rose again the third day and ascended to the Father, at whose right hand he ever lives to make intercession for his people. He is the only mediator, the Prophet, Priest and King of his people, and Sovereign of the universe. *Isaiah 42:1; John 3:16; 1 Timothy 2:5; Acts 3:22; Luke 1:33; Ephesians 5:23; Galatians 4:4; Hebrews 4:15; 5:5-6; Colossians 2:9.*

• **Regeneration** is the implanting of spiritual life by the Holy Spirit. God calls us into fellowship with Messiah Jesus by his Word and his Holy Spirit, our minds being spiritually enlightened and our wills and affections being renewed. *1 Peter 1:23; 2:9; James 1:18; Ephesians 2:4-5; Galatians 6:15; 2 Corinthians 5:17; Romans 6:13.*

• **Repentance** is a saving grace in which the repentant person is convicted of his sinfulness by the Holy Spirit, and then humbles himself because of his sin, showing godly sorrow, hatred of sin and a willingness to walk before God so as to please him in all things. *Job 42:6; Psalms 51:4-9; Romans 3:20.*

• **Faith** is a saving grace, by which we receive and rest upon Messiah Jesus alone for salvation as he is freely offered to us in the gospel. *John 7:38; 1*

Corinthians 2:5-12; Galatians 2:16.

• **Justification** is an act of God's free grace, by which he pardons our sins, and accounts us righteous. This is not based on anything we have done, but only on the righteousness of Messiah imputed to us and received by faith alone. Once justified, we are adopted into the family of God. *Romans 3:24; 4:5; 8:30; Titus 3:5; Ephesians 1:5; 2:8; Galatians 4:5; John 1:12.*

• **Sanctification** happens to those who are united to Messiah Jesus and are renewed in their whole nature after the image of God. It is a progressive work of the Holy Spirit, who dwells in all believers. We are thus enabled to pursue a life of holiness in obedience to all the commands of Messiah, though never attaining to perfection in this life. *1 Corinthians 6:11; 1 Thessalonians 5:23; 2 Thessalonians 2:13; Titus 2:14; Romans 7:14-25; Hebrews 12:14; 13:21.*

• **The Last Things**
We believe in the visible, personal and bodily return of our Messiah the Lord Jesus. *Matthew 16:27; 24:30; 24:36; 25:31; 26:64; Mark 8:38; Luke 21:27; Revelation 1:7.*

The bodies of men and women return to dust after death, but the bodies of all the dead, both just and unjust, will be raised at the judgement seat of Messiah. *Revelation 20; John 5:21-27; 1 Corinthians 15:51-52; 2 Corinthians 5:10.*

God has appointed a day in which he will judge the world by Messiah Jesus, when everyone shall receive according to his deeds. The wicked will go into everlasting punishment in hell with the devil and his angels. The righteous, with glorified bodies, will live and reign with Messiah forever. *Matthew 5:8; 25:41; 2 Corinthians 3:18; 2 Timothy 2:11-12; John 3:36; 2 Thessalonians 1:9; Revelation 3:21; 21:8.*

God in his mercy, grace and faithfulness has ordained that his purposes with his ancient people the Jews are not finished with nor transferred to another people. The new covenant will not be complete until it embraces the people of the old covenant *(Rom. 11:26)*. *Romans 9–11.*

Statement of Purpose

Leeds Messianic Fellowship is neither a church nor a synagogue. Those Jewish and Gentile believers in Jesus are encouraged, if they are not already, to become members of local churches in the Leeds and West Yorkshire area. We are not in competition with any church and urge that every believer involved in the ministry of *Leeds Messianic Fellowship* be a member of a local church and attending worship on the Lord's Day.

(*Leeds Messianic Fellowship* is a stepping-stone for non-believing Jews, who ordinarily could not or would not enter a church and hear the claims of the gospel of Messiah Jesus. If Jewish people are brought to faith in Jesus, then we would seek to integrate them into the wider body of Messiah by feeding them into gospel churches in Leeds where they would receive a more holistic discipleship than *LMF* could provide. The obvious place to go would be churches where *LMF* people are already in attendance.)

Those who attend are urged to lay their denominational particulars to one side. Therefore we encourage those who attend to *keep the unity of the Spirit in the bond of peace. Ephesians 4:3.*

(By the mere fact that so many denominational interests are present in *LMF* it is obvious that we could not become a church. Plus the fact that it would then become a church based on race, which is unbiblical: we believe in grace not race.)

We are not a synagogue, but we employ certain Jewish symbolism and celebrate the feasts of the Old Testament (Hebrew Bible). In the pluralistic society of modern Britain today we recognise that we must contextualise the gospel or, in our case, take the gospel back to its original Jewish context. Therefore, we have sought to create a forum where Jewish people can come, feel comfortable and hear the gospel presented in a culturally appropriate manner. We want to function in a way whereby Romans 11:11 can be said to be true and we would begin to *provoke them to jealousy.*

Although *Leeds Messianic Fellowship* has a certain cultural specific nature, we are Christocentric rather than ethnocentric. We believe that Messiah Jesus has broken down 'the middle wall of partition' and makes Jew and Gentile one in our Lord and Messiah Jesus. There is no saving merit in being the member of any ethnic group (Rom. 3:9-10), the only saving merit is in Messiah Jesus.

We deplore all forms of racism and anti-Semitism, we particularly grieve over the complicity that many of Europe's church leaders gave to National Socialism during World War Two. We recognise that there were certain views taught by some churches that aided the Nazi attempt at the genocide of the Jewish people. What is more grievous is that some of these views are still taught within the Christian church, which often does not realise that these views are so stained with innocent blood and have no biblical basis. *Leeds Messianic Fellowship* seeks in its teaching to educate against these non-biblical ideas and to fight against all forms of anti-Semitism and racism. In this way we honour our fellow human beings and glorify Messiah Jesus among Israel and the nations.

Leeds Messianic Fellowship wants to encourage Christians to recognise that Christianity is Jewish. Jesus was a Jew, he did not live in a cultural vacuum, he lived and taught in a particular time in history among a particular people. Therefore, to gain a better understanding of Scripture we must look at it through the cultural eyes of that time. In our teaching, we seek to look at Scripture through Jewish eyes, recognising that the Bible is a record of real historical events. For many centuries the church has over-spiritualised the Old Testament and often cannot see what it is really teaching because of an overriding desire to make a spiritual application of the Old Testament text to the 'New Testament believer'. We believe the Old Testament to be as inspired and as important to the Christian as is the New Testament, and seek to reflect that belief in our teaching.

Leeds Messianic Fellowship is not a political organisation and though we have a love and concern for the modern nation of Israel this in no way takes away our love and concern for the Arab people.

Leeds Messianic Fellowship also has a concern to pray for and make known the needs of the indigenous Israeli, Hebrew and Arabic-speaking church. They are encompassed around by those who seek their harm and are often forgotten or politicised.

Summary

Leeds Messianic Fellowship seeks to act as a bridge between non-believing Jewish people and believing Jews and Gentiles, that is, to the true church of Messiah Jesus.

We seek to present the gospel in a culturally acceptable way and though we may use Jewish symbolism and terminology, this is in no way the language of disassociation. We are proud of the heritage for which many Christian martyrs have died cruel deaths. We also recognise that many terms that are precious to Gentile Christians have been twisted by Satan during 2,000 years of history and are not always appropriate in seeking to effectively communicate the gospel to Jewish people.

Leeds Messianic Fellowship wants its members to take back to their churches the truth that Christianity is Jewish and encourage their church leaders to take a stand against anti-Semitism.

Leeds Messianic Fellowship is not political; we are for both Jews and Arabs. We want to encourage churches to wake up to the needs of the indigenous Israeli congregations. Although the Jews are back in unbelief, we believe the modern State of Israel to be part of God's dealings with the Jewish people today.

APPENDIX B

Israel and the Gospel in Paul's Letter to the Romans
Prepared by the author for the Banner of Truth Escondido Ministers' Conference May 30 – June 1, 2000. All quotations are from the New American Standard Version.

A Question of Motivation
Paul was a man of deeply felt spiritual passions. He was unlike many halfway people, who undertake a Christian calling while seeking to serve themselves. Though he clearly yearned for a wife and had given the topic much thought, he had forgone the right of marriage. One can almost hear the aching pain that racked him when he asks, *Do we not have the right to take along a believing wife, even as the rest of the apostles, and the brothers of the Lord, and Cephas?* (1 Cor. 9:5).

Speaking from undoubted personal experience he explains that *it is better to marry than to burn* (1 Cor. 7:9). Yet, *in view of the present distress ... it is good for a man to remain as he is* (1 Cor. 7:26).

Very early in his missionary career he understood that flight from persecution may well serve the interests of his own welfare, but it threatened the life of the churches. He therefore concluded that he would remain wherever possible and suffer the circumstances, and that he would return as early as he could to the cities he had been forced to leave.

Paul also knew that the Lord had ordained that those who preach the gospel should also live by it (1 Cor. 9:14), and had himself determined that those who teach well should receive a double stipend from the churches they served (1 Tim. 5:17). Yet he had forgone this right in order to forward the interests of the churches in whose founding he was involved. Logic insisted, *Who at any time serves as a soldier at his own expense? Who plants a vineyard and does not eat of the fruit of it? Or who tends a flock but does not use the milk of the flock?* (1 Cor. 9:7).

Certainly, if others had this right, he all the more so, for if he had sowed among them spiritual things, would it have been strange for him to reap from them some material benefits? After all, others who did not found the churches did so! But Paul was motivated by a different logic, an intensely spiritual one in which the gospel was paramount and therefore the absolute welfare of the churches God had used him to establish overwhelmed any other legitimate considerations. He endured everything in order to avoid the slightest hindrance to the gospel of Messiah (1 Cor. 9:12). There was a driving sense of compulsion that gave him no rest: *woe is me if I preach not the Gospel* he said, *I have a stewardship entrusted to me* (1 Cor. 9:18).

He had made himself a slave to all, so that he would win the more to Messiah. Family ties, personal health and interests, national and cultural identities – all these and more were forsaken, having been valued by Paul as worth no more than dung, so long as he could serve Messiah and be found in him. He tells the Corinthians: *I think that God has exhibited us apostles last of all, as men condemned to death, because we have become a spectacle to the world – both to angels and to men ... to this present hour we are both hungry and thirsty and we are poorly clothed and are roughly treated and are homeless, and we toil, working with our own hands. When we are reviled, we bless. When we are persecuted, we endure. When we are slandered, we try to conciliate. We have become as the scum of the world, the dregs of all things, even until now* (1 Cor. 4:9-13).

Paul was motivated by this one concern: to glorify Messiah by faithfully preaching the gospel to all, so that God's elect might be gathered in. He had crucified the flesh and its natural ties, and could declare with an honest conscience that the self sacrifice of Messiah had so transformed his thinking that he had been taken over by it: *Messiah died for all, that they who live should no longer live for themselves but for him who died and rose again on their behalf* (2 Cor. 5:13-15).

From this all-consuming passion there could be but one conclusion: *Therefore,* Paul states, directly relating what he is about to say to the previously described spiritual motivation, *from now on we recognise no man according to the flesh – even though we have known Messiah according to the flesh, yet now we know him thus no longer! ... If any man is in Messiah, he is a new creature, the old things passed away. Behold: new things have come!* (2 Cor. 5:16-17).

Among these new spiritual considerations, innocent of any personal interests or family ties, was a burning desire to which Paul refers in his letter to the Romans: *I am telling the truth in Messiah, I am not lying, my conscience bearing witness in the Holy Spirit, that I have great sorrow and unceasing grief in my heart, for I could wish that myself were cursed from Messiah for the sake of my kinsman according to the flesh* (Rom. 9:1-3).

Why is Paul so grieved for his fellow Jews, so much so that he speaks of his willingness even to be cut off from Messiah, if that could change their condition?

What is the cause of his perpetual sorrow? Let us

allow Paul to answer for himself. *Brethren, my heart's desire and prayer to God for them is for salvation* (Rom. 10:1).

Is Paul's earnest desire for the Jewish people the consequence of his natural love for the nation to which he belongs – a form of selfishness – or is there a deeper, more worthy reason? In light of what Paul has already said about his having divested himself of self-serving motivations, we ought to be very careful before we attribute to the great Apostle anything that runs contrary to this professed consequence of the renewal of his heart.

Paul's concern for the Jewish people is not primarily motivated by kinship. He is not concerned for the Jews because they are his kinsmen, although his grief is certainly compounded because of that. He refers to his close relationship with the Jewish people in order to provide us with a sense of the poignancy of his sorrow, not an understanding of its motivation.

Israel and the Gospel

Paul's desire for the salvation of Israel had to do with how he perceived the purpose of salvation, the goal of the gospel and the end for which Messiah had come. His passion had to do with the gospel, not with natural national affections. His desire was that, whether by his life or through his death, God in Messiah might be glorified, his amazing mercies seen and acknowledged by all, and his perfectly wise purposes worked out. That is why his discussion of the gospel fate of Israel concludes with such an exuberant doxology. Having reviewed God's past, present and future dealings with Israel, Paul breaks out in a paean of praise and worship:

> *Oh the depth of the riches both of the wisdom and knowledge of God! How unsearchable are his judgements and unfathomable his ways! For who has known the mind of the Lord or who has become his*

counsellor? Or who has first given to him that it might be paid back to him again? For from him and to him are all things, to whom be the glory forever! (Rom. 11:33-36).

This praise is the consequence of how Paul understood God's purpose and the outworking of that purpose with regard to the Jewish people. Perhaps, if we saw things as Paul saw them, we too would worship as he did. May it please God to make that worthy end the product of our present review of the book of Romans.

In Paul's view, the salvation of Israel had to do with the glory of God. Because he loved God, Paul longed for the salvation of the Jewish people. To Paul's way of thinking, the wisdom, grace and justice of God's dealings with Israel were not issues incidental to the gospel but related to its very essence. That is why those who consider chapters 9–11 of Paul's letter to the Romans as a natural and understandable digression fail to grasp the point that Paul has laboured to make. Far from being tangential, chapters 9–11 of the letter to the Roman Christians have to do with the very heart of the gospel, its internal essence. They have to do with what makes the heart of God throb, and therefore moves the heart of every man of God who is instructed in the Scriptures.

Romans 1:16
The point is made at the outset of Paul's letter to the Romans, when the Apostle states, *I am not ashamed of the Gospel, for it is the power of God for salvation to everyone who believes, to the Jew first and also to the Greek* (Rom. 1:17). It is spelled out in the remainder of the epistle. But it remains at all times in the forefront of Paul's thinking. Romans 1:16 is, I propose for your consideration, a summary of Paul's letter to the Romans.

What does Paul mean when he says that he is not ashamed of the gospel, and why is he not ashamed?

Paul's response is simple and must be taken into account in order to meet the expectations of the text and to render it comprehensible. Paul informs us why he is not ashamed of the gospel. He begins by telling us that he is not ashamed because *of what it is*: *the power of God for salvation to everyone who believes, to the Jew first and also to the Greek*. In other words, Paul here addresses the essence of the gospel, what the gospel *is*. Before we explore what Paul has to say about this subject, let us consider for a moment what we has to say about his attitude to the gospel:

'I am not ashamed'
I am not ashamed of the Gospel, says Paul. An understatement if there ever was one. Under these simple words, *I am not ashamed*, Paul encompasses an entire life of sacrifice, suffering, dedication and consuming devotion that drove him from one country to another, from one city to another, from the comfort and security of his home city, Tarsus, to Antioch, and thence from a pleasant ministry which was evidently blessed to Cyprus, to the rugged mountains of Southern Galatia and thence ever onward, to the north of what is nowadays known as Turkey, to Greece, Rome, Crete, and the far western corner of the Roman empire, ever returning to visit churches he founded or sending emissaries to ensure their spiritual welfare. Paul's prodigious travels are amazing, his correspondence voluminous, his labours beyond imagination and the price he paid to promote the gospel beyond comparison with anything but that once and for all magnificent sacrifice that his Lord, Jesus, made to ensure the salvation of all those whom the Father had given him. Humbly, but all the more forcibly because of the way he chose to put it, Paul sums this up with the pedestrian non-statement, *I am not ashamed of the Gospel!*
Not ashamed! He was driven, found himself to be under inescapable constraint, moved with a passion

that knew and could know no respite until it was at last fulfilled in its final consummation, as he poured out his life for the gospel he had served with such dedication. May God give us many more such men who, like Paul, are *not ashamed.* May he transform us to be so taken up with the glories of Messiah that nothing else can hold our attention or command our devotion.

In these words Paul has opened to our gaze something of his heart throb, the heart throb of a spiritual man. Why do we lack such devotion? Could it be due to the fact that we do not have such clear perceptions of the gospel? Why are our hearts so cold? Could it be because we have not yet been captured by such a clear view of the glory of God in the face of Jesus Messiah?

The Logic of the Gospel
Paul further instructs us why he is not ashamed of the gospel. *I am not ashamed of the Gospel because ...* there is reason, there is logic, there is a good cause why Paul is unashamed of the gospel.

Unlike many of the world's religions, the message of the Bible is eminently reasonable. It reflects the wisdom and rationality of God himself and therefore has an inner logic. It commands man to relate to it in a logical way. The message of Messiah is no irrational experience, incapable of description or comprehension. While there are elements that transcend human understanding, the gospel easily fits in to the natural order of things – apart from sin. Hence, in order to understand the Bible, we need to seek out and follow the logic of its message. There is a cause and an effect to the gospel, there are reasons and consequences. Paul states, *I am not ashamed of the Gospel because...*

As we have noted, the cause for Paul's unabashed view of the gospel has to do with its essence, with what the gospel is in and of itself. Let us now turn to that essence and discover what Paul has to say about it.

The Gospel Is God's Power to Save
First, *it is the power of God for salvation.* Unlike the world's religions, the gospel proclaims and affects a divine intervention of the course of human life. It is not man reaching into his own resources; pulling himself up by his own shoestrings; achieving his salvation by his own efforts, merits and natural abilities. No, the gospel humbles man as much as it exalts God. Indeed, it humbles man in order to exalt the God who saves.

The message of Jesus, the Messiah, has the only true view of man, as spelled out in the first few chapters of Paul's letter to the Romans: man is a rebellious sinner who took the good things of God and transformed them into a lie. He refuses to acknowledge even the little he knows of God and prefers darkness to the light of God's truth. Having been given over to impurity and to degrading passions, man has run headlong toward utter perversion *being filled with all unrighteousness, wickedness, greed, evil, full of envy, murder, strife, deceit, malice, they have become gossips, slanderers, haters of God, insolent, arrogant, boastful, inventors of evil, disobedient to parents, without understanding, untrustworthy, unloving, unmerciful* (Rom. 1:29-32).

This leaves man – *every man* (Rom. 2:1) – without *excuse* (ibid.) before him *who will render to every man according to his deeds* (Rom. 2:6), whether perpetuated by Jews under conscious jurisdiction of the Law, or by Gentiles who knew nothing of such covenantal obligations. Jewishness in itself cannot serve to excuse a man because true Jewishness involves the internalisation of the covenant by the work of the Spirit (Rom. 2:17-29). Jews and Gentiles are equally sinful and therefore liable to divine justice (Rom. 3:9-18). So, man is driven to the dust.

The gospel also exalts God, who is declared by it to be true to the covenant although all men have been proven awfully untrue. God has revealed to man a righteousness which fulfils all the requirements of the Law, but which is provided by a means other than the Law, that is *the righteousness of God through the faith of Jesus the Messiah for all those who believe, for there is no distinction* (Rom. 3:22-23). The gospel exalts the Lord God, who has shown himself rich toward all in salvation, apart from any covenantal Law-keeping on their part, because he is not the God of the Jews only, but also of the Gentiles (Rom. 3:26-30).

While not dependent upon Law-keeping, that salvation is not contrary to the Law given beforehand by God. Rather, it is in fulfilment of it, just as the Law itself served as a stage in the fulfilment of the promises given to Abraham. As we shall see, the gospel also leads inexorably to the fulfilment of the Law in yet another sense. Abraham himself was not justified by keeping the covenantal Law, nor was David. Salvation now comes as it did before: *through the righteousness of faith* (Rom. 4:13) and not that *of the Law* (v. 14).

Why so? Because such a method of salvation ensures that salvation is the gracious product of divine and sovereign kindness rather than the deserved reward of human merit. It is grace and not human merit that ensures *that the promise may be certain to all the descendants, not only those who are of the Law, but also to those who are of the faith of Abraham* (Rom. 4:16), who was promised by God that he would become *the father of many nations* (Rom. 4:17), not just the father of Israel.

Finally, the gospel is the power of God rather than of man because it does for man what man can never do for himself. In the very teeth of his difficulties, both physical and moral, man has *peace with God through our Lord Jesus the Messiah* (Rom. 5), for God has shown his love toward us while we were yet helpless sinners (Rom. 5:1-8). Having thus been saved by grace apart from human desert, is there any doubt that we will now be secure from the righteous wrath of God?

The gospel declares that salvation is all God's doing. Just as sin came into the world, and death through sin, by the agency of one individual, so too shall sin be vanquished and banished from the world by the feat of one individual. Jesus is the New Adam, the head of a new human race (Rom. 5).

Of course, there are terrible struggles, defeats and failures. But these cannot remove God from his throne. No condemnation awaits those who are in Messiah Jesus (Rom. 8:1-3). Moreover, the Spirit of God will fulfil in each redeemed individual all the potential of the gospel, meanwhile supporting him in his struggles and praying through him according to the will of God. The very groans we utter in the course of our conflict are the prayers of the Holy Spirit on our behalf. So, the victory is secure. The gospel is the power of God for salvation, God intervening in human life in order to secure the salvation of all the elect.

The same Spirit that raised Jesus from the dead resides in us. He will not only bring us to conform to the image of God's Son, reflected in the Law, but will also raise our very mortal bodies and refashion them to live in eternity. The whole creation is to be renewed, reintroduced to *the adoption, the glorious freedom of the sons of God* (Rom. 8:20-21).

This hope is so fantastic, so full and so secure that all we can say is, *glory to God in the highest,* and acknowledge with much gratitude that the gospel is indeed *God's power for salvation.* None but God can do it. None but God has undertaken to do it, and none but God will do it, in spite of present realities.

What shall we say to these things? If God is for us, who stands against us? (8:31). What can overcome us? Nothing, for in everything we are, by the power of God, made to *overwhelmingly overcome through him who has loved us* (Rom. 8:37), and nothing in this world or the next, in heaven or in hell can change that! The gospel is God's power for salvation and Paul exults in that wonderful truth. That is why he is *not ashamed* of it. If we, by the grace of God, had such a view of the gospel, we too would be as unashamed as he was. Our depressions, our moral and spiritual failures, and the weakness of our devotion to God are indeed the product of a shallow, unfeeling understanding of the gospel.

God's Power to Save

There is yet another reason why Paul is *not ashamed of the Gospel* and it is to be found in words already quoted. The gospel is not a naked manifestation of divine power, a kind of spiritual circus set up to wow and astound all who see. No, it is *the power of God for salvation*. Now, is this not remarkable: that God would choose to save? Why should he? He is in debt to no man, under no form of obligation or need. Paul is thrilled with the gospel because it is, in its very essence, not only a declaration of divine intervention in the course of human life and destiny, transforming him, lifting him out of bondage to sin and liability to punishment, securing his full and utter salvation so that he is sure one day to bear the likeness of Messiah to the end that Jesus will be the firstborn among many brothers. It is also a declaration of God's goodwill – no! of his amazing love – toward sinful man. It is not God's duty to save, but an act of his divine kindness.

We have already related the facts concerning the terrible sinfulness of man. Yet God has deigned to save him. He is good, kind, gracious, loving and merciful to the wholly unworthy, and the gospel is the declaration of that kindness. By the Holy Spirit who has been given to us, God has poured out his love toward us into our hearts *for one would hardly die for a righteous man – though, perhaps, for the good man someone might even venture to die. But God demonstrates his own love toward us in that while we were yet sinners Messiah died for us* (Rom. 5:7-8). 'Amazing love! How can it be!' That is why Paul is in no way ashamed of it. The gospel declares God's free and independent kindness.

It discloses man's worth in the sight of God by disclosing beforehand his unworthiness. It is a gospel conceived in the divine bosom, worthy only of the highest devotion and praise.

Gentiles Too

Paul has not concluded his description of what the gospel is. There is yet another reason why he is *not ashamed* of it, and it too relates to the essence of the gospel. The gospel is God's power to save *everyone*. Now, this was a remarkable discovery in those days, the impact of which we have lost because of our familiarity with it. That familiarity has robbed us of another opportunity to behold the glory of God in the face of Jesus Messiah by weakening our perception of the wonder of the gospel. Until then it had been assumed that God had saving favour only for the Jews. Peter describes it as an astounding discovery when he first understood, while hearing Cornelius recount to him the tale of the angel's message, that God is *not one to show partiality, but that in every nation the man who fears him and does what is right is welcome to him* (Acts 10:34-35) and that, henceforth, he was to consider no man unholy or *unclean* (ibid. v. 28).

Returning to Jerusalem and being accosted by his fellow apostles, he is forced to retell the story of his vision and of his visit to Caesarea. His story leads the apostles to one simple but earth-shattering conclusion that will revolutionise their lives from that moment on: *Well, then,* exclaim the flabbergasted apostles, *God has granted to the Gentiles also the repentance that leads to life!* (Acts 11:18).

That is what Paul celebrates in his letter to the Ephesians. The mystery hidden from the ages is now revealed: God loves and saves Gentiles too. They who were once afar off are drawn near by the blood of Messiah and made, together with the Jews, into one new man! Paul is thrilled with the gospel because it is the great equaliser, drawing both Jew and Gentile to God, making them both adopted children, the objects of everlasting grace.

Man's Transformation
Further, Paul is *not ashamed of the Gospel* because of what it does in and to man. Here too the gospel differs radically from all the religions of the world. Having taught man that he can do nothing for his salvation, it calls upon him to work out his salvation with fear and trembling. While altogether logical, the gospel is unafraid of seeming contradictions which resolve themselves in reality, simply because that reality is more profound than can be comprehended by a superficial view.

Having taught man that God does everything necessary for man's salvation, the gospel now calls upon man to do his part in response and as an essential ingredient of the salvation accorded him by grace. Man must believe. The gospel is *God's power for salvation to everyone who believes.* God, through the gospel, enables and motivates man to respond in faith to the goodness of God. But then it calls upon man to do so. Salvation puts men and women into action. The Holy Spirit's regenerating power transforms them into spiritually and active alert individuals who are not only bound to moral duties in the love and fear of God, but who desire to be increasingly more and more like their Saviour.

First, they leave off any effort to storm heaven's gates in their own strength. They recognise their utter sinfulness and cast themselves on the mercies of God. They forgo all attempts at human spiritual valour and all grounds for later boasting (Rom. 3:27). They seek and find a righteousness which is not their own, the product of their feeble efforts, but which is the gift of God. *They are justified as a gift, by [God's] grace, through the redemption that is in Messiah Jesus* (Rom. 3:24).

Second, there suddenly appears a new, driving,

motivating, all encompassing power in their lives, which creates a painful inner contradiction: having died and risen with Messiah by the power of God (Rom. 6:1-22), they now live *in newness of life,* reflecting the resurrection life of Jesus. The body of sinful motivations that formerly governed their lives has been destroyed and, they are now the slaves of righteousness, *living to God* (Rom. 6:11). But the habits of sin remain, constantly aggravating regenerate man, seeking to drive them back toward sin. Just as the Law had formerly served to expose their sinfulness before conversion, it now exposes their sin as children of God's grace.

This evokes a terrible yet altogether wonderful conflict, a groaning, a yearning after righteousness. A new principle is now at work. Christians are actively engaged in a struggle for spiritual and moral purity, in an unceasing quest for the renewal of the image of God in them.

Here too, they believe. They recognise that there is a great deal more to their salvation than the present conflict, with its all too few moments of victory and its frequent experiences of pain and sorrow. But they are saved *in hope* (Rom. 8:24) and *with perseverance, wait eagerly for* that hope's sure fulfilment (Rom. 8:18-25).

That is one important aspect of what the Bible calls 'faith'. Having been condemned to death by the Law, and having died in Messiah according to the Law's decree, man is now a regenerate servant of the Law, delighting in it in his inward man and eagerly seeking to fulfil the righteous obligations it imposes (Rom. 6-8).

Regenerated believers know that their struggle is not in vain, and that it is not to be conducted with merely human strength. Messiah lives by his Spirit in the believer, and he who raised Jesus from the dead undoubtedly has the power to bring about the full and final redemption of all who have believed in Jesus.

Their very bodies will be raised and they will at last *be conformed to the image of [God's] Son* (Rom. 8:29).

At the present, they groan, and their very groans are evidence of regeneration because they are the interceding of the Spirit on their behalf, praying according to the will of God. They therefore exult in the hope of the glory of God and are willing to take on death and life, angels and heavenly powers, the present and the future – anything created. And they are sure to overcome. They do so, not by their own presumed abilities, but *through him who loved* them (Rom. 8:37) and who has secured their salvation with his blood.

Nothing changes the world like the gospel!

To the Jew First
We come to Paul's last enumerated reason for exulting as he does in the wonderful message of God's love to sinners through Messiah and his saving work for and in them. Once again Paul explains his unabashed attitude to the gospel by describing what the gospel essentially is, that is to say, by referring to its essence.

The gospel *is the power of God for salvation to everyone who believes, to the Jews first.* This, too, refers to the core of the Gospel. There is no hiatus here, no pause, no logical gap to close. Rather, it is enfolded within the succeeding enlargement of Paul's earlier term, *everyone*, by spelling it out in specific terms: *To the Jew first, and also to the Gentile.*

This aspect of the gospel also refers to its essence because it best illustrates the utter mercy of God toward sinful man. Its inner logic is also clear. Has any nation apart from Israel ever been given the promise of a Saviour? To whom were given the adoption as sons, the glory, the covenants, the giving of the Law, the temple service and the promises (Rom. 9:4)? Whose are the fathers? From which nation did Messiah, who is God over all and blessed forever, come according to the flesh (v. 5)?

Of course the gospel is *to the Jew first*! It is the fulfilment of every blessing, promise and commandment given to them. It is the accomplishment of the covenant made with them. It is the inevitable outcome of the order God has established in the world, according to which he renders to every man according to his deeds (Rom. 2:6): *There will be tribulation and distress for every soul of man who does evil, of the Jew first and also of the Gentile, but glory and honour and peace to every man who does good, to the Jew first and also to the Gentile* (Rom. 2:1-10).

This priority of duty, or accountability, of reward and of grace is written into the very constitution of the gospel. God has entered into covenant with Israel, having determined to bless the world through that nation. His decision was, like everything else he does, based on his own kindness, not on human merit. It was also, like everything else God does, an act of unilateral sovereignty, for God owes account to no man.

That is why Paul is repeatedly engaged throughout his letter to the Romans with the issue of Israel. Since the gospel is such a unilateral act of divine power, how is it that Israel is not saved? Since the gospel is the merciful and vicarious fulfilment of the covenant made by God with Israel, how does it stand alongside those other covenants?

Paul demonstrates that merely being Jewish secures nothing but heightened responsibility (Rom. 2:1-16). He points out the failure of the Jewish people and their consequent guilt (Rom. 2:17-29). He hastens to remind us that such a failure does not, cannot, annul the faithfulness of God (Rom. 3:1-20), and that the mode of salvation is altogether consistent with the grounds and means by which Abraham, the father of the Jewish nation, was brought near to God.

In other words, rather than nullifying the covenantal Law later given, the gospel establishes its validity

(Rom. 4:21-31). Like those redeemed since the coming of Messiah, Abraham was made righteous through faith and not through human prowess – and the promise was made at a time when Abraham was not even circumcised! That is to say, it was made before God had entered into covenant with him. He then promised to make Abraham into a father of many nations, not just of the Jewish people.

That is also why Paul devotes so much time in chapters 9–11 of his letter to the Romans, discussing the fate of Israel as regards the gospel. In the light of increased Gentile acceptance of the message of Messiah, Paul intimates that the amazing grace of God toward unworthy sinners, as declared in the gospel, will be ultimately accomplished in Israel as well as among the Gentiles, and that God will work out his purposes however great be Israel's sin, *for this is my covenant with them* (Rom. 11: 27).

Just as God will not forsake the struggling, sinning believer, so will he not turn his back to the people whom he foreknew, and who are now in obvious sin. *God has shut up all in disobedience that he might show mercy to all* (Rom. 11:32). *From the standpoint of the Gospel they are enemies for your sake, but from the standpoint of God's choice they are* (note, please, *are*, not *were*) *beloved for the sake of the fathers* (Rom. 11:28). He has the power, he has the mercy, and the gospel declares the power of God to save both Jew and Gentile.

The gospel and all its benefits are described as the natural tree from which Israel has been cut off and onto which, contrary to nature, the Gentiles have been grafted. But God is able to graft them in again and *If you were cut off from what is by nature a wild olive tree and were grafted contrary to nature into a cultivated olive tree, how much more shall these who are the natural be grafted into their own olive tree?* (Rom. 11:24).

Note, please, that Paul does not speak in the past tense, 'what *was* once their own olive tree', but in the present tense. He frankly admits a present contradiction between what is natural and what actually exists. God, he informs us, will yet resolve that contradiction by bringing reality into line with what is natural. *For I do not want you, brethren, to be uninformed of this mystery, lest you be wise in your own estimation, that a partial hardening has happened to Israel until the fullness of the Gentiles has come in* (Rom. 11:25).

That is the sense in which Peter in Acts 3 appeals to his own Jewish people to put their trust in Jesus, when he insists:

1. That the acts of Jesus are the acts of the *God of Abraham, Isaac and Jacob, the God of* [their] *fathers* (Acts 3:13),
2. That the career, suffering, death and resurrection of Jesus are *the things which God announced beforehand by the mouth of all the prophets* (Acts 3:18),
3. And that true and ultimate belonging to the Jewish people is wholly wrapped up with faith in Jesus (Acts 3:23).

Peter reaches the climax of his appeal when he states in their hearing: *It is you who are the sons of the prophets and of the covenant which God made your fathers ... for you first God raised up his servant and sent him to bless you by turning every one of you from your wicked ways* (Acts 3:25-26). Peter uses a term we have also encountered in Romans 1:16: *For you first*, or, as Paul put it, *the Gospel is the power of God for salvation ... to the Jew first.*

This term, *first*, then, does not refer to an historical priority that, having been fulfilled, is not longer pertinent. It has to do with the essence of the gospel. God raised Jesus from the dead *for the Jew first*. He sent Jesus to bless the *Jew first* by turning every one of them from their wicked ways. The gospel is *the power of God for salvation to everyone who believes, for the Jews first*. If it were otherwise, God would have been discovered to be untrue to his word. His covenants would have been evacuated of all their content and his promises void of any substantial worth.

If it were otherwise, salvation would be unsure, grace would become mere goodwill unsupported by unlimited ability, and we would have been left to struggle with our sins in the vain hope that some day we might be good enough to reach out and grasp the heavenly blessing. If it were otherwise, Jesus would be no Saviour because, if he is unable to save those with whom he has entered into covenant, whom can he save? If Jesus is not the Messiah of Israel, he is not the Messiah at all.

Glory Be to God!
Paul exults in the glories of the gospel because it glorifies God, leaving no room for praise to man. So should we. It declares God's ability to save, his willingness to do so and the exquisite wonders of a grace that is altogether undeserved but all the more for that reason secure.

What shall we say to these things? If God is for us, who can stand against us? He who did not spare his own Son but delivered him up for us all, how will he not also with him freely give us all things? Who will bring a charge against God's elect? – God is the one who justifies! Who is the one who condemns? – Jesus the Messiah is he who died, yes, rather, who was raised, who is at the right hand of God, who shall also intercede for us! Who shall separate us from the love of Messiah? Shall tribulation, or distress, or persecution, or famine, or nakedness, or peril, or sword? … But in all these things we overwhelmingly conquer through him who loved us (Rom. 8:31-37). *Oh the depth of the riches both of the wisdom and knowledge of God! How unsearchable are his judgements and unfathomable his ways! For who has known the mind of the Lord, or he become his counsellor? Or who has first given to him that it might be paid back to him again? For from him and through him and to him are all things. To him be the glory forever, Amen* (Rom. 11:33-36), and amen.

Such was the heart-throb of Paul, a deeply spiritual man. Does our heart throb with his for the glory of God? May it be so!

APPENDIX C

God's Promises and the Prospects of Jewish Evangelism
Originally prepared by the author for the Banner of
Truth Escondido Ministers' Conference May 30 – June
1, 2000. All quotations are from the New American
Standard Version.

We have looked at Paul's letter to the Romans from
the portal of chapter one verse sixteen and have seen
that it is possible to understand that verse as an
introductory summation of the letter's theme. While
so doing we have learned that the question of Israel's
relation to the gospel and – more important – the
gospel's relation to Israel, is not a minor one,
incidental to the gospel Paul preached. It has to do
with the very essence of the gospel. In this short paper,
I propose to discuss the prospects of Jewish evangelism
in the light of God's promises as given in Paul's letter
to the Roman Christians.

Paul did not write in a vacuum. Underlying all of
his theology are two important factors: the revelation

of God in the Old Testament, and the revelation of God in Messiah. In order to proceed in our undertaking we must, therefore, remind ourselves of some Old Testament first truths.

The Sovereignty of Grace and the Covenants – the Biblical Background

A proper theology of covenants is fundamental to any faithful understanding of the Word of God. God has always framed his relations with mankind in covenantal forms. Adam was in covenant with God (Hosea 6:7). Noah was in covenant (Gen. 6:18). Abraham's relations with God were overtly and fundamentally covenantal (Gen. 17). That latter covenant was worked out in the relationship that God established at Sinai between himself and Israel.

Israel's relationship with God was wholly based on the covenant with Abraham (Gen. 17:7-14; Exod. 2:24; 6:4-5; Lev. 12:1-3; 26:42, 45; Deut. 4:31; 7:12; Ps. 105:9-10). We could go on to discuss the Davidic covenant and that which God made with Messiah for the salvation of his people, but these are not fundamental to our present discussion, so we will forebear.

The covenant of Sinai was a very important exposition of the Abrahamic covenant. From the moment it was established, every aspect of Israel's relationship to God and to the world, every aspect of the way the nation viewed itself, was to be governed by the covenant.

Israel repeatedly transgressed the covenant, but the gifts and the calling of God are irrevocable. God's purposes cannot be frustrated by the foolish wickedness of man, nor can his purposes be blocked or altered. He overrules man's wickedness and uses it for the furtherance of his eternal and gracious purposes: will Israel's stumbling at the message of the cross result in permanent disfavour? God forbid! Israel was temporarily broken off so that the Gentiles might be grafted in (Rom. 11:11, 19).

God foreordained Israel's rejection of Messiah so that the gospel would go to the Gentiles, and that he would have equal mercy on all. The Almighty is indeed Lord over all. Unaltered, unfettered, uncontingent, eternal in his glorious person, his purposes and all his works, God rules over the free actions of man in order to accomplish his eternal and gracious will. Salvation is never a matter of human desert or of human worth. It is a product of the sheer mercy of God, who grants redemption to whomsoever he wills, and who does so in a manner that unequivocally displays the wonder of his grace. No man can ever boast of his own salvation.

No man can attribute it to anything resident in him or in his deeds. It is all a work of God, who rules over his kingdom by sovereign, undeserved grace.

The Sovereignty of Grace in Paul's Letter to the Romans
That is the fundamental assumption that informs Paul's letter to the Roman Christians. It underlies the whole of that letter, serving as a foundation for his description of salvation in the widest sense of that term. Salvation, according to Paul, includes the initial forgiveness of sins through the mercy of God, which mercy introduces man – be he Jewish or Gentile – into the kingdom of God. The redeemed are *justified as a gift by his grace through the redemption that is in Messiah Jesus* (Rom. 3:21-24). There is no room, nor any need for works, except as the product of what God has done in and for man, for *how shall we who died to sin still live in it?*

It includes much more than forgiveness. It includes re-creation into the image of God, formerly scarred and distorted through the sin of Adam. Our baptism presupposes our prior regeneration, including our participation in Messiah's death to sin and our resurrection with him through the glory of the Father, so that we might walk in a newness of life (Rom. 6:1-11).

Grace does what the Law could never do because of the weakness of our flesh: it redeems men from the reign of sin (Rom. 6:12-14). The newness of life into which grace introduces us has everything in the world to do with the Law because the Law defines *righteousness* in the sight of God and grace transforms us from *being slaves of sin* to being the willing *slaves of righteousness ... resulting in sanctification and the outcome: eternal life* (Rom. 6:15-23).

We therefore conclude that salvation includes man's ongoing moral transformation whereby he is *made righteous* by Messiah's single act of obedience as the New Adam (Rom. 5:19). It includes the final consummation of that redemptive change wrought in man (Rom. 7:14–8:39), leading to his ultimate glorification when he is at last to be *conformed to the image of [God's] Son, that [Jesus] might be the firstborn among many brethren* (Rom. 8:29).

Salvation also includes God's sustaining grace for man in the face of man's many failures and of his terrible moral and spiritual weakness. It includes the Spirit evoking in man's heart a groaning after the righteousness of the Law, which is nothing less than the Spirit himself praying through us according to the will of God (Rom. 8:26-27; cf. Rom 7:24): *wretched man that I am! Who will deliver me from the body of this death?* and then evoking in his heart a triumphant recognition of the answer: *thanks be to God through Jesus Messiah!*

It also includes the assurance of eternal life in the face of repeated failures, for *there is no condemnation for those who are in Messiah Jesus... We have not received a spirit of slavery leading to fear again, but ... a spirit of adoption as sons by which we cry out, 'Abba! Father!'. The Spirit himself bears witness with our spirit that we are children of God, and if children, heirs also, heirs of God and fellow heirs with Messiah, if indeed we suffer with him in order that we may be also glorified with him* (Rom. 8:1, 14-17).

Nothing, no event, no creature and no circumstance

can separate us from the love of God, which is in Messiah Jesus our Lord (Rom. 8:31-39). God is the Lord and he will abdicate his throne to none, nor hand over those whom he has chosen to the just reward of their sin. Jesus has died for them, and that is enough. God rests, and we should rest on Jesus.

The Sovereignty of Grace in Israel's History
A similar view of God informs Paul's attitude to the prospects of Jewish evangelism. In the course of his outline of Israel's rejection of Messiah as a nation, Paul intimated Israel's unworthiness alongside God's determined grace: *all the day long I stretched out my hands to a disobedient and obstinate people* (Rom. 10:21). He describes God's persistence as equal to their consistent sin.

But it is not as though the word of God has failed (Rom. 9:6). God has not been defeated by the stubbornness of man. He has been using that obstinacy in order to show forth his glory both *through* Jews and Gentiles and *to* Jews and Gentiles.

At the present, Israel is blind to the wise goodness of God, but God has not rejected his people any more than he would reject one of the redeemed for their many and awful sins. Nothing can separate us from the love of God, which is in the Messiah, Jesus our Lord. He is working out in the history of Israel a sovereign purpose of grace, meanwhile preserving for himself and by his own initiative, *a remnant* within the nation *according to God's gracious choice* (Rom. 11:5). He himself stands behind Israel's stubborn refusal to accept the yoke of Messiah. Only *those who were chosen* have submitted *and the rest were hardened* (Rom. 11:7-10). Such is the mystery of God's working in Israel.

To what end? *Have they stumbled so as to fall? God forbid it!* A change is yet to come. God will bring it about, *for God is able to graft them in again* (Rom. 11:23). He is able to do everything he wants for he is ultimately, absolutely and altogether Lord, majestically ruling over all.

Please note here that the initiative is God's and God's alone. He blinded Israel so that the nation would reject Messiah, and he will open the nation's eyes so that the people might see and believe. He will graft them in again, *for I do not want you, brethren, to be uninformed of this mystery, lest you be wise in your own estimation, that a partial hardening has happened to Israel until the fullness of the Gentiles has come in and thus all Israel will be saved, just as it is written, 'The Deliverer will come from Zion, he will remove ungodliness from Jacob, for this is my covenant with them when I take away their sins'* (Rom. 11:25-27).

Redemption is an act of divine sovereign mercy, not of human religious ingenuity or insight.

Who Is Israel?

But who is this Israel of which Paul speaks? Many have claimed that we must identify the Israel that is the object of God's determined saving mercy, as the church. Such a view flies in the face of the biblical teaching concerning the faithfulness of God in spite of human sin. It contradicts the argument in Paul's letter to the Romans, as we have seen in the previous study. It also partakes of an exegetical inconsistency.

Let us briefly review this last point. In order to do so, we are forced to engage in some repetition. Perhaps that in itself could be helpful because reiteration is a good way to help us first comprehend and then remember the facts:

Paul uses the term 'Israel' in chapters 9–11 consistently, never with another meaning. He identifies them as *my brethren, my kinsmen according to the flesh* (9:1-3) for whom he grieves so much that he could wish himself accursed from Messiah if that would in any way assist them. He then goes on to describe Israel as those to whom belong the adoption, the Shekinah glory of the Lord, the covenants, the giving of the Law, the temple service and the promises, who are of the fathers *and from whom is the Messiah* (9:3-5). Obviously, Paul is speaking here of the Jewish people.

However, he says, *not all* who belong to the physical Israel necessarily belong to the spiritual body as well. He does not say here that there are some who belong to that spiritual body but are not part of the national Israel. Rather, he insists that it is not enough to be merely a child of the nation in order to belong to the true Israel of God (Rom. 9:6).

The proof of Paul's statement is to be found in biblical history, to which he refers: not all of Abraham's sons were partakers of the promise. Ishmael and Esau were rejected while Isaac and Jacob were *the children of the promise* (Rom. 9:7-13). None of these references can be related to the church. 'Israel' here is the Jewish people.

Paul again refers to Israel in 9:27-28, where he speaks of Isaiah crying out concerning the nation that, although its sons be as many as there are grains of sand by the sea, only a remnant of them would be saved. Here again it is clear that Paul has the people of Israel, the nation, in view.

In 9:30-32 he contrasts *the Gentiles* (v. 30) with *Israel* (v. 31), of whom he says that they are *pursuing a law of righteousness*, but are doing so not by faith, and have therefore stumbled over the stumbling stone who is Messiah, Jesus himself. Obviously, this refers to the people of Israel.

In chapter 10 Paul reiterates his heart's desire and prayer for Israel: he longs for their salvation (v. 1). Their zeal for God is *not in accordance with knowledge* (v. 2) because, instead of subjecting themselves to God's righteousness, of which they know nothing, they are endeavouring to establish their own (v. 3).

In verses 19-21 Paul describes Israel as a *disobedient and obstinate people* whom God will provoke *by that which is not a nation* – that is to say, by the church, consisting largely of Gentiles – as Isaiah makes bold to say, *I was found by those who sought me not. I became manifest to those who did not ask for me.* In none of these cases can the church be thought of as Israel.

Chapter 11 follows the same logic. It opens with the question: *God has not rejected his people, has he?* and responds with an avowal that such an event is impossible. It is impossible because of who God is and because of the nature of the gospel itself. Paul finds evidence for the fact that God has not forsaken his people in that he, a redeemed man, is *an Israelite* (v. 1) and concludes: *God has not forsaken his people whom he foreknew* (v. 2).

The term *foreknew* is important in Paul's argument concerning the nature of God's faithfulness according to the gospel and concerning the security of he who puts his trust in Jesus though he repeatedly fails.

Paul used this concept in Romans 8:28-30, where he argued that there is a complete and perfect identification between those whom God has foreknown and those who will ultimately partake of glory, who are undoubtedly to be shaped into the image of Jesus. Paul is here intimating what he there expounded: nothing can separate us from the love of God, which is in Jesus, not even the rejection of Jesus. If God has a purpose for the nation of Israel, he will accomplish it regardless of any opposing factors.

Well, you might ask, where is proof of that faithfulness in the present history of Israel? Ah, says Paul, *do you not know what the scripture says in the passage about Elijah, how he pleads with God against Israel? 'Lord, they have killed your prophets, they have torn down your altars, and I alone am left and they are seeking my life!' What is the divine response to him? – 'I have kept for myself 7,000 men who have not bent the knee to Baal'. In the same way, then, there has also come to be at the present time a remnant according to God's gracious choice* (11:2-5).

God's choice is on the basis of grace and not of any

human worth, so that the rejection of Messiah by the majority of the people of Israel in no way imposes upon God to reject his people. The gospel declares God to be one who rules over mankind's destiny by grace and not on the basis of human works. This is the way he has chosen to glorify himself. Again, 'Israel' here is the Jewish people.

Such is the case in verses 11:7-15: Paul speaks there of Israel which *has not obtained ... but those who were chosen obtained and the rest were hardened* (v. 7). *The rest* of whom? Of the nation of Israel. Those within the nation who are the true Israel obtained what the nation as a body has not because *they did not subject themselves to the righteousness of God* (10:3). *God gave them a spirit of stupor, eyes to see not and ears to hear not* (11:8).

But *they did not stumble so as to fall, did they? God forbid! But by their transgression salvation has come to the Gentiles* (v. 11). Paul once again contrasts the Jewish people, who transgressed by rejecting the righteousness of God in Jesus, with those among the Gentiles who believed in Messiah.

According to this verse, the purpose of such a work by God still has Israel in view, because Paul says that the Gentiles' participation in the righteousness of God through faith is directed by God to a purpose that he describes as *to make them*, Israel, *jealous*. That is why, Paul says, *I magnify my ministry* (to the Gentiles), *if somehow I might move to jealousy my fellow countrymen and save some of them* (vv. 13-14). This is also part of the outworking of God's intentions for the people of Israel.

There is another reason why Paul is determined to be demonstrative about his labours among the Gentiles: if the transgression of Israel by their rejection of Messiah has been such a blessing to the world, *how much more will their fulfilment be? ... If their* (apparent, temporary) *rejection be the reconciliation of the world, what will their acceptance be but life from the dead?!* Again, there is no room to doubt that Paul is speaking here of natural Israel, some day to be transformed by the sovereign, merciful act of God so that the majority of the nation will become the true Israel.

Continuing with the same theme, Paul speaks in verses 16-24 of branches being *broken off* (v. 19) and of these being *natural branches*. Would we make such a reference to the church or to Israel, especially when the text says that they were *broken off for their unbelief* (v. 20)? Indeed, we are informed that they were broken off so that the Gentiles, who stand by their faith, might be grafted in (vv. 19-20).

The branches broken off are the very ones to *be re-grafted in* (v. 23), *for God is able to graft them in again – for if you*, Gentile believers in Messiah, *were cut off from what is by nature a wild olive tree, and were grafted in contrary to nature into a cultivated olive tree, how much more shall these who are the natural branches be grafted into their own olive tree* (v. 24).

Once again Paul is speaking of the people of Israel in contrast to the Gentiles, and he summarises by stating that *a partial hardness has happened to Israel* as a nation, although there still are those very few who belong to the remnant.

This hardness is temporary, set by the hand of God to last *until the fullness of the Gentiles has come in – and thus all Israel will be saved just as it is written* (vv. 25-26). *From the standpoint of the Gospel they,* the Jewish people, *are enemies* but have been made to be such *for your sake*, that is, for the sake of the Gentiles. *But from the standpoint of God's choice they* – the national of Israel – *are beloved for the sake of the fathers, for the gifts and the calling of God are irrevocable.*

For just as you – Gentiles – *were once disobedient to God but now have been shown mercy because of their* – Israel's – *disobedience, so these also* who belong to national Israel *have been disobedient in order that, because of the mercy shown to you, they may also now be shown mercy, for God has shut up all in unbelief that he might have mercy to all.*

In the light of the above, I am at a loss to understand how anyone can doubt that the term 'Israel' in Paul's letter to the Romans designates anything but the people of Israel, presently known as the Jewish people.

Israel's unworthiness reflects that of all mankind, and the way Israel is saved is altogether identical to the way of salvation opened to every man: by sovereign grace. It is precisely such a view of the gospel that motivated Paul to weep and to pray for Israel. He knew the terrible holiness of God. He knew the terror of divine judgement. He certainly recognised the grievousness of Israel's sin. He also knew God. He knew how gracious God actually is.

He had learned from the Scripture to think in terms of covenants and understood full well that God, having bound himself to Israel by covenant, would never go back on his word. God's aye is an aye to be relied upon and his nay is unalterable. He is true though every man a liar. Heaven and earth will pass away, but his word stands as sure as the heavens, nay – surer – for the heavens and the earth will pass away and will be folded up as a garment, but God and his word fail not, they shall stand forever.

It is in this sense that Paul's view of the gospel is theocentric. It focuses upon God in his sovereign mercy, not on man's failure or his success.

The Prospects of Jewish Evangelism
Now, what does all this have to do with the prospects of Jewish evangelism? Everything in the world, both this world and the one to come, because those prospects do not depend on the wisdom, methods, winsome personality or powerful preaching of those engaged in that work. Nor does it depend on the social, political or economic conditions of the Jewish people, or on their willingness to consider religious matters.

The prospects of Jewish evangelism have to do with God and with his will. If he chooses to save, who can stay his hand? If he chooses to convince a nation of its need of Messiah and move it to cry out for saving mercy, no machination of the evil one, no hardness of heart, no measure of sin can stem the tide of repentance that will burst the bonds of sin and cause that nation to turn to God for salvation in Jesus' name.

Of course, all that is true of the evangelisation of any nation. God has worked throughout history, at times breaking forth in stupendous power upon large numbers of people, ushering them into the kingdom and transforming the life of the nation. I need not bring examples here – we are studying the Word of God, not the history of revival. But it is, surely, possible to state without reserve that both biblical teaching and the history of revivals testify to the saving power of God among nations. God is able to turn a nation to himself. He has done so in the past and there is every reason to believe that he will similarly act in the future.

We are not now discussing the power of God as such, but the prospects of Jewish evangelism in the light of God's ability and intention to keep his promises. Here we have solid grounds upon which to stand because the Word of God leaves us in no doubt as to his promises concerning Israel or of his ability or covenant faithfulness.

In terms of the gospel, Israel is unlike any other nation. As sinful as any nation, as much in need of the gospel as any nation, as capable of being saved as any nation, yet unlike any other nation, Israel has a past and a future that the Word of God declares is inextricably bound up with the gospel and with its prospects. Those prospects have to do with the covenant between God and Israel.

Although *Israel, pursuing a law of righteousness, did not attain at that law ... because they did not pursue it by faith but as though it was by works,* and although *they stumbled over* Messiah, *the stumbling stone* which God laid in Zion (Rom. 9:31-32), God has not rejected his people. Although they are ignorant of *God's righteousness and, seeking to establish their own, they did not subject themselves to the righteousness of God* (Rom. 10:3), yet God will display his sovereign mercy among them. As in Elijah's day, *in the same way ... there has also come to be ... at the present time a remnant according to God's gracious choice* (Rom. 11:2-7), preserved by the unilateral action of God.

Israel's present partial spiritual blindness has a predetermined terminus. It is to continue *until*, says Paul (Rom. 11:25), and then *all Israel will be saved, just as it is written: the deliverer will come from Zion. He will remove ungodliness from Jacob, for this is my covenant with them when I take away their sins* (Rom. 11:25-27).

Once again, God is to be revealed as sovereign in all matters pertaining to salvation, while salvation is to be revealed as a matter of sovereign grace and of divine unilateral initiative. There is no synergism here. *All Israel will be saved* because God *the deliverer will ... remove ungodliness from Jacob.*

He will transform the nation or, as Isaiah put it, *a nation will be brought forth all at once. As soon as Zion travailed, she also brought forth her sons. 'Shall I bring to the point of birth and not give delivery?', says the Lord. 'Or shall I who gives delivery shut the womb?', says your God. Be joyful with Jerusalem and rejoice for her, all you who love her. Be exceedingly glad all you who mourn over her, that you may nurse and be satisfied with her comforting breasts, that you may suck and be delighted with her bountiful bosom.*

For thus says the Lord, 'behold, I extend peace to her like a river and the glory of the nations like an overflowing stream. And you shall be nursed, you shall be carried on the hip and fondled on the knees. As one whom his mother comforts, so will I comfort you, and you shall be comforted in Jerusalem. Then you shall see this and your heart shall be glad and your bones shall flourish like the new grass. And the hand of the Lord shall be made known to his servants' (Isa. 66:10-14a).

Salvation, from its beginning to its very end, is of

the Lord and of none else. *The hand of the Lord shall be made known to his servants.* How? *The deliverer will come from Zion. He will remove ungodliness from Jacob.* There will be a shaking of the dead bones. God will cause breath to enter them and sinews to grow on the dead bones, and flesh, and skin, that they come alive, and they will know the Lord. Breath will come into them and they will stand, an exceeding great army (Ezek. 37:1-6).

What we have here is an act of gracious power, transforming an ungodly nation to which God had stretched out his hand of grace all the day long to no apparent avail. God will *pour out on the house of David and on the inhabitants of Jerusalem the Spirit of grace and of supplication, so that they will look on [him] whom they have pierced, and they will mourn for him as one mourns for an only son. They will weep bitterly over him, like the bitter weeping over a firstborn.* Indeed, *there will be great mourning in Jerusalem* (Zech. 12:10-14).

This is my covenant with them, says the Lord, when *I will take away their sins* (Rom. 11:27). We learn, then, that God is still in covenant with Israel. Note that the text is again in the present tense, not in the past: *This is my covenant with them,* not 'this was my covenant'. As we have said, biblical history is a history of covenants and biblical theology is, in the best sense of the term, covenantal theology. God's relations with mankind have always been framed in terms of covenants and, though man has repeatedly proven himself a consistent covenant breaker, God remains true to his undertakings because he is God, uncompromised by the obstinacy of human sin. He had promised Abraham, *I will establish my covenant between me and you and your descendants after you throughout their generations for an everlasting covenant, to be God to you and to your descendants* (Gen. 17:7). *Their unbelief will not,* can not, *nullify the faithfulness of God* (Rom. 3:3).

God is to be exalted in the salvation of Israel because he is true to his word and because he is able to do all that he desires. He is not like modern politicians, who promise more than they can ever deliver. God is in total control of all events, guiding them all to the accomplishment of his eternal purposes. His workings in the history of the world have a gracious purpose in view because he has chosen to be exalted in the world by the salvation of unworthy sinners. To that end he *has included all* – Jew and Gentile – *in unbelief that he might have mercy on all* (Rom. 11:32).

Dare we doubt his right to act in such a way in the hearts of his creatures? *Does not the potter have a right over the clay* (Rom. 9:21)? *He has mercy on whom he desires, and he hardens whom he desires* (Rom. 9:18). He has worked in the history of Israel and of the Gentile nations so that Hosea's words, originally intended for Israel, might be as true of Israel as they now are of the Gentiles: *I will call those who were not my people 'my people', and her who was not beloved, 'beloved'. And it shall be that in the place where it was said to them, 'You are not my people', there they shall be called 'the sons of the living God'* (Rom. 9:25-26).

What are the prospects of the gospel among the Jewish people in the light of divine promises? By way of understatement, very good. Better than the prospects of the gospel in any other nation of the world, because no other nation's future is so intertwined with the outworking of the purposes of God and because God has not entered into covenant with any other nation. The salvation of Israel has to do with God's glory, with his sovereign grace, with his faithfulness to each of his undertakings. It has to do with God revealing himself to mankind as sovereign in his grace and sovereign over his grace, as a God who saves in spite of sin and is willing to be merciful to the greatest of sinners – or to a nation of sinners.

When discussing the prospects of the gospel among

the Jewish people, our focus ought not to be on Israel, nor on Israel's sin or Israel's ill desert. It should be on God, on his grace and on his ability to accomplish all that he has purposed.

God's workings among the people of Israel have the world of nations in view. Just as *their transgression* has turned out to *be riches for the Gentiles* (Rom. 11:12) and *their rejection ... the reconciliation of the world* (Rom. 11: 15), so will *their acceptance ... be* as *life from the dead* (Rom. 11:15; see also v. 12).

God will yet work among Israel and use that nation to be a blessing to the world. *In that day the Lord will punish Leviathan, the fleeing serpent, with his fierce and great and mighty sword, even Leviathan the twisted serpent, and he will kill the dragon who lives in the sea. In that day a vineyard of wine – sing of it! I, the Lord, am its keeper. I water it every moment. Lest anyone damage it, I guard it night and day. I have no wrath. Should someone give me briars and thorns in battle, then I would step on them, I would burn them completely. Or let him rely on my protection, let him make peace with me, let him make peace with me. In the days to come Jacob will take root, Israel will blossom and sprout and they will fill the whole earth with fruit* (Isa. 27:1-6).

Practical Implications
There are practical implications to this wonderful work of God. Above all, the gospel should be reflected in our lives. *Just as you were once disobedient to God, but now have been shown mercy because of their disobedience, so these also now have been disobedient in order that, because of the mercy shown to you, they may also now be shown mercy* (Rom. 11:31). We must reflect the mercy that God has shown toward us. This we should do in at least three ways:

1) We should learn from God to show mercy as pastors and elders, as parents, and as individual Christians. No one is beyond the pale of God's merciful

reach. No one is irredeemable. We should, therefore, despair of none. Instead, we should seek God for grace to love and be kind to the worst of sinners, as the pattern of the gospel works itself out in our lives by that same grace. It is not our work to save sinners or persuade the congregation about this course or that. We are all in the hand of God and even blindness serves in the working out of his purposes.

2) We must walk humbly, in the fear of God, recognising that we do not participate in the blessings of the gospel because we are any better than anyone else but only because God has deigned to show us mercy. *Some of the branches were broken off, and you, being a wild olive, were grafted in among them and became partaker with them of the rich root of the olive tree* (Rom. 11:17). Note, **some** *of the branches were broken off*, not all of them. *And you ... were* **grafted in among them** *and became partaker* **with them**. Israel has not been replaced. Gentiles in Messiah *were grafted in among them* (the Jews) *and became partakers with them.*

Do not be arrogant toward the branches. But if you are arrogant, remember that it is not you who supports the root, but the root supports you. You will say then, 'Branches were broken off so that I might be grafted in'. Quite right, they were broken off for their unbelief, but you stand by your faith. Do not be conceited, but fear, for if God did not spare the natural branches, neither will he spare you (Rom. 11:18-21).

All too much damage has been done to the reputation of the church and to Jewish evangelism by an arrogant attitude toward the Jewish people adopted by some who profess the name of Messiah, as if Christians are in any way better than the Jewish people. The history of the church has done little to commend the gospel to the Jews. Quite to the contrary, while the church has repeatedly shown itself to be as humanly prone to sin as are the Jewish people, it has often considered itself to be a paradigm of virtue instead of an example of God's grace to unworthy sinners.

JUDAISM IS NOT JEWISH

3) We should shoulder some of the responsibility of expounding the gospel to the Jewish people both by our lives and by a faithful verbal declaration. Paul testifies, *I am telling the truth in Messiah, I am not lying, my conscience bearing me witness in the Holy Spirit that I have great sorrow and unceasing grief in my heart ... My heart's desire and prayer to God for Israel is for their salvation... I am speaking to you who are Gentiles: inasmuch, then, as I am an apostle of Gentiles, I magnify my ministry if somehow I might move to jealousy my fellow countrymen and save some of them* (Rom. 9:1; 10:1; 11:13-14).

Surely, if we seek to be apostolic in our faith and in our practice, we should partake also of some of the Apostle's *great sorrow* as well as of his *desire and prayer to God for Israel*. We too should long and labour *for their salvation*.

4) Sinful as we are, we should take courage in the wonderful grace of God. He is truly able to save!

May it please God to glorify himself through our lives and through our verbal witness and in the accomplishment of all his gracious purposes.

Amen.

APPENDIX D

Following are a number of texts representing the Messianic Movement. The first is published by Beth HaShofar, a Messianic congregation in Seattle Washington, and is an example of the problems described in this book. The second is a letter written by a Gentile who has joined the Messianic Movement. The third is a defence of the Messianic Movement.

The fine line of Messianic Judaism
by Roger A. Lundington

There is, somewhere between rabbinic Judaism and Christianity, a very fine line. It is Messianic Judaism. When getting into a subject such as this, you soon have opposition. Men and women raise up against change, or the unknown, many times before they even partially know what it is. This could be one of the greatest obstacles to what God is doing in this dispensation. It could be prejudged before being understood.

There are some that come from a Jewish background who immediately throw up a wall at the first mention of the word Messianic, in connection with Judaism. Then there are those from a Christian upbringing who refuse to even consider anything of Judaism, as being *'under the Law'*. The sad thing is that both sides are so closed minded that they will fail to see the beauty of this restoration.

There are cases where a Jewish man or woman seeking for Messiah would recognize his or her fulfilment in Yeshua (Jesus) and end up in a Christian church. There he or she would be thoroughly de-Judaized and be the token Jewish member of the congregation. Warned against his or her past Jewish customs and lifestyle, they close their eyes and ears to their past and end up with a Gentile picture of the Jewish Messiah.

Some of these believers end up in leadership positions or even may go on to become pastors or spiritual leaders of Christian churches and only refer to their Jewish background, customs, feast days and past lifestyles to build that particular denomination or sect, or for personal gain or position. Many have innocently labored in this manner having been taught erroneous doctrine handed down from days of pagan worship among the nations. It takes a real call from heaven to renounce the religious errors around us and stand for the truth. Historians are sometimes more unbiased and truthful than religious leaders.

On the other hand, there is an element of Judaism that has dedicated its efforts to disproving Yeshua as the Messiah. We write this article with the full knowledge of the great persecution suffered by the Jewish people during the last 1,900 years. But this Jewish Rabbi Yeshua should not be blamed for these deeds done by the Gentile Christian community. Had they seen and followed Yeshua's teachings (from the Torah) they would have gone to the Jewish community with love and compassion as must be done today.

The sad problem is those, who labor so hard to keep

their Jewish children from recognizing Yeshua as their Messiah, are losing them to Hari Chrishna, Moonies and other eastern cult religions. If the same effort had been given to objectively and honestly examining the prophesies about Yeshua being Messiah, Messianic Judaism would have flourished years ago.

From these observances, one would say that the distance between Christianity and Judaism is ever so vast, but let us look closer. Yeshua (Jesus), the focal figure in Christianity, was not only Jewish, but a Rabbi. He never taught against the Torah (Law) but upheld it and brought more light through it. He kept all the customs and feast days of Israel, and never once taught against Moses or the prophets, but this anointed one, who was born to a Jewish woman, in a Jewish community, attended the synagogue, fulfilled all of the Laws of Moses and promised he would return to his people Israel. He is no doubt the greatest gift Israel has ever given to the nations of this world.

Now, the Gentiles are ever so quick to judge Israel for not keeping the Torah (G*d's instructions), and condemn her for turning to the gods and idols of the nations over 2,000 years ago. But what have the Gentile nations done with the even greater light of the Messiah? There is not one truly righteous nation after all these years.

In the foggy twilight of the last 1,900 years, Yeshua (Jesus) has been transformed into a Gentile image surrounded by the trappings of pagan holidays and celebrations, and his name has become a common curse word among men.

Truly, it is high time both Jew and non-Jew, zealot and Christian acknowledge their errors and misconceptions of this precious man and the prophecies concerning him, and come before him with weeping and a repentant heart.

This is where the fine line of Messianic Judaism brings the precious truths together. We must fall upon the Rock and be broken, and seek his will. In Messianic Judaism, you will see the fulfilment of the Messianic prophecies. Witness in the Scripture and in person the restoration of the land of Israel after over 1,900 hundred years of neglect and abuse.

We must come together in unity where both Jew and non-Jew worship the promised Messiah. Here you can feel free to keep biblical customs, true biblical feast days, with better understanding. Sing and worship in Hebrew as King David did. Read Torah as it was in Acts 15:21. Experience the joy of welcoming the Sabbath and Yeshua's return by lighting the Sabbath candles.

Some have referred to Judaism as bondage. So a Jewish believer, one who has accepted Yeshua as Messiah, who was raised in a synagogue, wore a prayer shawl (tallit), wore a kippa (yarmulke), fasted on Yom Kippur and lived a joyous Jewish lifestyle, feels out of place following his customs in a new religious environment. There are even some that view these customs as bondage, not knowing they are a joy, and in many instances, fulfilling the commandments (guidelines for life) given by the Almighty himself to this people Israel, *throughout your generations.*

On the other hand, dear Christian friend, do you realize your roots are in Judaism? The writers of the Holy Book were Jews, and on second review you may see it as a book of instruction, most joyous, and a path to freedom not bondage. Please don't judge too quickly, but rather, take time to pray and meditate about these things. Your life could depend on it! If you come from a Jewish background, or a Christian way of life, or if you haven't believed in anything, it's worth your time to visit a Messianic synagogue or fellowship. Come with an open mind and heart, and the Ruach HaKodesh (Holy Spirit) will witness the true joy and freedom there is in serving the L*rd as Messianic believers.

Truly, the fine line of Messianic Judaism is the best of both worlds.

Published by Beth Ha Shofar, 13001 – 37th Ave. So. Seattle, WA 98168 USA

Messianic Gentile
by Michael DeHaven

First, I must confess: I am a Gentile. I was brought up in the Assemblies of God and have attended churches from several Christian denominations. It has only been a year since I started to actively study the true *Roots* of Christianity, and this last Rosh Hashanah I began to actively practise those *Roots*. In this short time, God has put a burden on my heart concerning the identity of Messianic Judaism, and especially of the Gentile believer in our Messianic Jewish congregations.

It has become apparent to me that mainline Christianity tends to view us as little more than Christians who gather together to do Jewish things. The reasons commonly attributed to our Jewish behaviour are either to learn about the Jewish *Roots* of our religion or to provide a Jewish-friendly way to win Jews to Yeshua. For whatever reason people believe we 'act Jewish', Messianic Judaism is not viewed as being truly Jewish. This implies an insincerity in our Judaism. Although being Messianic does make us, by definition, Christian, our lives, worship and identity need to be Jewish if we are going to call our faith Messianic Judaism.

Many of us practising Messianic Judaism, or at least attending Messianic services, are Gentiles who have little understanding of what it means to be Jewish. Although it is our spiritual heritage, it is not and can never be our physical heritage. This means we don't have the upbringing necessary to understand Jewish culture or to understand or appreciate Jewish worship. Our lack of Jewish heritage also makes it difficult for

JUDAISM IS NOT JEWISH

us to understand the pain associated with such vital issues as the Holocaust or anti-Semitism in our culture.

Many Gentiles who attach themselves to Messianic congregations are content to attend just to learn about the Jewish *roots* of Christianity, and those who do so should be encouraged in their efforts. I sincerely believe learning about Christianity's Jewish roots is good and is something the church needs to grab hold of.

This is an important ministry if we want to rid the body of Messiah of anti-Semitism or to help the Christian fully comprehend his or her faith. But as important as this is, it is not as important as Messianic Judaism's mission to reach out to the Jewish people with the good news of their Messiah.

In order to be totally effective in this ministry, we need to be certain of our identity. Those of us Gentiles who attach ourselves to a Messianic ministry, who desire to be active in the ministry and not just learn about our spiritual heritage, need to remember we are part of a Messianic Jewish ministry.

As a Jewish ministry, it is important that we learn to fully identify with and understand Judaism and what it means to be Jewish. Consequently, we need to learn to think, live, worship and pray as a Jew and to take our Judaism seriously: to take on the identity of a Jew and be as a Jew to the Jews. It is vital to the overall identity of Messianic Judaism for the active Gentiles to fully and sincerely identify with Judaism. If we Gentiles don't willingly take on that identity, our congregations will never be truly Messianic Jewish congregations.

A major step in this direction is to willingly take on the yoke of Torah, which is the heart and soul of Judaism. We need to diligently study it, love it and live a Torah-observant lifestyle. Many may think this is legalism or 'being rabbinical', but if we learn to live Torah with an attitude of faith, out of love for and devotion to G-d, if our mitzvot (the fulfilling of the commandments, BM) are done as a willing act of devotion, and not out of a legalistic attitude, then we will finally delight in Torah the way the Psalmist did. I sincerely believe that being Messianic shouldn't make us less observant than the traditional Jew, but the fact that we know our Messiah and that Torah is written on our hearts and minds should compel us to be more observant, Jew and Gentile alike.

There has been an inexplicable pull on my life since I first came in contact with Messianic Judaism. I feel drawn to it in a way I can only explain as the L-rd leading me in this direction. I know I am not alone in this. I have communicated with many Gentiles who are feeling drawn to it, but most of us are left wondering what our place is within this move of G-d. I urge the Gentiles who wish to be a part of Messianic Judaism's ministry to take hold of your spiritual heritage. I also encourage the Jews around them to be supportive of those Gentiles who are sincere in their efforts and desire to learn. The change will be difficult. It is something foreign to us. It is also very likely we will be subject to ridicule and rejection for our decision, even by friends and family who don't understand the reasons for our change. In this case, we need to remember our sufferings are temporary and insignificant when compared to our goal of the salvation of the Jews. In the end, I believe we will find joy and peace in our chosen identity as we become a part of a major move of G-d to reach out to his chosen people.

Shalom b'Shem Yeshua!

Michael De Haven

A Defence of Messianic Judaism
by *Pari Johnson*, February 1997,
Edited by Eric Wilson and Tim Hegg.

Introduction
When the followers of Yeshua were expelled from the synagogues in which they worshipped, they formed

new congregations. The first ones began in Jerusalem, led by the disciples of Yeshua with the membership and worship styles being characteristically Jewish. From these congregations, the message of Messiah Yeshua (Hebrew name of Jesus) went worldwide.

Currently many believers, both Jews and Gentiles, are returning to this form of worship and study of the Torah (the first five books of the Bible) and Tanakh ([The Torah – the Law or teaching], Neviim [the Prophets], Ketuvim [the Writings]). They are finding joy by being reconnected to their Hebraic *Roots*.

Why Study Jewish Roots?

The first Messianic congregation met in Jerusalem at the time of Yeshua. It didn't take long, just a century or two, for the Messianic Jewish flavor to dwindle, primarily because of persecution and anti-Semitism, something that continues today.

Since the Reformation, Christians have been trying to discover and replicate the early church. With this desire has come the awareness that the early church was basically Jewish.

Seeking to recover these 'roots' forces us back to Torah and biblical Judaism. In the process, we also learn how to think Hebraically. This gives new insights into the Apostolic Writings (New Testament) and the teachings of Yeshua that have been missed or misunderstood. The final result is freedom and growth in *the grace and knowledge of our L-rd and Deliverer, Yeshua the Messiah.*

Is This a Return to 'the Law'?

This common question concerning Messianic fellowships reflects a misunderstanding of the terms 'law and grace', and an incomplete knowledge of the Tanakh.

Torah, properly translated 'teaching', expresses the relationship and covenant between G-d and Israel by spelling out the lifestyle for his chosen people so they would be a witness for him to the other nations. Over the centuries, men added to G-d's Law in an effort to help the people keep the Laws. It is these additional laws that Yeshua questioned, not the original, God given Laws. Yeshua kept Torah and instructed his followers to do the same (Matt. 5:17-20).

Grace abounds in the Tanakh as well as in the Apostolic Writings. Law and grace exist side by side throughout the Scriptures with salvation always coming from God's grace through faith and not by works lest any man should boast (Eph. 2:8-9).

Why Use Messianic Terms?
Messianic believers want to express their faith in the Messiah in a manner consistent with Jewish heritage and culture. Special terms communicate biblical truth without the excess baggage of historical anti-Semitism.

Messianic: The expression of faith in the Messiah in a Jewish manner

Congregation: In our times, the word 'church' too often carries with it 'baggage' which the biblical word never conveyed. 'Congregation' reinforces the truth that the church is PEOPLE, not a building or institution.

APPENDIX E

A Short History of the Messianic Movement

In an effort to provide the Messianic Movement with historical roots, Messianic Jews have bought into statements such as that found in Jeff Wasserman's *Messianic Jewish Congregations*:

> 'There is little debate that the earliest church was essentially a Jewish church and that the incorporation of Gentiles on any large scale basis (sic) was a second generation phenomenon' (Wasserman, p. 19).

Regretfully, there is ample room for debate on this undebatable subject. If 'second generation' means those churches established among the Gentiles later than the founding of the church in Jerusalem and Judea, there is nothing wrong with such a statement. But the New Testament clearly shows that, by the time Luke completed the book of Acts, the majority of those who followed Jesus was no longer Jewish and the majority of Christian churches worldwide was decidedly Gentile.

John Fischer insists,

'some people may view the Messianic Jewish movement as something new. Perhaps it is new for our generation, but it is really very old. The movement has merely returned to a New Testament pattern. After all, Jesus and his early followers lived as Jews' (John Fischer, *The Olive Tree Connection: Sharing Messiah With Israel*, Inter Varsity Press, Downers Grove IL, 1983).

Of course, none would controvert the truth that Jesus and his first followers were Jewish and that he followed a Jewish lifestyle. But neither can it be questioned that he challenged many aspects of Jewish tradition. There is no doubt that his followers followed suit.

Supporters of Messianic Judaism assume that the early Jewish Christians in Jerusalem wholly participated in Jewish worship, including sacrifice in the Temple. The letter to the Hebrews makes it clear that there were indeed some such tendencies among Jewish Christians prior to the destruction of the Temple, but it also decries these tendencies, calls for a more substantial loyalty to Jesus and describes those who are inclined to follow the temple worship as 'falling away' (see above our discussion of the letter to the Hebrews). The willingness of many Messianic Jews to support their historical views by quoting Hugh Schonfield's works is a grave and unfortunate error, because Schonfield's works are signposts that led to his ultimate rejection of the gospel. They are not to be trusted, and many scholars have found fault with his historical assertions.

The Jewish people began to emerge from the shackles of rabbinicism in the Napoleonic period, at the turn of the 19th Century, when the Emperor allowed them to come out of their ghettos and encouraged them to develop a cultural independence of their own. He proposed to settle them in a defined part of his dominion, and there accord them a measure of political and economic independence. In Jewish history this period is called 'the Emancipation'. Jews began to be accepted in society, and a growing number of Jewish people in Europe aspired to such acceptance. One of the results was a growing interest in the common religion of Europeans, not all of which interest was spiritually motivated.

Jacob Jocz, in *The Jewish People and Jesus Christ After Auschwitz*, 1981, writes:

'The most remarkable development in Jewish culture is the increasing acceptance of Jesus the Jew. There is a genuine effort made to incorporate the Nazarene into the history of Jewish spirituality, not as the Christ of the Church but as a teacher in Israel.... Jewish (and even Christian) writers frequently speak of Christianity as the daughter of Judaism, meaning rabbinic Judaism. But ... the claim to "Jewishness" cannot be sustained any more as a prerogative of rabbinicism. On historic grounds it will be difficult to substantiate the claim that Hebrew Christians have abandoned Judaism. Rather, they have opposed rabbinic Judaism with their own brand, as did the monks at Qumran.'

In 1813 England witnessed the first attempt to bring Jewish Christians into an alliance that would serve to encourage them, present the gospel to their people and assist them in their relations with the churches to which they belonged. The association was called 'Bnei Abraham' (Hebrew for Sons of Abraham). In 14 May 1867 Dr C. Schwartz proposed the organisation of a Hebrew Christian Alliance of Great Britain, which later initiated and assisted in establishing similar Alliances in different parts of the world.

The Hebrew Christian Prayer Union was founded in England in 1883 in order to unite Jewish believers in Jesus for prayer. Within less than seven years, membership rose from 147 to 600 and branches were to be found in Russia, Norway, Germany, Romania, Palestine and the United States. By the end of the 1800s it is estimated that some 250,000 Jews professed conversion to Christianity in one form or another. Among these arose prominent individuals such as the British Prime Minister Disraeli, the Old Testament commentator Franz Delitzsch, composers such as Felix Mendelsshon and Gustav Mahler, the first Anglican Bishop of Jerusalem, Michael Solomon Alexander, and others. Bishop Alexander was appointed to his post in Jerusalem with the express hope of creating a Jewish Christian community in Palestine.

In the early and mid 1900s there arose a number of leading Jewish Christians. Among these we could mention Rabinowits in Kisheneff (who, in 1882, established a community called Israel of the New Covenant), Rabbi Isaac Lichtenstein (who continued to officiate as a rabbi and who wrote a number of commentaries on the New Testament) in Tapio-Szele, Hungary, and Daniel Tsion in Bulgaria (who served as Chief Rabbi of the country and was instrumental in saving many of the Jewish community from the Nazi killing machine).

Adat Hatikvah was founded in Chicago, USA in the 1930s. The first Hebrew Christian Church in Buenos Aires was formed in 1936. Many of these laboured for a distinctly Christian entity within the nation of Israel – an important distinction in comparison with the Messianic Movement which, following its failure to find acceptance in the Jewish community, has largely become a distinctly Judaised entity within the body of Messiah, seeking to call the church back to what is believed by the Movement to be the church's Jewish roots. In America, the Movement evolved from what was originally known as 'Hebrew Christianity' into today's 'Messianic' Jewish Movement.

Mission societies dedicated to Jewish evangelism played a significant role in forming what is now the modern Messianic Movement. In 1898 the (British) Mildmay Mission to the Jews founded a Jewish Christian congregation in London, which is now claimed by the Messianic Movement as one of its early modern harbingers. The congregation had few Jewish trappings and was overtly a Christian congregation among the Jews.

In America, the Movement evolved from what was originally known as 'Hebrew Christianity' into today's 'Messianic Jewish Movement'. This process was hotly contested by the earlier American Hebrew Christians, who immigrated from Europe and most of whom died by the middle of the 20th century. It was also strenuously opposed by the British Hebrew Christians until 1975. The old guard of American Hebrew Christians were largely fundamentalist Christians of Jewish origin who were very conscious of their Jewishness, avidly supported the Zionist Movement, were active in their opposition to anti-Semitism and eagerly sought to promote the gospel within the nation of Israel. But most of them saw no room for what is now the Messianic Movement.

On 22 May, 1901, Mark Levy, a Jewish Christian from Britain, convened what was known as the Boston Conference of the Messianic Council. He proposed at the conference to create a formal means of association for all Jewish believers in Jesus in North America. The participants agreed to organise another conference which would be designed to create the Hebrew Christian Alliance of America (HCAA). On 28-30 July 1930, the Alliance was formed with the declared primary goal of promoting the spread of the gospel among the Jewish people. Louis Meyer, who helped edit the famous Fundamentals of the Christian Faith, served as corresponding secretary.

In 1913 another meeting was held in Pittsburgh, with Maurice Rubens, a businessman, and Sabbati Rohold, a colourful, adventuresome and highly competent converted Orthodox Jew from Palestine who later led the work of Christian Witness to Israel in the land under its previous name, The International Society for the Evangelisation of the Jewish People. These men had founded the Hebrew Christian Alliance in America (the HCAA) in 1915. Rohold was elected to serve as the Alliance's first president. The Alliance was to serve as a fellowship of Jewish believers who worshipped in their various Christian churches. Heated discussions as to the wisdom, biblical grounds and feasibility of establishing distinctly Hebrew Christian congregations were held, and the idea was firmly rejected.

In 1917, the HCAA published the first issue of the HCA Quarterly, in English with a Yiddish supplement. Dr Emmanuel Greenbaum was called to be the Alliance's first missionary. He did not continue long in that position, and in 1932 new missionaries were called. At the instigation of the HCA, Moody Bible Institute established in 1923 a chair of 'Jewish Studies', first held by Solomon Birnbaum, who left Moody for Israel in 1936 and was responsible for a time for the Bethel Mission School for Children in Haifa.

Hirnbaum was followed by Max Reich until he went to be with the Lord in 1945, then by Nathan Stone in 1947. Stone was followed by Dr Louis Goldberg in 1965. At the instigation of Dr Goldberg, a revamped program of the program was inaugurated. This is a full-fledged academic program today led by Dr Goldberg until 1995, and since by one of his star students, Michael Rydelnik.

Hebrew Christians were eager to play an active role in the Zionist Movement because they sincerely believed in that political body's goals. The HCAA was finally rebuffed. HCCA support was welcomed, but not active participation. Nevertheless, the Alliance and other individual Hebrew Christians took part in various endeavours to settle the land in Sinai, near the Dead Sea, in Gaza and elsewhere in the country.

In 1925, the Hebrew Christian Alliance was broadened to form the International Hebrew Christian Alliance (the IHCA), with its main offices in London. Within a decade it had formed affiliated alliances in some twenty countries in North and South America, Europe, Australia, New Zealand and South Africa. Hugh Schonfield, a Jewish Christian scholar who later developed Ebionite views and denied the deity of Messiah, wrote of the founding of the International Alliance: 'Since 1925, the history of Jewish Christianity becomes in effect the history of the IHCA.' In 1927, Sir Leon Levinson, first president of the IHCA, claimed in The Hebrew Christian Quarterly, the official organ of the Alliance, that there were some 147,000 Jewish believers in the world: 17,000 in Austria, 35,000 in Poland, 60,000 in Russia, 30,000 in America and Canada, and 5,000 in Great Britain. These all held to an evangelical faith.

As of the 1920s, the HCAA had played an active role in the struggle against rising anti-Semitism in the USA and in Europe. The Alliance spoke out forcefully against Henry Ford's distribution of the so-called *Protocols of the Learned Elders of Zion*, a famous anti-Semitic book that purported to describe international Jewish machinations to take over the world. Upon its founding, the IHCA joined the fray and protested the treatment of Jews by Nazi Germany. During the war it ransomed and repatriated Jews and Jewish children from Germany to the British Isles, where they were granted asylum.

The European Alliances largely disappeared during the Second World War, their members persecuted for being Jewish by the Nazis while they were disowned by the Jewish community for being Christian. The American HCA helped some of these to relocate and, after the War, assisted in the founding of a mission to the Jews in Hungary.

Following the war and due to the anti-Semitic atmosphere created by the Nazis, initial efforts were made to establish separate Jewish Christian congregations. One such was attempted by David Bronstein in Chicago in 1934. This congregation became an independent Messianic congregation in the early 1970s under the leadership of Daniel Juster, and its name was changed to Adat Ha Tikva.

The American HCA established the 'Haven of Grace', a home for elderly Jewish Christians, which functioned between the years 1953–1966. In the 1960s a new generation began to make its presence felt in the American Alliance. Impacted by the anti-Establishmentarian views of those years, they had little allegiance to the church and a strong desire to distinguish themselves. They began to call for the adoption of Jewish traditions and for the more aggressive assertion of Jewish identity as believers in Jesus.

In 1966, the Young Hebrew Christian Youth Organisation (YHCYO) was established, which changed its name in 1967 to the Young Hebrew Christian Alliance (YHCA). Many leaders of the Messianic Jewish Movement in America today came from the ranks of the YHCA.

Martin Chernoff became the president of the HCAA in 1971, spearheading a stronger move in the YHCA toward rabbinic tradition. He served until 1975 and was later followed by his two sons, Joel (who served as president during the years 1979–1983) and David (who served for the years 1983–1987). During this time a new terminology was forged: Jews were no longer to be converted; they were to be 'completed'. Jesus became Yeshua, the Law became the 'Torah', the church was 'the congregation' or even 'the synagogue', biblical names were to be pronounced in their supposed original Hebrew form, and so on.

The late Manny Brotman (1939–1999) and his wife-to-be, Sheila Shishkin, founded a Messianic congregation in Washington DC in 1974. Manny was one of the modern pioneers of the Messianic Movement. He established the Young Messianic Jewish Alliance of America (MJMI) in 1965, and laid the groundwork for The Union of Messianic Jewish Congregations, founded in the mid-1970s.

Another prominent leader was Joe Finkelstein who, with his wife, Debbie, was active in Philadelphia from the late 1960s. Unlike the majority of Messianic leaders, Joe came from a Conservative Jewish background and Debbie was Orthodox. They attracted many Jewish and Gentile young people, some of whom professed conversion and joined together in worshipping at the Finkelstein's home. Joe repeatedly insisted that there is no contradiction between being Jewish and believing in Jesus. He and his wife maintained a Jewish traditional lifestyle, which was soon adopted by many of their young adherents.

In June of 1973, a motion was made to change the name of the HCAA to the Messianic Jewish Alliance of America (MJAA). The motion was supported by a small minority of Alliance members. In June 1975, the name of the Hebrew Christian Alliance of America was changed to the Messianic Jewish Alliance of America (MJAA).

Among the associations incorporating Messianic Jewish congregations and individuals are the Union of Messianic Jewish Congregations, the International Alliance of Messianic Congregations and Synagogues, the Fellowship of Messianic Jewish Congregations, the Canadian Fellowship of Messianic Congregations and Ministries, and the Southern Baptist Messianic Fellowship.

The Messianic Jewish Alliance of America, formerly the Hebrew Christian Alliance of America, was founded in 1986 and now has daughter alliances in 16 other countries.

The International Messianic Jewish Alliance (IMJA) is the worldwide alliance that seeks to represent the common interests of Jewish believers throughout the world, whether they belong to the Messianic Movement or to traditional evangelical churches. It carries out ministries through the work of its affiliated national alliances who unite their efforts to fulfil the aims of the international body. The professed purpose of the International Alliance is to care for the spiritual and material welfare of all Jewish believers and to maintain within the Jewish people a witness to Yeshua the Messiah.

The alliance is involved worldwide in bringing relief to any Jewish believer or group who has been ostracised because of their faith in Jesus, educating churches towards an understanding of the Jewish people, and establishing alliances in every region of the world where there is a community of Jewish Christians. The IMJA also acts as a unifying body for many organisations involved in evangelism among Jewish nations. In Israel, the IMJA shares in the running of the Ebenezer Home for elderly Jewish Christians near Haifa.

The Union of Messianic Jewish Congregations was founded in 1979 and today claims a membership of some 70 congregations located in North and South America and around the world. This movement sponsors the Messianic Yeshiva, which provides Messianic theological education. The UMJC Agency distributes financial aid to Jewish believers in Israel as well as to the new immigrants – a meaningful gesture to the government of Israel, whose resources are strained by the waves of immigrants from Russia and Ethiopia. The UMJC has also established a joint group of American and Israeli businessmen to help both foreign investors and Israelis who desire to begin businesses in Israel. They are working with different government agencies to get through the 'red tape' that is usually involved with such endeavours.

An example of one of the more extreme forms of Messianicism is OMJRA – the Observant Messianic Jewish Rabbinical Association, a theologically conservative association of Messianic Jewish rabbis who believe that they ought to keep the rabbinical law. One of the goals of the association as described in the OMJRA booklet is 'to promote the validity and necessity of Torah observance amongst the leadership of the Messianic Movement in general'. The association was founded in 1995 by 'Rabbi' Yehoshua M. Othniel, who had

'become disillusioned with the lack of Torah within the congregations where he studied and worshiped, felt the need to promote the richness of a Torah-observant lifestyle amongst his fellow believing Jews. Rabbi Othniel was convinced that the modern Messianic Jewish Movement suffered from a chronic identity crisis. Are we Jews or Christians? The response to this question was far from clear. Rabbi Othniel believed that a strong foundation of Torah along with Jewish culture, customs and traditions would transform the movement giving it a solid identity upon which to build for the future.'

According to Jeff Wasserman (p. 3), there are now about 300 Messianic congregations worldwide. Most of these are in the United States, with two in England, one in Holland, two in Germany, and a growing number in the former USSR and its satellite countries. The so-called Messianic congregations in Israel are largely made up of Jewish people who profess a saving faith in Jesus but most of whom do not adhere to rabbinic traditions in their congregational and private lifestyles, although the traditional Jewish holidays are celebrated as a matter of national culture. The greater majority of the Messianic congregations in Israel, the USA and elsewhere are charismatic.

APPENDIX F

Jesus in the Talmud

Some Christians – Jewish and otherwise – insist that Judaism is essentially biblical ('the roots of our New Testament faith') and that a truly biblical faith can exist within the context of Judaism. In light of Orthodox Judaism's views of Jesus, this is a very strange claim. True, among the rabbis one can find almost every idea, opinion and decree imaginable, but Judaism as such is directly opposed to the gospel of Jesus. As stated earlier in this book, Judaism is, in fact, the most consciously, most premeditatedly anti-Christian religion man has ever devised simply because Judaism as it developed since the death and resurrection of Jesus was in constant overt conflict with Christianity.

Of course, most of the forms of Christianity with which Judaism conflicted were themselves deviations from biblical norms. Roman Catholicism, Russian and Greek Orthodoxy, and the various forms of Christianity which developed in the ancient Middle East (such as

Nestorianism and Monophysitism) are poor representatives of the gospel of Jesus Christ. Those which were not persecuted soon became avid persecutors of the Jewish people, creating for the persecuted nation a situation in which it became extremely difficult to consider the claims of the gospel in a cool, objective manner. But Judaism's antagonism toward the gospel has much earlier origins. The New Testament itself tells us of Pharisaic opposition to Jesus and recounts the persecution of those among the Jews who forsook the synagogue and embraced faith in him as Messiah – the cases are too many to recount and too well known to need referencing.

On the one hand, while never justified, such an attitude is to be understood sympathetically in the context of the religious and national struggle which was then taking place. Two views of the faith of Israel were locked in mortal combat: the faith of Christ and Pharisaism. The Pharisees, firmly established in the synagogues on Palestine and the Diaspora, looked upon the upstart faith as a mortal threat to their influence and to the continued existence of the nation of Israel as they perceived it should be. Where opportunity allowed, they manipulated civil authorities and themselves engaged in physical and social harassment of Christians.

Evidence of this antagonism is found both in the Mishna* (compiled in the Second Century CE), the Talmud (both the Jerusalem and the Babylonian, whose composition was completed by the year 500) and in the Midrashim – Jewish interpretations. Many examples of this antagonism may be found in the Talmud.

All our references are from the Babylonian Talmud, and the primary sources are the collations of Gustav Dalman (1885–1941) and R. Travers Herford. Dalman taught at the Delitzschianum in Leipzig between 1895 and 1902. He then directed the German Protestant Institute for Archeology in Palestine until 1917, taught again in Germany and returned to Palestine in 1925 to direct an institute of his founding, the Institute for the Study of Antiquity in the Holy Land, until his death.

Hereford (1860–1950) was a doctor (Dr), a Unitarian minister at the Chapel in Stand, England, who devoted his life to the research of the Second Temple Judaism, particularly Pharisaical Judaism, and the Talmud. Basing his research on liberal theological views, he sought to present Pharisaic Judaism in as positive a light as possible. His important works included: Christianity in Talmud and Midrash (1919); Pharisaism, its Aim and its Method (1912); What the World owes to the Pharisees (1919); The Pharisees (1924); Talmud and Apocrypha: A Comparative Study of the Jewish Ethical Teaching in the Early Centuries (1933); an edition of Pirkei Avot with English translation, introduction and commentary (1962); The Separation of Christianity from Judaism (1927); and Judaism in the New Testament Period (1928).

Jesus' Origin
Shabbat 104b informs us that Jesus was a bastard son of 'one (who) has been unfaithful to her husband'. Mishnah Yevamot 4.13, quoted again in the Talmud (Yevamot 49b) states: 'Rabbi Shimon ben Azai said, "I have found a roll of pedigrees in Jerusalem, and therein it is written, A certain person (Ploni – a term used of Jesus in the Talmud, which generally prefers not to call him by name) is of spurious birth; to confirm the words of Rabbi Yehoshua".' Similar reference is found in Yoma 66b. In another instance Mary is described as one who 'played the harlot with carpenters' (Sanhedrin 106a). On this Rashi (the most influential of Jewish commentators) states, 'Paphos ben Yehudah was the husband of Mary... Whenever he went out of his house into the street, he locked the door on her, that no one might be able to speak with her. And that is a pattern of behaviour which became him not, for on this account there arose enmity

between them and she in wantonness broke her faith with her husband'.

Kallah 18b goes so far as to describe Jesus as 'both a bastard and the son of a woman in her separation', that is to say, one conceived during the time when, in the course of and immediately after a woman's monthly period, she is considered unclean – 'the most disgraceful origin possible' (Dalman).

Jesus Repugnant
The Talmud, as we have noted, is so adverse to Jesus that it usually avoids naming him. Instead, it calls him 'that man', 'Ploni', 'a certain man', 'Ben Stada' (Son of a harlot) and Balaam – the one-eyed prophet who brought upon Israel one of its greatest moral failures.

So strong is the revulsion that Judaism has for Jesus that the Tosefta to Hullin ii, 22-23 tells the following story: 'The case of Rabbi Elazar ben Dame, whom a serpent bit. There came in Jacob, a (Jewish Christian) man of Kfar Sama, to cure him in the name of Yeshu ben Pandira, but R. Ishamel did not allow it. He said, "You are not permitted, ben Dama". He (ben Dama) said, "I will bring you proof that he will heal me". But he had not finished bringing a proof when he died. R. Ishmael said, "Happy are you, ben Dama, for you have departed in peace and have not broken through the ordinances of the sages; for upon everyone who breaks through the fence of the sages, punishment comes at last..."'.

A similar story is told in the Jerusalem Talmud, Shabbat 14d, of the grandson of Rabbi Yehoshua ben Levi. Something stuck in his throat. 'There came a man and whispered to him the name of Yeshu Pandera, and he recovered. When he came out, He (R. Yehoshua) said to him, "What did you whisper to him?" He said to him, "A certain word (that is, the name of Jesus)". He (R. Yehoshua) said, "It had been better for him that he had died than thus"'. Finally,

Avodah Zarah 28a tells of Rabbi Abahu and Jacob the Heretic, previously mentioned. Jacob applied a drug to Rabbi Abahu's leg, 'and if it had not been for Rabbi Ami and Rabbi Assi, who licked his leg, he could have cut his leg off'.

Jesus – a Magician, Not a Sage

Jesus is described as one who 'practised magic and led astray and deceived Israel' (Sanhedrin 107b), much as did Balaam. His magical powers were supposed to have been learned in Egypt (Tosefta Shabbat XI 15), which was considered in those days the primary source of magical knowledge. According to Sanhedrin 43a, in a passage since expunged, when Jesus was being led to his death, a crier went before him calling out: 'He goes forth to be stoned because he has practised magic and deceived and led astray Israel. Anyone who knows anything in his favour, let him come and declare concerning him. And they found nothing in his favour. And they hung him on the eve of Pesach (Passover).'

Why was he put to death? Another reason is given in the Tosefta to Sanhedrin ix 7: 'The one who took to robbery was caught, and they crucified him on a cross.' And everyone who passed to and fro said, 'It seems that the king is crucified'. Therefore it is said, 'A curse of God is he who is hung'.

For that reason, Jesus is not to be considered a sage: 'from the time he is deceived, he is no longer a sage' (Tosefta Sanhedrin x 11). Instead, he is numbered among the seven who 'have no part in the world to come' (Mishnah Sanhedrin 10.2; Mishnah Avot 5.19).

Jesus' Followers to Be Rejected

All contact with Jesus and with his followers was eschewed. According to Tosefta Hullin ii 24, Rabbi Eliezer was troubled. 'Rabbi Akiva came in and said to him, "Shall I tell you why you are perhaps grieving?". He said to him, "Say on". He said to him, "Perhaps one of the Minim (a pejorative used of Jewish heretics, particularly of the followers of Jesus) has said to you a word of minut (heresy) and it has pleased you." He (Rabbi Eliezer) said, "By heaven you have reminded me! I was walking along the street of Sephoris and I met Jacob of Kfar Sichnin, and he said to me a word of minut in the name of Yeshua ben Pantiri, and it pleased me... I transgressed the words of Torah (Prov. 5:8): 'Keep your way far from her, for she has cast down many wounded'". And Rabbi Eliezer used (henceforth) to say, 'Ever let a man flee from what is hateful and from that which resembles that which is hateful'.

How were the Christian books and houses of worship to be treated? The books are to be burned, and never saved from the fire, they and every mention of the ineffably divine name in them (Tosefta Shabbat 18.5): 'May I lose my son! If they come into my hand I would burn them... If the pursuer were pursuing me, I would enter into a house of idolatry and not enter into their houses ... [the books of the Minim] put enmity and jealousy and strife between Israel and their Father who is in heaven should be booted out... Concerning them the scripture says, 'Do I not hate them with a perfect hatred, O Lord, which hate you, and I loathe them that rise up against you. I hate them with a perfect hatred, and they have become to me as enemies". And even as men do not save them (the Christian writings) from burning, so they do not save them from falling, nor from water, nor from anything which destroys them'. Hence they were called 'Aven Gilayon' and 'Avon Gilayon' (Shabbat 1116a) – a Hebrew pun on the Greek word for 'Gospel' (*evangelion*) meaning 'sinful parchment', or 'sinful writing'.

With such views of Jesus, his teachings and his disciples, how can Messianic Judaism ever hope to find acceptance among Orthodox Jews, who are brought up on the above-described teachings? Indeed, with such views of Jesus, why on earth would

Messianic Judaism seek acceptance by Jewish Orthodoxy? Is it not clear that any affirmation of Jesus and of his teachings is anathema to Jewish Orthodoxy and that, so long as Messianic Jews hold to any positive views of him, they will not be accepted as part of Judaism? Is it not further obvious that what we Jewish followers of Jesus should be doing is to challenge Judaism, not seek to come under its banner?

GLOSSARY

Abrahamic covenant the covenant God made with Abraham

Afikoman, Afikomen a ceremonially significant piece of matsa* kept for 'dessert' during the Seder* meal; traditionally, hidden and searched for by the children, who then hold it for ransom in order to receive a gift

Akiva Ben Joseph, Rabbi Ca. AD 50 – ca. AD 134, a Jewish religious leader; one of the founders of rabbinic Judaism; traditionally one of the first Jewish scholars to systematically compile the Mishnah*; executed by the Romans in the aftermath of the Bar Kochba* revolt ark

the sacred chest kept in the Tabernacle, and later in the Temple, holding Aaron's budded rod, the two stones of the Ten Commandments and a bowl of manna; nowadays, a special cupboard traditionally in or against the wall of a synagogue for the scrolls of the Torah*

Ashkenazic

a Jew of European descent, mainly from Poland, Lithuania, Russia, Germany, etc.

Baeck, Leo

1873–1956, Germany and England; a philosopher and teacher; leader of German Jewry during the Holocaust who remained in Germany by choice and continued to teach and guide even from Theresienstadt Concentration Camp; after the war, emigrated to England and became the president of the World Union for Progressive Judaism

bagel

a round, glazed, doughnut-shaped bread roll

Bar Kochba, Simon

died AD 135; a Jewish hero and leader of a major revolt against Rome under Hadrian in 132–135, whom Rabbi Akiva pronounced to be a Messiah, the Prince of Israel

Bar Mitzvah

when a Jewish boy reaches the age of 13 he becomes 'bar

mitzvah', that is a son of the commandments, and reaches spiritual responsibility

Ben Zakkai, Yochanan — an influential first century rabbi who is accredited with preserving the 18 Jewish traditional benedictions, in Hebrew, 'Shemoneh Esreh', which form the basis of the liturgy for the Daily Service, a kind of creed or declaration of faith

biblical holidays — those holidays which are commanded by God in the Torah

Birkat HaMinim — a malediction added to the 18 benedictions* in the second century against the 'minim'*

Bishop Alexander — Michael Solomon Alexander, a Jewish Christian; the first Anglican bishop of Jerusalem from 1841

Bnei Avraham — Hebrew for 'Sons of Abraham', an association of Jewish Christians in the 19th century

Bnei Brith — literally, 'sons of the covenant'; the oldest and largest Jewish service organisation in the world, founded 1843 in New York

Brit Chadasha — Hebrew for 'new covenant', or New Testament

cantor — the one in the synagogue who

'sings' the prayers, leading the congregation

Chanukah — the 'feast of lights' occurring in December, when each night a candle is lit in a special candelabra, to a total of eight lights celebrating the Maccabbean victory over the pagan Syrian conquerors over Israel ca. 164 BC and the re-dedication of the Temple in Jerusalem

Christocentric — a view that makes Christ its centre and focus

Christology — theological studies of the person and work of the Lord Jesus Christ

Clement of Alexandria — Titus Flavius Clement, c. 155 – c. 220; the first known Christian scholar, a prolific writer

Clement of Rome — Fl.c. 90–100; a prominent early Roman bishop, author of the earliest known non-apostolic Christian writing

Conservative — one of modern Judaism's major denominations in the USA; founded in 1845 from a split over Reformed Judaism

Davidic dance — dance purportedly reminiscent of Israel folk dance, used in worship in many Messianic congregations. Dances are reminiscent of

David's worship before the ark
(2 Sam. 6:16)

Day of Atonement   a day of prayer and fasting for
forgiveness of sins; the most
holy day in the Jewish
religious year

Delitzsch, Franz   1830–1890, a Jewish
Christian and scholar; his
translation of the New
Testament into Hebrew is still
used today in Israel

Diaspora   any country outside of the
land of Israel; also called the
'dispersal' or 'exile'

Ebionite   derived from the Hebrew word
for 'poor'; they exulted the Law,
rejected the Pauline epistles
and the deity of Christ

Edwards, Jonathan   1703–1758, considered one of
America's greatest philosopher
-theologians; under his
preaching America ex-
perienced great revival

erev Shabbat   the evening before the day of
Saturday: Jewish days begin at
sundown, so erev Shabbat is
the beginning of the Sabbath

eschatological   theology to do with the future,
the final events in the history
of mankind and the world

ethnocentric   focusing on ethnic identity

European Emancipation   also known as the 'Haskala'; a

Jewish Movement in Europe active from 1770s to 1880s that sought to speed Jewish emancipation by increasing secularisation, a concern for aesthetics and linguistic assimilation

forced conversions

throughout church history, Jews have been compelled to take on the religion of Christianity on pain of death

fringes

refers to the fringes on the tallit katan* worn under clothing

Gentile

someone not Jewish

gospel

the good news of salvation

Halacha

Jewish religious code of law

HCAA

Hebrew Christian Alliance of America; founded in 1915

Hebrew Christian

a Jew who believes in Jesus and is born again

Holocaust

refers to the murder of 6,000,000 Jews in Europe during World War II

IAMCS

International Alliance of Messianic Congregations and Synagogues

IHCA

International Hebrew Christian Alliance

Jewish Christian

a Jew who believes in Jesus, see Hebrew Christian

Jocz, Jacob	a third generation Hebrew Christian and theologian of the 21st century; Polish head of the London mission of the Church Missions to Jews
Judaism	the Jewish religion
kashrut	the dietary law of Judaism whereby certain foods may not be touched; and milk and meat are kept entirely separate to the point where religious homes will have separate dishes and pans for milk meals or for meat meals
Kehila	the Hebrew word for 'congregation'
Ketuvim	all the writings in the Old Testament other than the prophets and the Pentateuch
kippa	a 'yarmulke'
Law	refers to the Mosaic Law as understood today by rabbinic Judaism
Levinson, Sir Leon	first president of the IHCA
Lichtenstein, Isaac	a rabbi in Hungary in the mid-1900s who believed in Jesus and wrote a number of commentaries on the NT
Ma'ariv	the evening prayer
Maccabees	a priestly family that led a national revolt of the people in 168 BC against their Hellenist Syrian conquerors, resulting in

	the restoration and re-dedication of the Temple after decades of idol worship; reigned over Palestine until ca. 63 BC
Magyars	the dominant people of Hungary
Matsah	unleavened bread, like a big cracker
Melchizedek	the priest of Salem to whom Abraham gave a tenth of all his spoil after defeating the local kings and rescuing his nephew, Lot
Meschiach	Hebrew for 'Messiah', or 'Christ'
Meshichi	Hebrew for 'Christian' or 'Messianic Jew'
Meshummed	Yiddish for an apostate, a traitor
Messianic Jew	a Jew who believes in Jesus and is a member of the Messianic Movement
mezuza	a small ornamental box holding certain scripture and affixed to the front doorpost and to all the inner doorposts in the house
Midrashim	a tractate of the Mishnah*
Mincha	the afternoon prayer
Minim	'heretics'; Jewish Christians were called 'minim' in the first century

Mishna	Mishna *Mishnah, a Hebrew term meaning 'repetition' or 'study'; is the name given to the oldest post-biblical codification of Jewish Oral Law; together with the Gemara (later commentaries on the Mishnah itself), it forms the Talmud

Between 400 BC and the beginning of the Christian Era, the biblical Laws were intensively studied, applied to new situations, and supplemented by traditions of popular observance and by precedents established by prominent leaders. This material, long transmitted by word of mouth and known as the Oral Torah, defined the meaning of biblical Laws.

After the fall of Jerusalem and the destruction of the Temple in AD 70, the Jewish scholars and teachers called tannaim continued to elaborate and systematise the Oral Torah. About AD 200, Rabbi Judah HaNasi promulgated a collection of the most reliable traditions. This work, the Mishnah, became the official text out of which further Jewish legal development occurred.

Mitzva, mitzvot	Hebrew for 'commandment'; refers to the 613 laws of Halachic Judaism, or to a good deed

MJAA	Messianic Jewish Alliance of America, the new name of the HCAA
Montefiore, Claude	1858–1938, an influential Anglo-Jewish leader; founder of British Liberal Judaism
Nevi'im	the books of the prophets in the Old Testament
New Year	One of the High Holy Days of the Jewish Year; occurs ten days before the Day of Atonement and ushers in a period of soul-searching and intensive prayer which culminate in the day of prayer on the Day of Atonement; the Jewish Year is based on a lunar calendar, the first moon which begins in September/October
Niddah	a tractate of the Mishnah*
Notsrim	Hebrew for Christian; refers to any non-Jew from a nominal Christian background
Observant	a Jew who observes all 613 laws of the rabbinic code of law
Orthodox	a deeply observant Jew
Passover	a feast of seven days occurring within a month of Easter, celebrating God's miraculous deliverance of the people of Israel from Egypt; begins with the Seder on the first night (first two nights outside of Israel)

Patriarchs	the three fathers of the Jewish nation: Abraham, Isaac and Jacob
Pentecost	see 'Shavuot'
Pesachim	a tractate of the Mishnah*
Pesach	Hebrew for Passover
Pharisee	an Orthodox Jew in Jesus' day; this particular brand of Orthodoxy is the father of modern-day Judaism as we know it
phylacteries	small leather boxes holding scripture, bound on the forehead and right forearm of an observant Jew during prayer
Protocols of the Learned Elders of Zion	a forgery of documents purportedly written by Jewish 'Elders', describing their 'plot to take over the world'
Purim	a festival celebrated today, based on the events related in the biblical book Esther
Rabbi	a Jewish religious teacher and leader
rabbinic	pertaining to the teachings of the rabbis and halacha
Rabinovits, Joseph	1837–1899, the head of the Jewish Christian community in Kishineff, called 'Israelites of the New Covenant'

Rashi	Rabbi Shlomo Yitzhaqi, medieval French commentator *par excellence* on the Bible and Talmud, whose work is regarded as the most substantive introduction to Biblical and post-biblical Judaism
Reform Judaism	a denomination of modern Judaism marked by a liberal approach to religious tradition, resulting in non-observance of much that is considered irrelevant to modern life, and simplification of ritual
Reformation	a movement of the 16th century to restore the Christian faith to its biblical roots, and rejecting the faith and rituals of the Catholic Church
Replacement Theology	according to this theology, the people of Israel as referred to in the Bible are now the church universal; all the promises relating to Israel now belong to the church
Rohold, Sabbati	a Jewish Christian of Orthodox background who led CWI in Israel under its previous name, the International Society for the Evangelisation of the Jewish People
Ruach HaKodesh	Hebrew for the Holy Spirit
Seder	the traditional meal on the first night of the week of Passover

Sephardic	a Jew whose ancestors come from Spain; nowadays this definition extends to Jews from Arabic speaking countries, otherwise known as 'Eastern Jews'
Shabbat	the seventh day of the week on which God rested ('shavat') from the work of creation; the Jewish holy day of worship and prayer
Shacharit	early morning prayer
Shavuot	Pentecost, generally in May or June
Simchat Torah	literally, 'the Joy of the Torah'; the last day of the Sukkot Festival in which the yearly cycle of Torah readings is completed and celebrated; traditionally, the Torah scroll is paraded around the synagogue, accompanied by dancing, kissing of the scroll, and general expression of joy and delight
St Ambrose	c. 339 – 397, Bishop of Milan
St Augustine	354 – 430, Augustine of Hippo; Aurelius, bishop of Hippo Regius in Numidia in Roman N. Africa, considered to be one of the greatest of the church fathers
Sukkot	the Feast of Booths; observant families build a small booth on their porch or in the garden, eat all their meals there and

sometimes even sleep there, to commemorate the mercies of the Lord in preserving the people of Israel in the desert for 40 years after delivering them from Egypt; see Leviticus

synagogue

the Jewish house of worship in which the scrolls of scripture (the Torah, and the Haftorah, or prophets and writings of the Old Testament) are kept in an ark

synagogue readings

the Pentateuch is divided into 52 readings, each of which is read aloud during Sabbath services; the cycle begins and ends during the feast of Sukkot

tallit

a ritual prayer shawl worn by men during prayer

tallit Katan

a rectangular vest, sleeveless, worn under clothes by observant Jewish men

Talmud

'learning', 'study'; discussions on the text of the Mishnah by Babylonian and Palestinian rabbis from the third to the fifth centuries; comprised of the Mishnah* and Gemara, a commentary on the Mishnah

Talmud Torah

a school for young Jewish children where the Jewish religion is taught

Tanach

the Hebrew Bible, consisting of the Pentateuch, prophets and writings

temple	a Reform synagogue is often referred to as a temple
Ten Commandments	the commandments given by God to Moses (Deut. 5:6-19)
Theism	belief in the one transcendant God the Creator
the council in Jerusalem	the first council set up by the young church (Acts 15) was based in Jerusalem
Torah	the Pentateuch, the first five books of the Bible
Torah scroll	the Torah is written by hand on parchment and kept in a scroll, which is kept in the synagogue and read on Sabbath prayer
Trypho	a learned Jew of the first Century, quoted in Justin Martyr's* *Dialogue with Trypho*
Tsion, Daniel	the chief rabbi of Bulgaria during the 1900s; a Jewish Christian, instrumental in saving many from the Holocaust
tsitsit	the ritual fringes worn by observant Jewish men underneath their clothes
UMJC	Union of Messianic Jewish Congregations, based in Denver, Colorado
United Jewish Appeal	a fundraising organisation in support of Israel and Jewish causes

Yalkut	a book of the Talmud
Yalkut Isaiah	one of the sections of the Mishnah*
yarmulke	a kippa, a round cap worn by observant men at all times and particularly during prayer and eating
YCHYO	Young Hebrew Christian Youth Organisation, founded in 1966
Yeshua	the Hebrew name for 'Jesus'
YHCA	the YHCYO, which changed its name to Young Hebrew Christian Alliance in 1967
Yiddish	the language spoken by some European Jewish communities; a mixture of Hebrew and German or Polish; written with Hebrew letters
Yom HaShoah	Holocaust Memorial Day
Zion	a section of Jerusalem defined in the Bible as the city of David; later applied to the hill where the Temple stood and in time to denote the Temple itself; is symbolic of Jerusalem, of the Promised Land, of Israel's hope of return and of heaven as God's dwelling place
Zionism	modern secular movement focusing on the return to the Promised Land and the establishment of a Jewish state

BIBLIOGRAPHY

Aviad, Janet, *Return to Judaism: Religious Renewal in Israel.* University of Chicago Press, 1983.

Baeck, Leo, *Judaism and Christianity, Essays by Leo Baeck.* The Jewish Publication Society of America, Harper & Row, New York, 1958.

Bagetti, B., o.f.m., *The Church from the Circumcision.* Rome, 1970 ed. Fr. Eugene Hoade.

Barrett C. K. and Martin Hengel, *Conflicts and Challenges in Early Christianity*, edited by Donald Hagner, published 1999 by Trinity Press International, Harrisburg PA.

Bauer, W., *A Greek-English Lexicon of the New Testament and Other Early Christian Literature.* University of Chicago Press, 1957, Translated by Arndt and Gingrich.

Berkowitz, Ariel and Devorah, *Torah Rediscovered.* First Fruits of Zion, Littleton, Co., 1996.

Bikurei Tziyon, issue 64, May/June 2000, *Readers' Views and Comments.*

Levitz, Baruch Vos. 'Israel, Unique Amongst the Nations.' *Bikurei Tziyon,* issue 68, þ2001 .

Moshe, Michael, 'Whatever He Says, Parashat Mishpatim.' *Bikurei Tziyon,* issue 68, 2001.

Saal, Paul L., 'Let's Reason.' *Boundaries,* March/April 1999.

Dauerman, Stuart, 'It Seems to Me'. *Boundaries,* March/April 1999.

Resnik, Russel L., 'Torah for Today, the Festival of Exile'. *Boundaries,* March/April 1999.

Smolkin, Melinda, 'Creativity and the Soul.' *Boundaries,* March/April 1999.

Calvin, John, *Sermons on Galatians.* The Banner of Truth Trust, Edinburgh, 1997.

Christians and Jews, A Report of the Conference on the Christian Approach to the Jews, Atlantic City, New Jersey, 1931, International Committee on the Christian Approach to the Jews, International Missionary Council, New York City, 1931.

Colquhoun, John, *A Treatise on The Law and The Gospel.* Solio Deo Gloria Publications, Morgan, PA, 1999.

Danielou, Jean, *The Theology of Jewish Christianity: A History of Early Christian Doctrine Before the Council of Nicaea, Volume One.* Darton Longman & Todd Ltd., London and The Westminster Press, Pennsylvania, 1964.

Elgvin, Torleif, *Israel and Yeshua.* Caspari Center for Biblical and Jewish Studies, Jerusalem, 1993.

Feher, Shoshana, *Passing Over Easter: Constructing the*

Boundaries of Messianic Judaism. Alta Mira Press, Walnut Creek, 1998.

Flannery, Edward F., *The Anguish of the Jews, (Twenty Three centuries of Antisemitism)* revised and updated, Paulist Press, New York/Mahwah, 1985.

Morrison, Moshe, *Rejoice Sukkot. First Fruits of Zion,* September/October 1998 Issue 57.

Fruchtenbaum, Arnold G., *Hebrew Christianity: Its Theology, History, and Philosophy.* Washington, DC: Canon, 1974.

Goble, Philip E., *Everything You Need to Know to Grow a Messianic Yeshiva,* South Pasadena, CA: William Carey Library, 1974.

Gordon, Sheri Ross, *Inside Jews for Jesus.* Reform Judaism, 22 (Winter 1993), 22-27, 32.

Gartenhaus, Jacob, *Famous Hebrew Christians.* International Board of Jewish Missions, Inc., Baker Book House Co., USA, 1979.

Gruen, Erich S., *Heritage and Hellenism, The Reinvention of Jewish Tradition.* University of California Press, London, California, 1998.

Hagner, Donald A., *The Jewish Reclamation of Jesus, An Analysis and Critique of Modern Jewish Study of Jesus.* Academie Books, Zondervan Publishing House, Grand Rapids, Mich, 1984.

Hengel, Martin and Barrett, C.K. edited by Donald Hagner, *Conflicts and Challenges in Early Christianity.* Trinity Press, 1999, Harrisburg, PA.

Horbury, William, *Jews and Christians: In Contact and Controversy.* T & T Clark Ltd., Edinburgh, Scotland, 1998.

Hort, Fenton John Anthony, *Judaistic Christianity.* Baker Book House, Grand Rapids, Mich., 1980.

Jews for Jesus. *Mishpochah Message,* Fall 1993.

Jocz, Jakob, *The Jewish People and Jesus Christ: A Study in the Controversy between Church and Synagogue.* S.P.C.K, 1979.

Juster, Daniel C., *Growing to Maturity: A Messianic Jewish Guide.* Union of Messianic Jewish Congregations Press, Denver, Colorado, 1996.

Juster, Daniel, *Jewish Roots: A Foundation of Biblical Theology for Messianic Judaism.* Davar Publishing Co., Pacific Palisades, Rockville, 1986.

Kjaer-Hansen, Kai *Jewish Identity and Faith in Jesus.* Caspari Center, Jerusalem, Israel, 1996.

Kjaer-Hansen, Kai *Joseph Rabinowitz and the Messianic Movement.* The Handsel Press Ltd., Edinburgh, 1995; Wm B. Eerdmans Publishing Col, Grand Rapids, Michigan.

Levison, Rev. N., *The Jewish Background of Christianity, A Manual of the Political, Religious, Social and Literary Life of the Jews from 586 BC. to AD 1.* T & T Clark, Edinburgh, 1932.

Liberman, Paul, *The Fig Tree Blossoms: Messianic Judaism Emerges.* Fountain Press Inc., Harrison, Arkansas, 1977.

Lindsey, Robert Lisle, *Israel in Christendom, The Problem of Jewish Identity.*

Lipson, Juliene G., *Jews for Jesus: an Anthropological Study.* New York: AMS, 1990.

Longenecker, Richard N., *Paul, Apostle of Liberty: The Origin and Nature of Paul's Christianity.* Baker Book House, Grand Rapids, Michigan, 1976.

Longenecker, Richard N., *The Christology of Early Jewish Christianity.* Baker Book House, Grand Rapids, Michigan, 1970.

Marks, Michael W., *New Testament and the Law: A New Testament study on the Validity of Jewish Law.* Shammash Ariel Messianic Congregation, Pueblo, Colorado.

Mass, Eliezer, *Stand Firm: A Survival Guide for the New Jewish Believer.* American Messianic Fellowship, Lansing IL, 1990.

Nichol, Richard C., 'Messianic Judaism – So What Exactly is It?' *Messianic Jewish Life,* July–Sept. 1999 Vol. LXXII, No. 3. 'So Ask the Rabbi.' *Messianic Jewish Life* Vol. LXXIII, No. 2.

Fischer, Patrice, 'Tradition: Keeping the Faith.' *Messianic Jewish Life* Vol. LXXII, No. 3.

Rich, Lawrence J., 'Jewish Practices and Identity in the Book of Acts.' *Messianic Jewish Life,* Vol. LXXII, No. 3.

To the Editor, *Messianic Jewish Life,* April-June 2000 Vol. LXXIII, No. 2.

Fischer, Eve, 'Youth Perspective.' *Messianic Jewish Life,* July-Sept 2000 Vol. LXXIII, No. 3.

Metro VOICE Sept. 1999, Vol. 10 No. 9.

Montifiore, Claude, *Judaism and Hellenism.* McMill Co. 1918, London.

Murray, J. O. F., *Judaistic Christianity.* Baker Book House, Grand Rapids, Mich., 1980.

Prestige, G. L., *Fathers and Heretics.* S.P.C.K., London, 1940.

Rausch, David A., *Messianic Judaism: Its History, Theology and Polity.* The Edwin Mellen Press, Lewiston, New York, 1982.

Rosen, Moishe, and William Proctor, *Jews for Jesus.* Old Tappan, NJ: Fleming H. Revell, 1974.

Saperstein, Mark, editor, *Essential Papers on Messianic Movements and Personalities in Jewish History,* New York University Press, New York and London, 1992.

Schoeps, Hans Joachim, *The Jewish-Christian Argument: A history of theologies in conflict.* Faber and Faber, London, 1963.

Stendahl, Krister, *Paul Among Jews and Gentiles.* Fortress Press, Philadelphia, USA, 1976.

Stern, David H., *Messianic Jewish Manifesto.* Jewish New Testament Publications, Jerusalem, Israel, 1988.

Strickland, Wayne G., *Five Views on Law and Gospel.* Zondervan Publishing House, Grand Rapids, Michigan 1996.

Wasserman, Jeffrey S., *Messianic Jewish Congregations: Who Sold This Business to the Gentiles?.* University Press of America, Lanham, Maryland, 2000.

Whittaker, Molly, *Jews & Christians: Graeco-Roman Views.* Cambridge University Press, 1984.

Wilken, Robert L., *Judaism and The Early Christian Mind.* A study of Cyril of Alexandria's Exegesis and Theology, Yale University Press, New York, 1971.

Wilson, Marvin R., *Our Father Abraham: Jewish Roots of the Christian Faith.* W. B. Eerdmans Publishing Company Grand Rapids, Michigan and Center for Judaic-Christian Studies, Dayton, Ohio, 1989.

Winer, Robert I., *The Calling: The History of the Messianic Jewish Alliance of America.* Wynnewood, PA: MJAA, 1990.

Young, E. J., *The Book of Isaiah, Vol III.* W. M. Eerdmans Publishing Company, 1972, 1974.

THE FINAL WORD

There, I've said it! It has been sheer pleasure to contemplate the wonders of our Saviour and the fullness of the salvation he has accomplished. It has been a sorrow to have to disagree with some of my brethren. Now you, my dear readers, will judge the validity of the concerns expressed here and the fairness of my arguments. We may disagree, but the reason for our disagreements is our shared desire to glorify God by our loving obedience. In this holy, never-ending ambition, we are united.

There is nothing I long for more – short of the coming of Christ – than a move of God's Spirit among our people, many thousands of conversions and the emergence of a body of godly Jewish Christians who will call our nation back to him who is our only truly legitimate hope. May it please God to use this little book to that end.

You are invited to send me your comments, advice and criticisms – preferably by electronic mail at
bmaoz@attglobal.net.
Visit our website at
http:/**www.graceandtruthbulletin.org**

SCRIPTURE INDEX

SUBJECT INDEX

324, 326
   accepting, 256
   they are no longer Jews, 73
  leaders in, 308
  life in, 211
  Messianic Movement and, 239-240,
     245-246, 256
  of Constantinople, 73-74
  of God, 184, 228-229
  passion of, 203
  Paul's, 270
    dealings with the church, 206,
      211, 218, 274
    new term for synagogues, 85
  persecution, 270
  prophetic message of, 254
  reflects Christ in the world, 199-200
  roots of, 312, 320
  serving Christ, 211
  sin in, 134-135, 305
  synagogues, not, 250
  teaching on the Old Testament, 266
  terminology in, 256
  theology, 257
  unity in, 195, 207, 210-211, 218,
    222, 230, 249
  worship, 200
  see also congregations
'Church Growth Movement', 32
circumcision, 60, 122, 170, 195-196
  Abraham, 285
  and observing the Law, 25, 125, 131-
    132, 169
  cultural, 207
  has no value in Messiah, 58-59, 207
  Paul's, 88
  spiritual, 133, 207
  the Gentiles being, 59, 71, 122, 136,
    189-190, 206-207, 212
  uncircumcised men, 135
Clement of Alexandria, 92
Clement of Rome, 92
comfort, 30
  for Israel, 9, 11-12
  from God, 14-15
commandments, see Law of God
communism, 35
community, 30, 67, 84, 108, 127, 154,
  185, 208
  elements of faith vary within, 250
  Gentile Christian, 308
  Jewish, 21-26, 34, 74, 153, 179-180,
    219, 221, 225, 234, 308, 320
    Christianity in, 237, 320, 323,
     326
    does not accept Messianic Jews,
     236-237
    Jesus was a part of, 309
    Jewish Christian community, 34
    witnessing to, 239
  of faith, 129
  of Israel, 120, 129, 236

Torah community, 109-110
confession, 30
  of Jesus as Lord, 22
congregations, 35, 83, 220, 305, 308,
  313-314
  as church, 324
  communal framework of, 246-247
  congregational life, 47, 117, 197-200,
    204, 230, 257
    ethnic and cultural, 182, 186,
     199-201, 208, 210
    Messiah focus of, 257
  in Israel, 39-40, 144, 195, 267
  in the Messianic Movement, see
    Messianic
  congregations
  Jesus the focus, 197-199, 208, 230
  Jewish Christians, 197-198, 201,
    207-208, 210, 218-219, 228,
    321, 324
  mixing Jews and Gentiles, 37, 48,
    182, 186, 198, 225, 238
  in Diaspora congregations, 234
  nationally based, 182
  Orthodox Jewish, 224
  Paul founded, 85
  people, 315
  unity within, 198
Conservative Judaism, 154
  synagogues, 23
  see also Judaism
conversion, 35, 44, 58-59, 66-67, 71,
  110, 282
  and the Messianic Movement, 245
  Christians, 227, 320
  converts, 48, 75-76, 108, 145, 165,
    225, 244
    Jewish, 73-75, 238-239, 322
    Paul's, 85, 140, 206
  forced conversions, 60, 342
  fruit of God's power, 67, 181
  Gentiles, 229, 249, 251
  Jewish, 70, 153, 207, 224, 229, 250
  Messianic Jews, 225, 229, 240, 324
  of sinners, 68
  Paul's, 181
  to Judaism, 118
Corinthians, 140, 171, 195, 205-206,
  270
Cornelius, 47, 135-136, 280
covenant, 44-45, 55-56, 78, 82, 110-113,
  115, 151, 276-277
  Abrahamic, 77, 290, 302
  ceremonies of, 148
  Davidic, 290
  Gentiles outside of, 190-191
  God's, 224, 264, 287, 290, 302
    made with the church, 210
    made with the fathers, 56, 77, 97,
     98, 114-115, 117, 123, 125,
     156, 286
    Abraham, 285

as Lord, 68
his presence, 141
hoping for, 283
in Jesus, 93, 168, 187, 275, 280
in the salvation of Israel, 273,
    293, 303
in this world and to come, 258
living lives for the, 63-64
manifested in church unity, 211
moral Law reveals, 125
on Moses' face, 103
promoting, 30, 111
revealed in the Torah, 171
seeking, 32
we fall short of, 44
worship, 223
of the Messiah, 54, 67, 90, 183, 193-
    194, 200, 223, 247, 253, 291
unity in, 257
of the nations, 301
Shekinah, 294
to God, 273, 278, 288
God, 26, 32, 96, 122, 133, 147, 183,
    217-218, 223
Almighty, 291
anger of, 10-12, 51, 176, 277
    see also wrath
as a shepherd, 10,16
attributes of his Godhood, 13
authority of, 246
breaking his commandments, 262
broke down the dividing wall, 215
calling of, see calling
changes hearts, 63, 67, 99, 136, 182
    by the new covenant, 104
church of, 184
comfort from, 14-15
covenant, see covenant
Creator, 103, 117, 121, 188, 190,
    261
dishonouring, 149
drawing near to him, 149, 151, 167,
    203, 213, 215, 223, 284
dwelling of, 65
eschatological plans of, 245, 303
exalted, 276-277, 303
faithfulness of, 11, 35, 78, 192, 264,
    284, 294, 296, 300, 302-303
Father, 26, 64, 68, 77, 90-91, 121,
    189, 193, 199, 211, 214-216,
    253, 274, 291
in heaven, 334
Jesus ascended to, 262
member of the Godhead, 261
fear of, 29, 33, 83, 159, 202, 254,
    280-281, 305
forgives sin, 27, 33, 44, 60, 104, 208
frees us from the Law, 91
fullness in him, 133
gaining approval of, 25-26
Gentiles repent before, 44
gifts of, 14, 141, 193-194, 235, 298

gives us his Spirit, 54,135
glorifying, 30, 53, 99, 127, 211, 257-
    259, 272, 287
of himself, 36, 297, 306
glory of, see glory, of God
'God's people', 222
grace of, see grace, of God
guiding of, 24, 28
heals, 66
heirs of, 292
his foreknowledge, 296
his word stands forever, 299, 303
holiness, see holiness
image of, 59, 103, 124, 126, 203,
    252, 263, 282, 291
Jesus acknowledged as, 235
Jesus reconciles us to, see reconcilia-
    tion
Jesus sits at the right hand of God,
    134, 262, 287
Jewish themes of, 82
judgement of, 101, 159, 272, 287
justice of, 13, 273
knowledge of, 29, 46, 58, 66, 91-92,
    98, 105, 128, 132, 145, 171,
    211, 217, 272, 276, 287, 314
in Christ, 203
Israel's, 295
Paul's, 299
Law reveals, 61
lordship of, 228
love for, see love, for God
love of, see love, of God
majesty of, 185
makes all things new, 65
mercy of, see mercy, God's
nailing him to a cross, 253
nature of, 27, 46, 116
new life in, 109
offending him, 10
of Israel, 70, 109, 151, 296, 304
    does not reject them, 293,296-
        297, 300
    foreordained their rejection of
        Messiah, 291
    he favoured them, 191, 298
    the fathers, 286
    they apostatised from him, 213
of our fathers, 36
pleasing him, 36, 63, 185, 228, 262
power of, 17, 33, 68, 76-77, 120,
    180-181, 200, 277, 282
    for salvation, 273-274, 276, 278-
        281, 283, 285-286, 300, 302
    his word, 65-66, 167
presence of, 36, 38, 53, 59, 64-65,
    83, 98-99, 119, 128, 141, 147,
    164, 191, 213
promises of, 25, 43-44, 55, 71, 93,
    100, 110, 133, 180, 191, 213
    covenant with fathers, 36, 97, 277
    faith in, 104

126, 188-190, 196-197, 278, 283,
  299, 308
  blessings in, 287
  citizenship in, 199
  Father in, 334
  gates of, 281
  kingdom of, 238
Hebrew, 40, 45, 159, 175, 182, 184-185,
  226, 310
  believers' Hebraic roots, 314
  Bible, 82, 264
  church, 266, 320
  'Hebrew Christian', 37, 319-323, 342
  Paul, 88
  prayers, 248
  Scriptures, 70
  texts, 245
  the Hebrews, 95, 98, 110-111, 318
  words, 235, 240, 246, 314, 319, 324,
    334
hell, 64, 278
heretics, 155, 334
hester panim, 175
High Priest, 49, 95, 98, 105
history, 69, 75-76, 98, 112, 143, 150,
  160, 165, 256, 265-266, 286
  biblical, 295, 302
  Christian, 249, 305
  climax of, 64
  Gentile church, 250
  God has worked throughout, 300, 303
  historians, 308
  historical roots, 317-319
  Israel's, 14-16, 84, 88, 153, 293,
    296, 303
  Jewish, 106, 197, 221, 228, 315, 319
  Jewish Christian, 220-221
holidays, 147-148, 172, 207, 246, 250,
  327, 339
holiness, 116, 125-126, 149, 157, 181,
  185, 229, 235
  life of, 263
  of God, 14, 100, 125-126, 157, 185,
    229, 235, 256, 299
Holocaust, 21, 60, 78, 106, 166, 265,
  312, 342
holy places, 46
Holy Spirit, 10, 26, 98, 107-108, 121,
  168, 174, 189, 216-217, 271, 310
  access to God through, 193, 214-215
  baptism by the, 71
  called out 'Abba Father', 58
  changed by, 67, 182
  dwells in all believers, 263
  enlightens his church, 129
  fear of God by, 202
  forgiveness through, 61, 145
  gift of, 96, 107, 120
  gives life, 103
  God gives, 54, 135
  grieving, 122
  guides in obedience to rabbinic

dictum, 246
internalising the covenant by, 276
in the outworking of the new covenant,
  144
life by the Holy Spirit, 61-62, 110,
  114, 123
love of God through, 279
member of the Godhead, 261
Messiah acquaints us with, 91, 282
one body in, 195, 204
power of, 61, 67-68
  in Paul's preaching, 67
prayers of, 278, 283, 292
raised Jesus from the dead, 278
receiving, 54, 56, 58, 132
regenerating work of, 253, 262
removes the veil, 171
righteousness through, 59, 126
sanctification by, 67, 103, 263
saving work of, 32, 63, 104, 107
Torah does not give, 102-103, 114,
  132
transforming, 103, 117, 167, 171,
  176, 218, 281
Trinity and, 253
unity of, 71, 204, 264
witnesses with our spirit, 36, 306
Word of God
  he works by, 68, 167
  is his sword, 67
hope, 62, 64, 67-68, 70, 78, 98, 105,
  107, 119-120, 127, 155, 179, 189
  by grace, 203
  for Israel, 192, 197
  for salvation, 287
  for the glory of God, 283
  in Christ, 194, 213
  Jews and Gentiles, 254
  none without God, 191, 212, 216, 224
  saved in, 282
Hosea, 214, 303
hostility, 25-26
human needs, 29-30, 32-33
human reason, 29
humility, 134, 204, 276
hymns, 249-251
hypocrisy, 154, 163-164
idols, 46, 206, 213, 309
ingenuity, 30
inheritance, 55
iniquity
  Jerusalem's, 9, 11-12
Inquisition, 21, 244
International Hebrew Christian Alliance,
  144, 323
International Messianic Jewish Alliance,
  144, 248, 252, 326
Isaac, 44, 286, 295
Isaiah, 10, 12, 153, 296
  Book of Consolations, 11
  on trusting God, 14
  prophecies, 224

power of his word, 66
practised Jewish customs, 251
praying that Jews and Gentiles are
 one, 23
proclaiming, 64, 181
reconciles us to God, *see* reconciliation
redemption in, 281, 291
rejection of, 82, 96, 112, 155, 160,
 167, 176, 181, 220, 296
Judaism rejects him, 37, 150, 236,
 332-333
relating with, 96
religion of, 40, 171
religious traditions, 170
return of, 263, 309
revealed himself to Paul, 193
revolutionised Judaism, 166
righteousness of God in, 297
sanctification in, 53, 99, 102
Saviour, 25, 29, 49, 62, 107, 193,
 229, 252, 262, 274, 287
 by his name, 300
served in the Temple, 97
subservience to, 90
 world subject to him, 95
suffering, 176, 262, 286
Talmudic teaching on, 160
teachings of, 334-335
took the place of the Torah, 91-92, 97,
 100-102, 105-106, 110, 116-
 117, 126, 128, 133
 as the way, truth and life, 141
 fulfilled it, 262
trust in, 24, 102, 286, 296
truths of, 96,128
upheld the Law, 309
worshipping, 236
Yeshua, 226-228, 243, 250, 308-
 309, 314, 324
see also Christ; Jewish Messiah;
 Messiah; Son, the; Yeshua
Jewish Anti-Defamation League, 239
Jewish believers, 22, 25-28, 33, 38-39,
 48, 51, 108, 111, 123, 129, 155,
 157, 168-170, 180, 224, 256
apostatised, 181
as Christians, 71, 237, 246, 250
associating with non-believers, 74-75,
 78, 186, 229
 within Jewish nation, 233
challenging Judaism, 335
cultural and national identity, 256
division with non-Jewish believers,
 251
eternal inheritance, 194
evangelized, 239
faithful, 96-97
fellowship, 261, 322
Hebraic roots, 314
in conflict with the gospel, 81-82
in congregations with Gentile

Christians, 254, 264, 326
in the early church, 222
Israeli, 255, 327
Jewish authorities persecuted, 166
Messianic, 227-228, 326-327
 Movement as a spiritual haven for,
 241
mixed marriages, 240
'no longer Jewish', 73-74
not Jewish Christians, 245
observing Torah, 314, 327
spiritual home for, 233
still Jewish, 63, 69-71, 75, 81-83,
 87, 155, 167, 181, 186, 207, 225
 observing Jewish customs, 310,
 324
 taught to believe they were not,
 245-246
table fellowship, 137
uniting in prayer, 320
see also Jewish Christians; Messianic
 Judaism
Jewish Christians, 37, 48, 98-99, 155,
 248, 319, 323, 342
challenging rabbinicism, 153-155,
 160, 228
forsook traditions, 170
community of, 34, 221, 320, 326
congregations, 39, 85, 197-198, 207-
 208, 211, 218-222, 228, 319,
 321, 324
 in Israel, 255, 318
 culture of, 218-221
 Messianic congregations, 242
executed by stoning, 49
faith in Jesus, 63, 242
fellowship, 207-208, 220-221, 257
freedom in Christ, 116-117
Gentiles becoming, 251
identity of, 31, 76, 153, 183, 219,
 222, 242
 insecurity about, 242
 national identity, 145, 219, 227
in conflict with the gospel, 81
Jesus as the Law, 92
Jewish believers not, 245
Judaising, 220
lifestyle of, 106, 116, 208, 218
moral Law, 124
most are not a part of Messianic
 Movement, 241-242, 244
national culture, 127, 145, 168, 219,
 221, 254
no longer under the Law, 55, 106,
 116-117, 168, 177
 free from the Mosaic covenant,
 229
oppose Messianic Judaism, 251
persecuted, 153, 166
preaching the gospel to fellow Jews,
 68, 208
receiving the Holy Spirit, 136

still Jewish, 63, 75, 81-82, 167, 176-177, 199, 208, 220, 222, 251, 321
  forces to distance from, 246
  identifying with Judaism, 242, 318, 329
  within the body of Messiah, 35, 78
  within the nation of Israel, 78, 82, 153, 166
  see also Christians; Jewish believers; Messianic Judaism
Jewish Messiah, 21
  for all nations, 93
  Gentile picture of, 308
  life as a follower of, 23, 74
  trusting, 19-20, 27-28
  see also Messiah; Yeshua
Jewishness, 24-26, 33, 37, 44, 50, 64, 76, 101, 117-118, 140, 181, 198, 219, 238
  by following traditions, 84, 172
  choosing Saviour over, 36, 96, 100
  Christianity, 265-266
  congregations of Jews and Gentiles, 234
  culture of, 35, 86, 234
    cultural consensus, 228-229
  defined by the Bible, 69
  denial of, 75, 83, 181
  duties of, 84
  excuses Jews from the gospel, 63, 105
  faith in Jesus, 245-246
    threatens, 235, 242
  gospel affirms, 70, 181, 245
  in Messiah, 252
  internalises the covenant, 276
  Jesus is culmination of, 84, 153
  Jewish Christians, 176-177, 208, 219-220, 222, 225, 256, 321
    abandoning, 246, 308
    by embracing rabbinic customs, 242
  Messianic Movement, 87-90, 105, 156, 180, 225, 243
    congregational life, 198, 311-312
    liturgy, 184
    preoccupation with, 238, 247-248
    rabbinic traditions, 234, 243, 246
  national identity, 75, 81, 150
  nature not nurture, 221
  not Jewish, 150, 155, 157
  of faith in Jesus, 234
  of Israeli congregations, 40
  of patriarchs, 156
  Paul's, 193, 196
  persecution for, 238
  praying, 100
  proving to fellow Jews, 234
  rabbinic authorities determining, 70, 74, 93, 160, 234, 247, 319
  rabbinic customs, 234
  see also Jews, identity as a Jew

Jews, 21, 31, 50, 134, 176, 179-181, 183, 188, 211, 219-222, 224, 256, 267, 284, 293, 309
  American, 146
  apostles as, 50-52, 55-56, 70, 85, 88, 206, 222, 271-272, 286, 294, 318
    Paul calls Israel Jewish people, 295, 297, 299
  called by God, 34-35, 120
  Christianity's relations with, 60, 75-76, 145, 201, 265-266, 305
  circumcision, 59, 122, 139, 169-170
  congregations, 195, 198, 201, 208, 210, 224, 317
    with Gentiles, 37, 182, 212, 238
    worshipping as if in a first century biblical setting, 236
  conversion, 70, 153, 229, 238, 320, 324
  covenant people, 264, 277
  culture of, see culture, Jewish
  customs, see customs
  debating Jesus as Messiah, 70
  devout, 164
  dietary traditions, 215
  disciples of Jesus, 70
  Ethiopian, 153-154
  ethnicity, 243-244
  evangelising, 27, 33, 36, 39, 169, 181, 208, 236, 239, 289, 293, 299-300
    by the church, 257, 305
    impacting them with the gospel, 233, 255, 266, 306
    in the Messianic Movement, 321
    through the Messianic Jews, 240, 311-313
  faith
    in Jesus, 286
    in Yeshua, 239, 309, 311
  genocide, 265
  Gentiles becoming, 60, 70, 118, 235
    see also Messianic Judaism
  hearts hardened, 151
  heritage, 311, 315
  homeland in the Middle East, 222
  hope for Messiah, 119
    expectations of him, 213
  identity as a Jew, 20-25, 27-28, 34, 36-37, 73, 153-154, 180, 222, 228, 248
    accepting Jewish history, 106
    and a believer, 24, 81, 177, 181, 219, 324
    apostles identified with, 47, 108
    discontinuity with faith in Jesus, 75
    in Christ, 38
    in rabbinicism, 49, 100, 156, 172
    in the Messianic Movement, 38-39, 48, 87, 105, 183, 197-

Christian Focus Publications

publishes books for all ages
Our mission statement -

STAYING FAITHFUL
In dependence upon God we seek to help make His
infallible word, the Bible, relevant. Our aim is to ensure
that the Lord Jesus Christ is presented as the only hope to
obtain forgiveness of sin, live a useful life and look forward
to heaven with Him.

REACHING OUT
Christ's last command requires us to reach out to our world
with His gospel. We seek to help fulfill that by publishing
books that point people towards Jesus and help them to
develop a Christ-like maturity. We aim to equip all levels
of readers for life, work ministry and mission.

Books in our adult range are published in three imprints.

Christian Focus contains popular works including
biographies, commentaries, basic doctrine, and
Christian living. Our children's books are also
published in this imprint.

Mentor focuses on books written at a level suitable for
Bible College and seminary students, pastors, and
other serious readers; the imprint includes
commentaries, doctrinal studies, examination of
current issues, and church history.

Christian Heritage contains classic writings from the past.

For a free catalogue of all our titles, please write to
Christian Focus Publications, Ltd
Geanies House, Fearn,
Ross-shire, IV20 1TW, Scotland, United Kingdom
info@christianfocus.com

For details of our titles visit us on our website
www.christianfocus.com